A GEOGRAPHY

OF

BRAZILIAN DEVELOPMENT

JANET D. HENSHALL, M.A., M.Sc., Ph.D.

Research Associate in Geography,
University of Calgary, Canada

&

R. P. MOMSEN Jr, A.B., M.A., Ph.D.

Professor of Geography,
University of Calgary, Canada

BELL & HYMAN LTD
LONDON

Published by
BELL & HYMAN LIMITED
Denmark House
37–39 Queen Elizabeth Street
London SE1 2QB

First published in 1974 by
G. Bell & Sons Ltd.
Reprinted 1976, 1978

ISBN 0 7135 1812 X (hardback)
0 7135 1832 4 (paperback)

Printed in Great Britain by
A. Wheaton & Co. Ltd., Exeter

Contents

Maps

Figures

vi

Tables

Preface

A considerable amount of international interest has focused on Brazil in recent years both because of the extraordinary rate and momentum of its economic growth and because of the variety of growing pains, particularly social and political ones, that this has occasioned. Written expressions of this interest have, however, tended to concentrate on specific aspects of the country's developmental processes and problems such as those relating to industrialization, agrarian structures, social justice, political events, ecological disturbances or, more rarely, the status of a particular region. Such considerations should be seen as elements of a particular stage of development through which Brazil is passing. The nation cannot be expected to achieve equilibrium in all sectors of its social, economic and political life nor indeed should we expect balanced regional growth in such a vast country in which regional differences reflect both physical environment and the various legacies of historical antecedents.

The authors have chosen to examine these antecedents of current development processes in both a sectoral and a regional context, and then to focus upon the regional disparities which characterize Brazil's present geographical patterns and development efforts. The two principal problems faced were those of selectivity and of keeping up to date with rapidly changing events. One may hope that these difficulties have been overcome sufficiently to provide a comprehensive view of Brazil's progress along the road to development and of the problems that still block its path, as viewed in a geographic context.

To the extent that this may have been achieved, the authors are indebted to the many Brazilian friends and colleagues who have, over the years, shared their knowledge and insights with them. We are particularly grateful to Miguel Alves de Lima, Dorothea Momsen and Alicia L. Miller for regularly providing us with a variety of publications, maps, statistics and other items which have enabled us to keep abreast of developments in Brazil. We should also like to thank William Denevan, University of Wisconsin, and Scott Raymond, University of Calgary, for their useful suggestions on the chapter on pre-Columbian occupance. We are grateful to Dr. L. J. King, McMaster University, for advice on data analysis and to Ruth C. Park for computing assistance. Thanks are also due to Minnie Medwid for her care and helpfulness in drafting all the accompanying maps and figures. Last, but by no means least, we wish to thank Professor R. O. Buchanan for his infinite patience during the lengthy gestation period of the manuscript and for the innumerable improvements he made therein, not the least of which was the reconciliation of English and American writing styles.

Rio de Janeiro   J. D. H.
May 1974   R. P. M.

CHAPTER 1

The Land

Brazil has a great future—and always will have.
Popular saying

Brazil is among the world's largest countries, with an area of approximately 8·5 million square kilometres (3·5 million square miles). The potential productivity of this vast land has long been viewed with optimism. One of Brazil's leading geographers has pointed out[1] that for nearly five centuries observers have heaped praises upon this country.

Each generation has had its chronicler to predict a splendid future for Brazil. In the sixteenth century it was said to be, 'Undoubtedly the best of any place in the Americas for human life, having throughout good and fertile lands . . . being healthful and free of sickness',[2] and that this was a country that 'has the capacity to build itself into a great Empire, and to become at little cost the equal of any of the States in the world'.[3] Three hundred years later it could still be said: 'Happy is the State which possesses such space for the future, as it can therefore expand, colonize, and prosper in peace within its own frontiers'.[4] And only two decades ago the French geographer, Deffontaines, was moved to write, 'Every square kilometre here has real value. Brazil is, among all the countries of the world, the one which has the greatest spatial potential'.[5]

Yet it would seem that after 450 years of endorsement the Brazilians have yet to take full advantage of all the superlatives their country has been said to offer them. Many portions still remain, to all intents and purposes, to be occupied, and even larger parts are sparsely settled and but fitfully used. Most Brazilians, in fact, live within 600 kilometres of the Atlantic

Ocean and even within this belt, at times scarcely an hour's journey from a major metropolis, empty pockets exist in the landscape.

Viewed in the dispassionate light of resource availability, the Brazilian occupance pattern exhibits many anomalies. Areas of dense agricultural settlement in the northeast are subject to flood and drought while well-watered lands such as those of the Pantanal stand almost empty. Eroded and impoverished lands in Rio de Janeiro and Minas Gerais States are intensively cultivated while fertile and accessible areas along the Amazon River and its tributaries remain unused. Major lines of transport traverse incredible barriers[6] while many natural corridors to the interior, such as the São Francisco, the Doce and the lower Paraíba do Sul valleys, have been all but neglected. Valuable minerals like the nickel deposits of Goiás lie untapped for lack of transport, while in other cases few processing plants are found at the natural outlets or assembly points of raw materials, as for instance the iron ore and timber shipments through the port of Vitória. On the other hand, raw materials, capital, and people have been attracted over vast distances into certain localities such as the cities of São Paulo and Rio de Janeiro or their adjoining satellite towns, there to create centres of productivity and wealth surpassed by only a few megalopoli elsewhere in the world. In their shadow, however, such once-promising places as Caravelas, Paraíba do Sul, Ouro Prêto and Ubatuba lie almost neglected except by the curious outside visitor.

Many of these apparent anomalies may be explained by economic-geographic factors of the modern milieu; but an accurate comprehension of the present-day reality cannot be obtained without at least a cursory knowledge of Brazil's physical setting and a somewhat more detailed understanding of its historical evolution. From these, one can perhaps better appreciate the full meaning of the saying: *O Brasil tem um grande futuro—e sempre terá* (Brazil has a great future—and always will have)!

PERPETUAL FRONTIERS

One of Brazil's principal problems may be that it has too

much land for a population which was less than 20 million at the turn of the century, did not pass the 50 million mark until 1950, and today at about 100 million still has only twice as many people as the United Kingdom on thirty-five times the land area. As Brazil has no barren deserts, inhospitable tundras, or lofty mountains (the country's highest peaks are less than 10,000 feet above sea level) such as set finite limits to the effective areas of the world's other large nations, practically all of it is usable. Although it may not quite justify the superlatives that have been heaped upon it through the years, it has numerous mineral and fluvial resources and few areas will not support the farmer or stockman, if only at the subsistence level.

On the other hand, there is no extensive portion of Brazil which can be said to have so advantageous a combination of natural and locational resources as to make it, inevitably, the focus of a national oecumene. On the contrary, Brazilian history appears to consist of a seemingly endless series of discoveries leading to new foci of economic development, whether it be the opening of new lands, the introducing of new crops, the exploiting of new sources of mineral wealth, or the embarking on new business ventures. Yet the land and its resources seem never to have quite lived up to the original promises they were thought to hold, resulting in a dispersal of effort, a picking over of opportunities and the eventual neglect or abandonment of once-enticing areas or situations.

The wife of one successful pioneer on the Central Plateau, living not far from where Brasília now stands, captured it this way:

> The years have rolled by. Our land is now planted in bearing coffee trees. Highways interlace the frontier. . . .
>
> As I sat looking out the window on the horn of plenty that had become ours, my husband came up behind me and put his arm around my shoulder.
>
> 'Do you know what I've been thinking?' he asked. 'There is a new forest land beyond the Maranhão. There is no road leading to it. I was thinking . . .!'
>
> I saw a vision again of pushing through to, and opening another frontier in his eyes.[7]

Perhaps the restlessness that was once Portugal's, during its

great age of world exploration, has been transferred in per-
petuity to the inhabitants of this, its former colony. It is also
possible that Brazil's future has seemingly remained out of
reach on some distant horizon because there has always been
a new horizon across the vastness of its lands. Or it may be
that, lacking either highly productive or unequivocally repug-
nant areas, the Brazilians' cornucopia-like view of their
environment[8] has consistently faded under the realities of
sustained development in a setting that offers only the monotonous mediocrity of a tropical country.[9]

PHYSICAL REALITIES

Brazil's most accessible and historically productive lowlands,
along the banks of the Amazon and on the shores of the Atlantic
(Map 1), are restricted, non-contiguous and dominated by
hot, humid climates. In the Amazon, various types of *várzea*,
or seasonally inundated plains, are heterogeneous in composition, extremely variable in their usefulness and intercalated
with less fertile *terra firme* formations.[10] The estuarine and
coastal zones at the mouth of the Amazon are also of reduced
value because of either seasonal or tidal flooding.

The plains of Brazil's windward coast, sandwiched between
the mountains and the sea, are nowhere more than 160
kilometres wide. Their fertile alluvial soils are, furthermore,
restricted by swamps and by the dry *restinga* formations of
old coastal dunes; and they are interrupted by uplifted sedimentary mesas, known as *taboleiros*, crystalline hills, and spurs
of the coastal ranges which reach the sea in many places south
of the Guanabara, or Rio de Janeiro Lowland. Whereas to the
north of Salvador the coastal mountains are neither high nor
steep, and have the salutary effect of triggering orographic
precipitation from the Trade Winds in an otherwise moisture-
deficient area, to the south as the Serra do Mar they become
lofty and rugged, causing excessive precipitation along the
coast and a seasonal rain shadow in the interior.

In the far south, the highland rim bends westward and the
coastal plain merges with the northernmost extension of the
Uruguayan and Argentinean *pampas*. Although the native
grasslands of southern Rio Grande do Sul are also known by

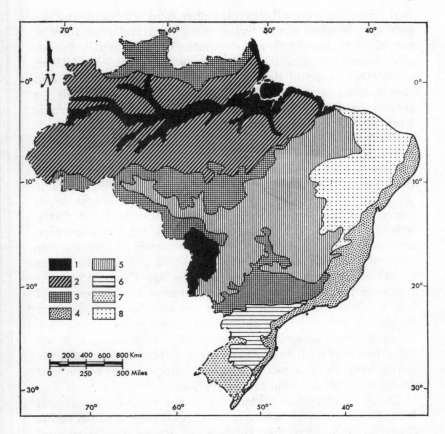

Map 1. PHYSIO-VEGETATION REGIONS OF BRAZIL. (1) seasonally inundated plains, woods and grasslands; (2) Equatorial *terra firme*, evergreen broadleaf forests with some scrub; (3) uplands under semi-deciduous forests; (4) windward coastal plains and mountains complex, predominantly tropical forest; (5) tropical wet-dry plateau, scrub predominant; (6) subtropical plateau, Araucaria pine and meadows at higher elevations, broadleaf suptropical forests in lower valleys and along the northern border; (7) subtropical plains and hills, grassland with gallery and coastal subtropical forests; (8) semi-arid plains and low plateaux, thorn scrub *caatinga*. Source: Conselho Nacional de Geografia, *Atlas Nacional do Brasil*, I.B.G.E., Rio de Janeiro, 1966, Plates II–1, 2, 3, 9, and 11.

that name, they are subtropical rather than temperate and the soils are therefore not so fertile nor the natural vegetation so nutritious as those further to the south. The Pantanal, a seasonally inundated alluvial plain along the Paraguay River, completes the list of the most extensive, albeit dispersed and varied, lowlands of Brazil. This 'great swamp' is used only for grazing, although the application of large-scale hydrologic work could, probably, turn it into a highly productive agricultural area.

Where the Brazilian Plateau extends into the subtropics and frosts occur, the natural vegetation consists of Araucaria Pine forests (*Araucaria angustifolia*) and meadowlands. The productivity of this region varies with the steepness of its slopes and the underlying rock formations. Its most fertile soils have developed over diabase, which occurs in the southern and western parts of the region and extends discontinuously under the *terra roxa* soils of the hilly uplands and semi-deciduous forests of northern Paraná and western São Paulo. Thence it continues into the 'Triangle' of westernmost Minas Gerais and into southern Goiás. Restricted on the east by steep slopes or by poorer soils overlying the sedimentary formations, the full value of these agriculturally productive volcanic soils is not uniformly realizable because of an intensifying dry season to the north, frosts to the south, and higher temperatures to the west where the plateau declines in elevation.

The bulk of the Brazilian highlands centres on Goiás and Mato Grosso where it is known as the Central Plateau (*Planalto Central*). An uplifted peneplain, it is deeply weathered and mantled for the most part with infertile lateritic soils. The predominant vegetation is a broad-leaved scrub of varying density and composition, mixed with tropical bunch grasses. Where semi-deciduous forests exist in galleries or in areas of recent down-cutting[11] they provide pockets of higher productivity and a ground water supply to last through the dry season.

To the northeast the dry season increases in duration and intensity, and precipitation becomes unreliable in the extreme, giving rise to a semi-arid land of endless thorn scrub: the *caatinga*. Although there is abundant sunshine here and soils which are agriculturally productive when water is made available, the latter is an organizational step which has yet to be undertaken in systematic and large-scale fashion.

To the north and west, as temperatures increase with lower elevations and as precipitation from the Intertropical Convergence Zone becomes more reliable, the scrublands are replaced by semi-deciduous forests which, in turn, become the evergreen types of the Equatorial region, a pattern that is mirrored north of the Amazon River, in the direction of the Guiana Highlands. Because leaching is less in the semi-deciduous forest belts than on the Equatorial *terra firme*, because of lower temperatures and longer dry seasons, the soils of the former are the more productive, although they do not compare with the best of those in the *várzea*. In contrast to the latter, which are readily accessible but suffer from discontinuity, use of the semi-deciduous forest zones, although they are fairly continuous, is hampered by steepness, remoteness and difficulty of access, since they are located above the fall-lines of the Amazon tributaries and are isolated from areas of expanding population by an international boundary in one direction and by vast expanses of scrub in the other. Nevertheless, they are now, with the growth of new and better surface transport facilities, becoming the focus for fresh frontiers of settlement and may turn out to be the key to rational re-occupation of the Amazon region which has remained outside the Brazilian oecumene since the white man took over this land from the Indian.

REFERENCES

1. Azevedo, Aroldo de, Ed. *Brasil a Terra e o Homem*, Vol. 1, Companhia Editora Nacional, São Paulo, 1964, pp. 4–6.

2. Gandavo, Pero de Magalhàes. *Historia da Provincia de Sãcta Cruz*, 1576, Ed. Melhoramentos, Rio de Janeiro, p. 63.

3. de Sousa, Gabriel Soares. *Tratado Descriptivo do Brasil*, 1587, Livraria Martins, Rio de Janeiro, p. 59.

4. Supan as quoted in Azevedo, *op. cit.*, p. 6.

5. Deffontaines, Pierre. *Geografia Humana do Brasil*, 2nd edition, Livraria-Ed. da Casa do Estudante do Brasil, Rio de Janeiro, 1952, p. 24.

6. Momsen, R. P., Jr. 'Routes over the Serra do Mar', *Revista Geografica*, Vol. 32, No. 58, Jan.–June 1963, pp. 5–167 (also published as a monograph by Industrias Graficas Taveira, Rio de Janeiro, 1964).

7. Lowell, Joan. *The Promised Land*, Duell, Sloan and Pearce, New York, 1952, pp. 213–214.

8. Reichmann, Felix. 'Brazil's Cornucopia', Chapter 6 in *Sugar, Gold, and Coffee*, Cornell University Library, Ithaca, N.Y., 1959, pp. 138–145.

9. For more detailed regional surveys of Brazil's physical geography, see, for instance, Chapters 26–31 in James, Preston E., *Latin America*, 4th Edition, The Odyssey Press, New York, 1969, or Conselho Nacional de Geografia, *Paisagens do Brasil*, 2nd edition, I.B.G.E., Rio de Janeiro, 1962.

10. For discussions of the physiographic characteristics and soils of the Amazon region, see Sombroek, W. G., *Amazon Soils*, Centre for Agricultural Publications and Documentation, Wageningen, 1966, which includes maps and cross-sections along the Belém–Brasília Highway, and Soares, Lúcio de Castro, *Amazônia*, Conselho Nacional de Geografia, Rio de Janeiro, 1963 (an English version was published in 1956 as Excursion Guidebook No. 8 for the 18th International Geographical Congress, Rio de Janeiro).

11. See, for instance, Faissol, Speridião. *O Mato Grosso de Goiás*, I.B.G.E., Rio de Janeiro, 1952, or Momsen, R. P., Jr., 'The Forest-Grassland Boundary between Jaraguá, Anápolis, and Goiânia on the Planalto Central,' *Comptes Rendus*, Vol. 3, 18th International Geographical Congress, Rio de Janeiro, 1965, pp. 82–89.

CHAPTER 2

The Indian

Die if necessary, but never kill. Motto of the Indian
Protection Service

Before the definitive arrival of the European, the land that
was to become Brazil was occupied by an Amerindian population that has usually been estimated at between one and two
million; but recent studies indicate that a figure on the order
of four million may be more appropriate.[1] The intensity of
this occupance ranged from nomadic hunting and gathering
in scattered bands, through a continuum of decreasing no-
madism and intensifying agricultural practices, to the advanced
farming techniques of sedentary Indians on the floodplains
of the main rivers and along the coastal plains (Map 2).

According to Denevan,[2] pre-Columbian densities produced
by these different occupational patterns in differing habitats
ranged from one person for every five square kilometres in
the forested interfluves of the *terra firme*, to one person for
two square kilometres in the savannas and the *caatinga*, to five
or more persons per square kilometre on the Amazonian
floodplains and nearly ten along the coast.

In broad terms, it can be said that Tropical Forest tribes,
who were roughly coincident with the sedentary agriculturalists
of Map 2, occupied the best-favoured coastal and riverine
lands and were technically more advanced than the nomadic
or semi-nomadic, predominantly Paleo-American tribes whom
they had pushed back into the less attractive interior regions.[3]
Bates[4] captures the essence of this two-fold division of the
Brazilian aborigine thus:

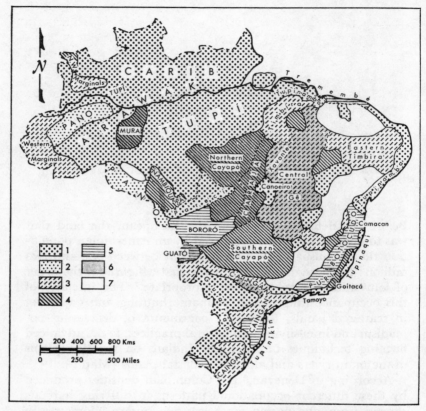

Map 2. GENERALIZED LAND OCCUPANCE IN PRE-COLUMBIAN BRAZIL.
(1) Sedentary: highly developed agriculture, with fishing; (2) Sedentary:
highly developed agriculture, without fishing; (3) Semi-nomadic with
well developed agriculture; (4) Nomadic hunters and gatherers with
rudimentary agriculture; (5) Nomadic hunters and gatherers; (6)
Fishing important; (7) Unoccupied or unknown. TUPÍ: Language
family; Tupinamba: Language group or tribe. Sources: Julian H.
Steward and J. Alden Mason, 'Tribal and Linguistic Distributions of
South America', *Handbook of South American Indians*, Vol. VI endpaper
map; Cestmír Loukotka, 'Ethno-Linguistic Distribution of South
American Indians', Map Supplement No. 8, *Annals of the Association of
American Geographers*, Vol. 57, No. 2, June 1967; others.

One fact seems to be well-established, namely that all the coastal tribes (and presumably those of the Amazon and its principal tributaries, *auths.*) were far more advanced in civilization . . . than the savages who inhabited the interior lands. They were settled in villages and addicted to agriculture. They navigated the rivers in large canoes made of immense hollowed-out tree trunks; in these they used to go on war expeditions, carrying in the prows their trophies and calabash rattles, whose clatter was meant to intimidate their enemies. The inland savages, on the other hand, led a wandering life, as they do at the present time, only coming down occasionally to rob the plantations of the coastal tribes, who always entertained the greatest enmity towards them.

RACIAL ORIGINS

Brazil's earliest inhabitants to be identified archaeologically, from caves in Minas Gerais and from shell mounds along the São Paulo coast, lived about 10,000 years ago and belonged to the Australoid division of mankind.[5] The coastal, or Sambaquí (from a Tupí-Guaraní word meaning 'shell hill'), people lived by gathering molluscs and hunting birds and small animals, and represent the archaic phase of a culture which survived in the south into relatively recent, although pre-European times when it included Guaraní cultural and racial elements.[6]

More widely known than Sambaquí Man is his racial cousin Lagoa Santa Man, also known as the Lácida, whose plentiful remains and rupestral paintings in the limestone caverns of the Rio das Velhas, Minas Gerais, have been studied since the last quarter of the nineteenth century. Similar paintings dating to about 3000 B.C.[7] have been found in northwestern Mato Grosso, where the Lácida may have been forced to take refuge by more warlike and culturally advanced peoples. The dolichocephalic, platyrrhine, occasionally wavy-haired Nambiquara Indians who inhabit this inhospitable region today approximate to the Australoid physical type and are believed to be fairly direct descendants of the Lácida.[8]

Small numbers of Indians belonging to the Archaic White stock within the Australoid racial division apparently still survive[9] among the decimated and amalgamated Western Marginal tribes, now confined to the remote headwaters of the Amazon near the Brazilian–Peruvian border. It is not unlikely that this group has been the basis for the tales of 'white Indians' coming from the Amazon since the sixteenth century when they roamed in fairly large bands, raiding along the principal rivers, as compared to their more recent appearance only as individuals who have strayed from their tribe.[10] Although a few surviving Australoids or near-Australoids are still found in the more isolated corners of Brazil, the vast majority of the aborigines are, and were in pre-Columbian times, mixtures to varying degrees of this race with later waves of brachycephalic Mongoloids, the Paleo-American tribes being physically closer to the earlier occupants and the Tropical Forest tribes more obviously Mongoloid.

The Tropical Forest tribes—the Tupí, Arawak, and Carib in particular—had by the time of the European arrival migrated over extraordinary distances from their culture hearth, which was probably situated between the Rio Negro and the Lower Amazon in the south and the Caribbean coast and the Lower Orinoco in the north. Expanding outward at the expense of the Paleo-Americans, who were forced further and further back into refuge areas, their canoe-based riparian civilization spread mainly into areas accessible to, and usable in conjunction with, riverine or coastal water routes, ultimately to encompass a realm that extended from easternmost Brazil (35° W) to the Gulf of Honduras (90° W), and from southern Florida (26° N) to La Plata Estuary (34° S),[11] where they established the southernmost extension of agriculture on the east coast of South America. Within what became Brazil, they took virtual possession of the Amazon and its major tributaries below the fall-line, and of the Atlantic coastal plain. Thence exclaves and fingers of occupance reached into the interior along the better riverine lands, including those of the São Francisco, the Paraíba do Sul, and the Jacuí, and spread across the subtropical broadleaf forest regions of southern Brazil to the Paraguay River, whence they raided as far west as the borders of the Inca Empire.

NOMADIC & SEMI-NOMADIC TRIBES

In contrast to the relative cultural, as well as racial and linguistic, homogeneity of Brazil's Tropical Forest Indians, the Paleo-American tribes within that country's present boundaries exhibited great variety, which was, no doubt, furthered by their longer history of occupance of a much wider range of environments. Some hunters and gatherers were scarcely above the level of the Lagoa Santa or Archaic Sambaquí cultures; other Paleo-Americans were nearly sedentary agriculturalists and fishermen with not a few techniques borrowed from the Tropical Forest tribes.[12]

The Paleo-Americans had fewer material goods than the Tropical Forest Indians, their ceramics were of inferior quality, with some groups making none at all, and they rarely used the otherwise ubiquitous hammock. Hunting was generally of much greater importance than fishing to the Paleo-American tribes, and some did not fish at all. The implements used in either pursuit tended to be less well developed than among the Tropical Forest tribes, even if the skills were not; neither blowguns nor fishhooks were known to the majority, and the ability to make and use canoes was very much restricted.

For the most part, gathering was more important to the Paleo-Americans than was agriculture. It included all manner of small animals, lizards, toads, worms, grubs, and shellfish, as well as honey, wild vegetables, and the fruits from a variety of palms. These last were important dietary staples, gathered during the dry season to make it a time of plenty, and conflicts over territorial rights were frequently over the possession of palm groves. Among the agricultural Paleo-Americans, yams and sweet potatoes tended to be more important than cassava. Sweet cassava was preferred to the bitter which, when eaten at all, was freed of its poison by means of simpler equipment than that used by the Tropical Forest tribes for whom it was the staple food.

Despite the importance of hunting and gathering to most Paleo-American tribes, by the time of the European conquest those who did not practice at least a rudimentary agriculture were not very important numerically and no longer occupied any very large portions of the present Brazilian territory. They were, however, among the most militant and intransigent of the aborigines, feared by both Indians and whites, and achieving posthumous legendary stature like their counterparts of the Argentine *pampas* or the North American plains.

Among the most warlike were the Tremembé, who maintained their hold over a large stretch of the northern coast despite its location in proximity to the Tupí heartland and athwart the latter's main axis of southward penetration. The Tremembé were nomads who wandered about in small bands, attacking their enemies from ambush whenever the opportunity presented itself. They were armed with spears tipped with sharks' teeth and with crescent-shaped stone 'anchor axes', the latter being found archaeologically along much of the Brazilian coast and indicating a far wider early range for the Tremembé. These axes were made without stopping during a crescent moon and were left ceremonially with the corpses of their victims. One such victim was a Portuguese seaman after whose murder the Tremembé were virtually wiped out by a punitive expedition mounted in 1674.

Midway along the windward coast, where the Serra do Mar is at its widest and most inaccessible, there lived a large number of Indian groups at various technological levels. Their arrangement, with hunters and gatherers at the core and agricultural tribes on the periphery, suggests a sequence of pressures from successively higher cultures. The most rugged and inaccessible part of these mountains was the domain of eastern Brazil's technologically most backward Indians, the Botocudo, or Aimoré. They were also the most feared by generations of Europeans, and Portuguese dictionaries today still include *botocudismo* as a synonym for savagery and barbarity. The end result of their fighting skills and belligerance, combined with occasional cannibalism, was that the Botocudo had the dubious distinction of being the only group to whom colonial laws protecting the Indians did not apply; and colonists shot them on sight and hunted them down at every opportunity (regrettably, many other Indians were also summarily exterminated under the guise of being the dreaded Botocudo, thereby avoiding possible chastisement by government agents).

The military prowess of the Botocudo undoubtedly derived from their spatial situation. They inhabited an area where game was not plentiful, so in order to survive they had developed hunting techniques based on stealth and including great skill at tracking. Scarce resources also caused each band to defend its own territory tenaciously and to seek out new sources of supply at the expense of others, leading to depradations and to the endless feuds for which the Botocudo were famous.

In the sixteenth century the Botocudo pillaged and laid waste towns along the Bahia coast, killing both Portuguese and Tupinaqui inhabitants. Although finally driven back into the mountains they continued to harass the coastal settlements throughout the seventeenth century. Fragmentation and feuding ultimately hastened the Botocudo's defeat when those who settled near the whites during the nineteenth century and served them as labourers, joined the fight against their untamed fellow tribesmen.

Even at the start of the Brazilian republic in 1889, some 5,000 Botocudos still remained and their unconquered territory in the Serra dos Aimorés was left unassigned when the state boundaries were drawn up. This resulted in endless litigation between Espírito Santo and Minas Gerais that has been resolved only during the last decade. After holding up settlement of the rich coffee lands north of the Rio Doce until well into this century, the remaining Botocudo have adopted agriculture from the whites, and their villages can be seen today in clearings along the forested banks of that river.

The many, but less numerous, minor tribes surrounding the Botocudo did not fare so well, having already been reduced to isolated and constantly shifting bands before the arrival of the Europeans. Some, like the Patashó, were hunters and gatherers to whom even fishing was unknown; most practised a rudimentary, at times only incipient, agriculture; and one group, the Camacan, were effective farmers with both inland and coastal settlements. Stronger and more cohesive than the others, they remained hostile to, and independent of, the Portuguese until 1806, when they were defeated and settled in government *aldeias*, or villages, there to be mistreated and exploited by white officials.

Occupying a more southerly position, in the Paraíba do Sul

drainage basin, about 4,000 Purí Indians and some smaller, related tribes were in many respects similar to the Botocudo: belligerent, nomadic, skilled at tracking and hunting, and in this case famous for the calls which they used to lure birds within range, to be caught by a noose attached to a long pole. They used bows and arrows or spears to do a certain amount of fishing, but this was unimportant and they had no canoes. In contrast, among their neighbours, the Goitacá, who occupied the coastal plain between the mouth of the Paraíba and the lagoons to the south (the Campos dos Goitacazes), spearing sharks near shore was almost as important as hunting, perhaps because their technique was to run game down by tracking it across the savanna until it was exhausted. Although it was secondary to gathering, the Goitacá practised some agriculture, growing tubers and maize but no cassava.

It took the Portuguese, at times assisted by Tupinamba warriors, from 1553 to 1630 to subdue the warlike Goitacá and complete their occupation of the Campos dos Goitacazes. However, from their jungle fastness in the Serra do Mar the Purí and affiliated tribes continuously raided the coastal settlements of the agricultural Tupí as well as the European sugar plantations, being especially fond of the cane they seized as a substitute for their favourite delicacy, wild honey. The Purí managed to delay the establishment of communications along the Lower Paraíba above the fall-line until the 1790s, and were not driven out of some of their territory until the middle of the nineteenth century.[13]

In the south of Brazil, the greater proportion of the Paleo-American Indians belonged to the Caingan linguistic family[14] who, at the time of the conquest, were a diverse and wide-ranging group whose territory extended from the Uruguayan *pampa* to the Campos de Piratininga, where the city of São Paulo now stands, and westward to the Pantanal. The range of the Caingan must have been even greater before they were pushed back by the Tupí-Guaraní; in fact, they are believed to have contributed the major element to the Southern Phase of the Sambaquí Culture. A relic of this still survived at the time of the first European occupance of the Santos–São Vicente area, in the seasonal movements of the Goianá tribe who in winter migrated from the Campos de Piratininga to shellfish-gathering grounds on the coast. In the 1530s their trails across the escarpment gave the first whites to settle in the interior access to the plateau.

The Caingan heartland was in the Araucaria forest region and the nut from that tree was their dietary staple from April to June. They climbed the trees to knock down the nuts by means of nooses around their feet and backs, a technique used also for robbing birds' nests and bee hives. The pith of the pindó palm (*Cocos romanzoffiana*) had also been a basic food, but after contact with the Guaraní it was replaced by cassava flour among some of the tribes. The Caingan collected wild tubers and numerous fruits, and the tambú beetle and its larvae, found in decayed palm and bamboo trunks, were prized delicacies. They ate snakes and lizards, and hunted the abundant tapir and peccary communally. With a few exceptions, fishing played a minor role and in some tribes was not done at all. In any case, the catch was obtained by primitive means, either by hand or with bows and arrows or, rarely, two-pronged spears. They had no canoes and crossed rivers by cutting down trees which they braced with poles stuck into the stream bed.

Agriculture, although widely practised among the Caingan, was at a low technical level. Their maize, pumpkin and bean crops were eaten as they matured, with no storage against the lean months. And their means of clearing the land was rudimentary in the extreme, being confined to breaking off brush, small trees, or bamboo by hand or with cudgels prior to burning. The Caingan were, therefore, restricted to cultivating meadowlands and savannas where they were not confronted with the problem of felling large trees. The Goianá, for instance, confined their farming to the open country of the Campos de Piratininga, which was not attractive to the more powerful, forest-dwelling Tupinikin who surrounded them. The last of the Caingan to occupy any extensive area of open land were those of the Campos de Guarapuava, in the middle reaches of the Iguaçu River on the western rim of the diabase plateau in southern Paraná. They were finally driven out by white settlers early in the nineteenth century and, although an estimated 2,000 Caingan were still living in Paraná at the beginning of the present century, only a handful now survive to lurk in the depths of the most remote forests.

Well adapted to a different type of grassland—the seasonally flooded Pantanal—the Guató, unlike most of the Paleo-Americans, were well versed in the use of canoes. With these they wandered continuously, even living in them during times of flood. Although their techniques for fishing were no more highly developed than among the other Paleo-American tribes, it was an important part of their livelihood, to which they added the hunting of caimans and jaguars from canoes when these were in the water.

The Guató also gathered nuts, fruits and aquatic plants, including wild rice (*Oryza*, sp.), which they harvested in large quantities during flood periods. They were particularly dependent upon the nut of the acurí palm (*Attalea*, sp.) which grew on the low mounds and levees above the marshes. Such was the importance of this palm that artificial mounds up to about two feet in height were built along the margins of the Pantanal in order to extend its growing areas above flood levels.[15] Today, the 50-odd Guató Indians who have survived continue to harvest and to grow the acurí, cracking the nuts on a flat rock with stone hammers as in the past; they also plant bananas and minor crops of maize, cassava and fruits, which they regard as delicacies rather than staples, on their artificial mounds in the Pantanal.

Among the many 'wild and warlike' Indians[16] who inhabited the Chaco and, in Brazil, the headwaters of the Paraguay River, the Bororó were among the most deadly. Although they were centred on the plateau, between the Pantanal and the Rio das Garças in Goiás where they may still be found today, their hunting and raiding expeditions took them westward into what is now Bolivia and as far east as the Minas Triangle. From the latter area they were, during the eighteenth century, enlisted by the Portuguese as a defensive force against the depradations of the Cayapó.

As might be expected, Bororó hunting practices were highly developed, often being communal affairs under the command of a medicine man. The task of the women was to gather seeds, nuts and roots, which they unearthed with digging sticks. Before contact with the Europeans, the Bororó grew cotton, gourds for containers and, unlike most Paleo-American tribes, tobacco, as well as some minor food crops, but this incipient agriculture was ephemeral in its relationship to the livelihood they gained from hunting and gathering.

The Nambiquara, who today continue to occupy the outermost margins of the Central Plateau in the northwest, were rudimentary farmers. They cultivated several kinds of primitive maize, beans, ground-nuts, cotton and gourds, as well as a variety of tobacco with very small leaves. They also planted cassava, both bitter and sweet, presumably introduced from the surrounding Tropical Forest tribes. But despite this considerable variety of crops, they were essentially nomadic bush dwellers whose overall pattern of living revolved around seasonal occupations.

The Nambiquara routine probably differed little in pre-Columbian times from that described by Lévi-Strauss in the 1930s;[17] during the rainy season, from October to March, they occupied make-shift villages of huts made of palm branches and leaves, tending their gardens in burned-over gallery forest-clearings; during the remainder of the year they roved across the savanna in small bands. From brief camps, the women went off in search of small animals, rodents, snakes, lizards, grasshoppers, spiders and grubs, and to gather roots, seeds, fruits and wild honey. Meanwhile, the men would set off on hunting expeditions armed with palm-wood bows and arrows of various designs: long ones without feathers for fish; shorter ones with blunted points for birds; and curare-tipped ones with broad, spear-shaped bamboo tips (to induce haemorrhaging and thereby render the poison more effective) for large game such as the tapir or the jaguar.

The preserve of the Nambiquara was not penetrated by Europeans until 1907, during the laying of a telegraph line between Cuiabá and the northwestern frontier posts, which until then had been accessible only by means of a lengthy journey up the Amazon River. Ironically it was a half-Indian, General Rondon, later the founder of the Indian Protection Service, who explored this territory over the following eight years and opened it up to whites. The contacts which followed, reduced the number of Nambiquara from an estimated 10,000 to only about 1,000 today.

To the east, where the Araguaia River cuts deeply into the Central Plateau, the Carajá Indians have a life style that is in many respects similar to that of the Nambiquara. But here, around Bananal Island, the gardening and gathering seasons are reversed, as the rainy period from December to March inclusive is also the river's high-water period, when they must move to higher ground. There they lead the typical gathering and hunting life, their practice of running down game having given them a reputation for physical prowess among the inhabitants of Goiás. During the dry, or low water, season they live along the beaches of the Araguaia in small villages consisting of insubstantial shelters of woven palm fronds and containing from a dozen to perhaps two hundred inhabitants, planting their crops and fishing.

Although in most respects the Carajá are typically Paleo-American in their technology and way of life, like the Guató they learned to make and use canoes—perhaps from the neighbouring Tupí Canoeiro, or 'Canoe People'—in order to exploit fully the rivers, streams and lagoons around Bananal Island. They used poison for their fishing, and spears and lassos for catching fresh water porpoise and pirarucu (*Arapaima gigas*), the largest of all fresh water fish. A further note on the adaptability of the Carajá is that they were the only major Paleo-American group to adopt the hammock from the Tropical Forest Indians, although they used it as a ground mat.

Although not unwarlike in defending their territory against other tribes, the Carajá were relatively docile during their first few centuries of desultory contact with white *bandeirantes* and prospectors. As a result, some 30,000 still survived within the traditional tribal boundaries as late as 1913. Since then, however, their tractability has stood them in little better stead than did the intransigence of other groups; although it perhaps postponed the inevitable, their number has since declined to but three or four thousand.[18] Their adaptability led them, when confronted with intensified contact with the whites, to seek employment as labourers during the construction of the telegraph line to Mato Grosso, as muleteers and ox-cart drivers, and as stevedores, deck hands and stokers on the steamships that, before the westward expansion of the railway, navigated the Araguaia. While some have, presumably, been assimilated into the Brazilian ethnic mix, decimation by disease has inevitably been the price the Carajá have had to pay for association with the white man. Today they act as guides and canoemen for fishing parties that come to Bananal Island, an increasingly frequented vacation spot thanks to the growth of Brasília not far away, while their clay figurines and feather handicrafts are on display in tourist shops, hotel lobbies and airports throughout the country.

THE GÊ

Of the many different Indians who inhabited Central Brazil at the time of the Conquest—one author lists 42 distinct 'tribes, groups, and hordes' in Mato Grosso, 12 in Goiás, and 172 in Minas Gerais[19]—by far the largest number, second only to the Tupí, comprised the Gê linguistic family. They included such diverse tribes as the Cayapó, the Xavante and the Timbira, extending over a vast area which embraced most of the Central Plateau and portions of the equatorial forests to the north and of the semi-arid region to the northeast.

Although the various Gê differed widely in their patterns of land occupance, there was unity not only in language, but also in their religious beliefs and their social organization and practices, which, curiously, are said to have corresponded in many respects with those of the forest and prairie tribes of North America.[20] They were, for the most part, organized as clans rather than tribes, with settlements based on kinship. Feuds were common, generally as a result of disagreements over territorial rights; but, as in North America, wider groups would occasionally unite against a common enemy, particularly if he were European.

Notable exceptions to this pattern were the Xavante, who were organized along well-disciplined, quasi-military lines. They manned their defences effectively well into the modern age, even shooting arrows into aeroplanes that passed over their territory, whereas the normal reaction of the aborigine is to scatter in fright. Despite some recent and tentative co-operation with the National Indian Foundation (successor to the Indian Protection Service), the land of the Xavante along the Rio das Mortes (River of Death) and in the Serra do Roncador still retains a special aura of danger and impenetrability to white and Indian alike.

The internecine wars of the Gê usually concerned babassú (*Orbignia*, sp.) and buriti (*Mauritia vinifera*) palm groves, the nuts from which constituted a major component of their diet, especially during the dry season. At this time of year, too, wild fruits and vegetables, gathered by women, were particularly plentiful; they also sought out the usual array of small fauna, including armadillos, which were dug from their burrows. The men were of course skilled hunters; with powerful bows that were up to three metres long they shot deer and other game from hides in trees or after it was flushed out by communal drives using beaters and grass fires, and were particularly adept at stalking the skittish and fast-moving rheas under the cover of tall grasses.

The palm groves that served as foci for the wanderings of the Gê were located as galleries in the valley bottoms, where, during the rainy season, crops were also planted. Although the character and intensity of their farming practices varied considerably, sweet potatoes and yams were generally the most important crops; they also grew maize, sweet cassava, and a creeper that was unknown to the Tropical Forest Indians, a species of *Cissius* the starchy tendrils of which were baked. Bitter cassava was grown by the Northern Cayapó, the Xerente, who inhabited the east bank of the Araguaia between the Xavante and the Carajá, and by the Timbira. The latter's large fields of this crop, their nearly sedentary habits, and their sizeable villages of 500 to 1,500 inhabitants, combined to make the Timbira the most advanced of all the Paleo-American tribes.

The location of these three tribes—Timbira, Xerente, and Northern Cayapó—along the northern tier of Gê territory is a clear indication that the knowledge of bitter cassava cultivation and, more to the point, the extraction of its poisonous juices, could have come only by diffusion from the Tropical Forest tribes. This despite the fact that their preparation process, by twisting in a band of buriti bast, was simpler than that used by the neighbouring Tupí. It is interesting to note, however, how strong a barrier to diffusion must have existed between the Tupí and the Gê, as the latter had no pottery to speak of (weaving waterproof baskets instead) and no hammocks. Nor did they use canoes or fishhooks, despite the fact that stream fishing was important to all the Gê except the technologically backward Southern Cayapó and the agricultural Timbira.[21]

THE SEDENTARY TRIBES

The knowledge of hammock making, advanced pottery techniques and the use of canoes[22] and fishhooks are among the traits that at a glance distinguished the Tropical Forest tribes' way of life from that of most of the Paleo-American ones. Differences in agricultural practices between the two, however, were of even more fundamental import in that they enabled the former to attain a more intensive use of their environment, thereby to achieve a more advanced social organization, higher population densities, greater concentrations of individuals in a given area and, ultimately, the capacity—even the necessity —to expand, usually at the expense of the Paleo-Americans but also at that of less advanced branches of their own ethnic group.

The basis for this high intensity of land occupance on the part of the Tropical Forest Indians was their dependence upon the root of the bitter, or poisonous, variety of cassava for basic nourishment. It not only exceeds all other crops in yield per unit area in tropical conditions[23] but it also has the unique property of not deteriorating as long as it is left in the ground unharvested, a capacity for self-storage that is an incalculable advantage in an environment where harvested crops are soon destroyed by bacterial, insect and animal agents.

On the other hand, in contrast to the more heterogeneous but well-balanced food supply of the Paleo-American groups, this dietary emphasis on the starchy cassava root with only minor recourse to such protein-rich crops as ground nuts and beans, made it essential that the Tropical Forest tribes obtain the necessary proteins and fats in the form of animal products. Since game was relatively scarce in the forested lands they inhabited, even though to obtain it they had developed the extremely effective blowgun and poisoned dart (which were more accurate and had a longer range than the ball and musket of their early conquerors), it was not unnatural that they should have turned to fishing as their principal source of protein, evolving for this a complex technology that included hooks, harpoons, nets, traps and weirs as well as drugs. This in turn made possible the large and permanent villages which distinguished their occupance patterns from those of the nomadic and semi-nomadic tribes. Although there were, of course, some differences among the Tropical Forest tribes in their emphasis on, and degree of perfection of, the various elements in their means of obtaining a livelihood, their nearly exclusive concentration on cultivable forest lands adjoining riverine or coastal fishing grounds demonstrates their basic technological homogeneity.

The principal differences within the Tropical Forest culture, setting one tribe apart from the other, were sociological and religious. The details of these practices need not concern us here even though they were, with territorial disputes, instrumental in maintaining antagonisms between, and fragmentation of, the many tribes and sub-tribes, and no doubt contributed to their failure to evolve a coherent 'civilization' along the lines of those in Andean and Middle America. Nevertheless, even though the required spatial and institutional cohesiveness was lacking among the Tropical Forest Indians, many of the basic elements of an incipient civilization were there, including artistic specialization (as among the potters of Santarém and Marajó Island), trade (for instance, in blowguns and curare), sedentary farming in an essentially permanent territory, and settlements of the proportions of small towns. These last frequently contained one or two thousand inhabitants, while some had over three thousand; and it is of interest to note that in 1808, the year the Portuguese Court fled to Rio de Janeiro, only ten European towns in all of Brazil had populations that exceeded two thousand, presumably because the rest had essentially to be supplied by locally produced foodstuffs using crops and agricultural practices which were basically those of the Tropical Forest Indians.[24]

An indication as to how the Tropical Forest tribes could, in pre-Columbian times, have attained such settlement densities in specific locales—in contrast to the crude population densities for overall habitat regions given above—may be gained by analogy from an examination of roughly comparable intensities of present-day aboriginal occupance of the environment. In a study of the Kuikuru tribe who practised a slash-and-burn, or land rotation, system of farming dominated by cassava, on quite unexceptional lands along the Upper Xingú, Carneiro was able to determine per capita acreage requirements for permanent settlement in relation to crop productivity levels using the formula

$$P = \frac{\dfrac{T}{R + Y}\, Y}{A}$$

where P is the population of the community, T is the total area of arable land (in acres) within practicable walking distance of the village, R is the number of years an abandoned plot must lie fallow before it can be recultivated, Y is the number of years a plot can be cultivated before it has to be abandoned, and A is the area of cultivated land (in acres) required to provide the average individual with the amount of food that he ordinarily derives from cultivated plants per year.[25]

Substituting data pertaining to the Kuikuru, but verified against information on the neighbouring Waura, who were known to have lived in the same place for a century or more, Carneiro obtained the following values for his equation:

$$P = \frac{\dfrac{13,350}{(25 + 3)}\, 3}{0 \cdot 7}.$$

That is, seven-tenths of an acre of cassava was required, on the average, to support one tribesman[26] cultivating a given piece of land for three years with a fallow of 25 years. The Kuikuru tribal territory of 13,350 acres would therefore be able to support some 2,000 people $(P = 2,041)$ on a permanent basis,[27] indicating that figures of that order for permanent pre-Columbian aboriginal settlements occupying a sufficient area of cultivable land such as that favoured by the Tropical Forest tribes, would not be in the least unusual. In fact, Carneiro states categorically that where 'the ethnographic or archaeological record reveals periodic relocations of villages of 500 persons or less, causes other than soil depletion should be assumed to have been responsible'.[28]

CONQUEST

It was, then, in such areas of relatively high population density, settlement concentration and intensity of land use along the Brazilian coast and Lower Amazon that European explorers, traders, and colonists first established themselves. Outright conquest such as the Spaniards carried out against the Aztec and Inca Empires did not, however, take place even though later slave-hunting expeditions into the interior assumed a military air. Treaties were not uncommon through which the white man and the Tupí united against marauding Paleo-Americans, Europeans assisted friendly tribes against traditionally hostile ones, and Portuguese, French, and other whites sought reinforcements through native allies against one another's encroachments.

But conflicts did arise between the races over lands once conquered by the Tropical Forest Indians, which were coveted by the Europeans because of their accessibility and their capacity for yielding tropical products. The Tupí, who occupied the best of these, bore the brunt of the first Portuguese impact and, as a result, disappeared from the colonial scene at an early date. They were not heroically vanquished like the Botocudo or Southern Cayapó, nor were they set upon and decimated like the Tremembé and the Timbira. Rather, the majority fell victim to the white man's ways and diseases in the same fashion as the Nambiquara and the Carajá have done in the present, supposedly enlightened, century.[29]

Before his demise, however, the Tupí who inhabited the coastal and riverine plains from Santos to Santarém delivered the forest products that would be sent to Europe; he provided his new master with a *lingua franca* which continued in use in many areas until the last century; he offered the isolated trader a home in his village; he taught the colonist about native crops and how these should be grown in this strange environment; he showed the new arrival the practicality of the hammock, which is still used throughout many regions of Brazil; he provided the lonely white man with women, whose blood continues to flow in the veins of one-third of all Brazilians. As a result, although only fifty to one hundred thousand

Indians survive in the country today,[30] the influence of their race on Brazilian genes, habits, language and culture lives on within the modern nation.

REFERENCES

1. Denevan, W. M. Personal communication, July 1970.

2. Denevan, W. M. 'The Aboriginal Population of Western Amazonia in Relation to Habitat and Subsistence', paper presented at the XXXVII Congreso Internacional de Americanistas, Mar del Plata, Argentina, 1966, 47 pp., mimeo.

3. This two-fold division of Brazil's Indians is used both in the Introduction to the *Handbook of South American Indians*, Steward, Julian H., Ed., Cooper Square Publishers Inc., New York, 1963, where original credit is given (Vol. 1, p. 11) to 'Cooper's 1940 and 1941 Fourfold Culture Divisions of South American Indians', and in Cestmír Loukotka's 'Ethno-Linguistic Distribution of South American Indians', *Annals of the A.A.G.*, Vol. 57, No. 2, June 1967, Map Supplement No. 8. It should be noted that the authors' suggestion that the Paleo-Americans represent an earlier population that was pushed out of the main Amazon by the Tropical Forest tribes is not shared by Lathrap, who says, 'There is at the present time little to suggest that the region was previously occupied by peoples other than these Tropical Forest cultures'. Lathrap, Donald W., *The Upper Amazon*, Thames and Hudson, 1970, p. 45.

4. Bates, Henry Walter, *The Naturalist on the River Amazons*, University of California Press, Berkeley, 1962, p. 45 (paper-bound issue, 465 pp., reprinted from the 2nd edition, John Murray, London, 1864).

5. Carbon-14 dates for the lower Minas Gerais (Lagoa Santa) strata provide the date 9,720 B.P. ± 128, as given by Haynes, C. Vance Jr., 'Carbon-14 Dates and Early Man in the New World' in *Pleistocene Extinctions*, Martin, P. S. and Wright, H. E. Jr., Eds., Yale University Press, New Haven, 1967, pp. 271 & 275. See J. B. d'Avila's 'Anthropometric' chapter in Steward, *op. cit.*, Vol. 6, p. 73, for a discussion of the contemporaneity and similarity of the Minas Gerais and São Paulo Australoids.

6. For a discussion of the shell mound cultures which ranged from the Amazon Estuary to the Lagoa dos Patos in present-day Rio Grande do Sul, see 'The Indians of Eastern Brazil', Part 3 (Vol. 1, pp. 401–408), of Steward, *op. cit.*, which includes a map of the 'Distribution of the Four Sambaquí Culture Phases' (p. 405). Detailed original studies of later shell mound phases in Paraná and Santa Catarina can be found in Vols. 4, 5, 6 and 8 of *Arquivos de Biologia e Tecnologia*, 1949–53, published by the Instituto de Biologia e Pesquisas Tecnológicas of the State of Paraná under the senior authorship of Guilherme Tiburtius and J. J. Bigarella.

7. *Brazilian Bulletin*, December 1969, Brazilian Government Trade Bureau, Brazilian Consulate General in New York, p. 4.

8. d'Avila, *op. cit.*, p. 73. For an overview of the physical range in types

between and within the sub-races of Australoids of Brazil and Australia, and for an interesting, if perhaps somewhat coincidental, persistence of very similar ways of life in approximately analogous environments, compare the Nambiquara of Plates 19–46 in Lévi-Strauss, Claude, *Tristes Tropiques* (John Russell translation), Hutchinson & Co., London, 1961, with photographs accompanying Chapter 6, 'The Australian Aborigines', in *Vanishing Peoples of the Earth*, National Geographic Society, Washington, D.C., 1968, pp. 114–131. A general discussion of racial characteristics and distributions as they relate to our area can be found in Cole, Sonia, *Races of Man*, British Museum (Natural History), London, 1965, pp. 9, 49 and 103, while a popularized summary appears in the *Brazilian Bulletin* of April 1970, p. 8.

9. Compare, for instance, the photograph of a chief of the Isconahua Indians, Fig. 3 on p. 90 of Whiton, Louis C., Greene, H. Bruce, and Momsen, R. P. Jr., 'The Isconahua of the Remo', *Journal de la Société des Américanistes*, Vol. LIII, Musée de l'Homme, Paris, 1964, with that of an Ainu chieftain on p. 268 of Life's *The Epic of Man*, Time Inc., New York, 1961. There are some, however, who believe that all such physical types in the area result from interbreeding with whites who have, it is true, been responsible for many of the reports of so-called 'white' Indian tribes.

10. See, for instance, Morrison, H. Stuart, 'White Indians', series of articles in the *Brazil Herald* (Rio de Janeiro), various dates in March 1953, or Fernando Pinto and Vieira de Queiroz, 'Indios Brancos: Uma Lenda na Selva', *O Cruzeiro*, September 1, 1971, pp. 4–18.

11. Loukotka, *op. cit.*

12. For sources of more detailed information on specific tribes or areas both within and outside the Amazon Basin, the reader is advised to refer to the nearly 500 ethnographic references contained in the massive work of the Instituto Nacional de Pesquisas da Amazônia, *Amazônia Bibliografia 1614–1962*, Instituto Brasileiro de Bibliografia e Documentação, Rio de Janeiro, 1963, 842 pp.; a number of ethnographic studies of specific tribes or on facets of Indian life have also been published as monographs since 1957 in the *Anthropology Series* of the I.N.P.A.

13. For details of European penetration of this region see Momsen, R. P. Jr., *Routes over the Serra do Mar*, *op. cit.*, Chapter I.

14. There is some confusion among different writers as to tribal names within the Caingan and with respect to the details of their means of obtaining a livelihood. The Goianá have, for instance, been described as sedentary agriculturalists in one source and as migratory hunters in the next; and the Aweikona of Santa Catarina (also known as Botocudos because of the *botoques*, or large cylindrical plugs they wore in their lower lips and ear lobes) were said to have practised agriculture at one time, although they later subsisted entirely by hunting and gathering; see Steward, *op. cit.*, Vol. 1, pp. 449–450.

15. This incipient form of cultivation may have some bearing on the origins of the once widespread practice of mound-building, presumably usually in association with farming, on the flooded savannas of the interior of South America. For a discussion of these and related earthworks see Denevan, W. M., *The Aboriginal Cultural Geography of the Llanos de*

Mojos of Bolivia, University of California Press, Ibero-Americana No. 48, Berkeley, 1966.

16. Steward, *op. cit.*, Vol. 1, p. 197.

17. Lévi-Strauss, *op. cit.*, pp. 265–266.

18. A description of the conditions and customs of the Carajá before most twentieth-century changes occurred will be found in MacIntyre, Archie, *Down the Araguaya: travels in the heart of Brazil*, Religious Tract Society, London, 1924 (?), while a somewhat later study is that of Brito Machado, O. X. de, *Os Carajás*, Conselho Nacional de Proteção aos Indios, Publication No. 104, Rio de Janeiro, 1947.

19. Artiaga, Zoroastro. *Dos Indios do Brasil Central*, Departmento Estadual de Cultura do Estado, Goiânia, 1940s (?).

20. Lévi-Strauss, *op. cit.*, p. 239; *Brazilian Bulletin*, May 1970, p. 8.

21. It is instructive to contemplate the eventual fate of these two tribes which were located nearly 1,000 miles apart and whose way of life differed so markedly. The Southern Cayapó, who unremittingly attacked colonists in southern Goiás and the Minas Triangle, were driven out in the 1780s by a combined force of provincial and Federal troops, bandeirantes, and Bororos. Leaving behind them a trail of carnage, they finally took refuge in the headwaters of the Xingú where the last 30 or 40 survivors were contacted in 1910, the tribe now being extinct. The Timbira survived relatively undisturbed until the first quarter of the nineteenth century, when slave-hunting expeditions fell upon them under the pretext that they were Botocudos. The survivors, numbering only a few hundred, fled their savanna habitat to take refuge in the forests to the west, where about 150 of their descendants remain today. For a detailed example of the process of attrition as it has affected another Indian group, the Western Marginals, not located in a direct line of colonization or conquest, see Momsen, R. P., Jr., 'The Isconahua Indians', *Revista Geográfica*, Vol. 32, No. 60, 1964, pp. 59–81, and especially the maps on pp. 64 & 65.

22. Although references to the canoe and its place in the aboriginal cultures of Brazil abound, only passing, if any, notice is usually taken of the role of the balsa raft, or *jangada*, in the Tupí culture whence it derives. This is in contrast to the detailed early descriptions and heated recent discussions of its Pacific counterpart (as in Thor Heyerdahl's *Sea Routes to Polynesia*, George Allen and Unwin Ltd., London, 1968, and his several earlier works), and despite the fact that this craft still constitutes one of the basic elements in any characterization of the Brazilian Northeast where the *jangadeiro* is, 'Like the gaucho of the southern plains, the most interesting and almost legendary human type who . . . daily writes his page of heroism noted only by the waters of the ocean', Santos, L. Bezerra dos, 'Jangadeiros', in *Tipos e Aspectos do Brasil*, Conselho Nacional de Geografia, I.B.G.E., Rio de Janeiro, 1949, p. 83). These fishing craft or their modern, planked derivatives are still frequently encountered in the shipping lanes off the Brazilian coast, sometimes several hundred kilometres from shore.

23. Cole, J. P., in *Latin America, an Economic and Social Geography*, Butterworths, London, 1965, p. 139, shows that in Brazil (1960) 1·3 million hectares yielded 17·6 million tons of cassava whereas it took 6·7 million

hectares to produce 8·7 million tons of maize. From this, it can be calculated that the yields of cassava and maize in Brazil today are, respectively, about 13 and 1·3 tons per hectare, or ten times higher for the former. This difference was probably even greater in pre-Columbian times as the methods of cultivation and the maize varieties grown have been considerably improved, but have remained essentially unchanged for cassava.

24. For a summary of the relationship between Brazilian farming practices and those of the Indian, see, for instance, Smith, T. Lynn, *Brazil, People and Institutions*, Louisiana State University Press, Baton Rouge, 1963, pp. 366–372.

25. Carneiro, Robert L. 'Slash-and-Burn Agriculture: A closer look at its implications for settlement patterns', *Selected Papers of the Fifth International Congress of Anthropological and Ethnological Sciences*, University of Pennsylvania Press, Philadelphia, 1956, p. 230.

26. This is not an unusually low figure, as Fauterau, Eric de, in *Etudes d'Ecologie Humaine dans l'Aire Amazonienne*, Fontenay—Le Compte, Vendée, 1952, p. 3, gives one-fifth of an acre as needed per head of population to support the Indians of French Guiana, and calculations from a map in Momsen, 'The Isconahua Indians', *op. cit.*, facing p. 72, indicate that the Shipibo of the Ucayali River require only about one-half acre for their subsistence crops, only a relatively small proportion of which is cassava. However, the latter inhabit fertile, seasonally flooded *várzea* land, which is permanently cropped, in which respect they probably closely approximate the farming conditions which prevailed in the most densely populated areas in pre-Columbian times.

27. Carneiro, *op. cit.*, p. 232.

28. *Ibid.*, p. 233.

29. An infinitely greater number of tribal Indians have died in Brazil from accelerated 'natural' causes during the present century than from atrocities perpetrated against certain isolated groups on the periphery of settlement, where the law is distant and its minions are easily corrupted by powerful landlords or intimidated by the hardened fugitives from justice who, between them, often control vast stretches of the outlying wilderness. It is, however, only the latter, more spectacular situation which has recently received widespread, indignant and often exaggerated coverage in the world press (as, for instance, abstracted in 'Brazil's Dead Indians: the killing of an Unwanted Race', *Atlas*, Vol. 19, No. 1, January 1970, the World Press Company, New York, pp. 22–29). In fact, the situation is more one of 'an underground war without quarter and with violence and excesses on both sides' (from a report from Rio de Janeiro by Joseph Novitski to the *Calgary Herald*, Canada, June 30, 1970, p. 18). A report by a group of ethnologists appointed by the International Red Cross who visited Brazil in 1970 states that 'nothing has been found to corroborate rumours about massacres, or even individual acts of cruelty against Indians in Brazil'. It does, however, recommend that the government pay more attention to protection of the Indians against 'disease, malnutrition, and adverse results of their contacts with civilization' (*Brazil Herald*, February 26, 1971). A useful survey of the current situation among Brazil's tribal Indians and

the outlook for their future will be found in Brooks, Edwin, 'Twilight of Brazilian Tribes', *The Geographical Magazine*, January 1973, pp. 304–310, with map of the tribes' locations.

30. A sociological statement on the present situation of the Indian *vis-à-vis* the white in Brazil may be found in Oliveira, Roberto Cardoso de, *O Indio e o Mundo dos Brancos*, Difusão Européia do Livro, São Paulo, 1964; a useful summary of the course of white expansion in the Amazon and the legalistic framework within which it took place is Reis, A. C. Ferreira, *Os Indios da Amazônia*, Instituto Nacional de Pesquisas da Amazônia, Publicações Avulsas No. 3, Manaus, 1963 (16 pp., mimeographed); and a statement of current official policy towards the Indian appears in the *Brazilian Bulletin* for December 1969, p. 7.

CHAPTER 3

Evolution of the Economy

Deus é brasileiro. Popular saying

The history of the economic evolution of Brazil is frequently characterized as a series of booms and busts attributable to the periodic rise and decline of a sequence of valuable export commodities. The country is said to have prospered whenever it has been in a monopoly or near-monopoly situation with respect to world markets, only to collapse at the earliest signs of competition. Economic disaster has in each case been narrowly averted, thanks to the fortuitous advent of a new product which initiated another cycle of prosperity. 'God', it is often said appreciatively, 'is a Brazilian'.

Thus simplified, the country's economic history can be divided into brazilwood–sugar–gold–coffee–and rubber periods. While these may have a certain validity in *grosso modo* and as frames of historical reference, for several reasons they leave much to be desired as descriptive vehicles. They do not, for one thing, account for the economic evolution of Brazil since World War I and particularly during the last few decades; they tell us little about the nation's internal economic growth and changing organization; they imply a uniqueness to the Brazilian production pattern, whereas in fact such booms and busts have been characteristic of most tropical and extractive economies; and they fail to take into account the continued production, and even perhaps the economic impor-
_____ commodity to the country after its replacement as
_____ attention by the product of the next boom.
_____ he traditional, cyclical view of Brazil's evolution,
_____ pon the commodity production aspect of these

booms, relegates the spatial component to an undeserved secondary role, when, in fact an exploratory and exploitive approach to its new lands has been a dominant theme in the country's sequence of occupance, any particular commodity being, at any given time, as much a means to this end as an end in itself.

It might be expected that Brazil, in any case, being a large country with a diversity of physical environments, would have had more than its share of highly productive periods based upon different minerals and tropical products. Any single one of these might have constituted the economic apogee of a more modestly endowed nation. Even its production of lesser-heralded items—indigo, diamonds, cattle, palm oils, timber or iron ore, for instance—would have sufficed to bring praises of the Lord's bounty from many a smaller country.

The diversity of Brazil's natural resources, the size of its home markets and the spectacular volume and value of the exports generated by its booms have all served to mask the gradually expanding diversity of her economy and the filling in of her oecumene: first the coastal plains, next the eastern highlands, followed by the interior plateaux of São Paulo and the west, the southern plateau and the plains of Rio Grande do Sul. Product has been added to product throughout the continuous expansion of the Brazilian frontier into the *sertão*, or backlands, in an historical process which is only now coming to a close in the distant reaches of the Amazon.

EARLY FOOTHOLDS

The first permanent European footholds in Brazil, so far as is known, were trading posts established at Salvador and Cabo Frio in 1502,*, to implement a contract granted the previous year for the shipment of 750 tons of brazilwood to Europe. This tree of the genus *Caesalpina*, which could be as much as a metre in diameter and 10 to 15 metres tall, was used for the manufacture of a natural red dye. The heavy logs, cut into 2 metre lengths, were brought out of the coastal

---

* The discovery of Brazil is officially attributed to Pedro Alvarez Cabral in the year 1500. However, it is not unlikely that Phoenician traders landed on the northeastern coast in the sixth century B.C.[1] and it is almost certain that Portuguese exploration took place along the Amazon in 1498 and 1499, and possibly earlier elsewhere.[2]

forests by Indians, who exchanged them for axes, adzes, mirrors and trinkets from the traders, whom they also supplied with food.

A haphazard occupation of the Brazilian coast followed, but, in contrast to the wealth that was flowing into the Portuguese coffers from southern Asia, the prospects for Brazil seemed meagre indeed. It has been said when Cabral died in 1520, 'the navigator was forgotten by the courts, and his discovery remained nearly abandoned'.[3]

But others, especially the French, were encroaching upon the activities of Portuguese merchants who had been granted the right to trade and maintain factories in Brazil. To protect its interests and to consolidate and systematize its hold on this new land, Portugal in 1530 divided the coast up into twelve *capitanías*, each from 200 to 600 kilometres in linear extent, which were to be run by representatives of the Crown. The first official colony was established in 1532 under this system at São Vicente, adjacent to present-day Santos. Also in that year, a sailor from a Portuguese ship made his way over the coastal escarpment and established the European presence in the interior by settling down in an Indian village near what was to become the city of São Paulo, where he was subsequently joined by others of his ilk. Five years later a second colony was founded on the coast at Olinda, now a suburb of Recife.

Meanwhile, both the Portuguese and the French traffic in brazilwood had been expanding, largely thanks to the relatively dense and co-operative Indian population along the coast. This did not give rise to permanent European settlements, if one excepts the occasional trader who established himself in an Indian village, as the ships would lay to in a sheltered anchorage while the natives hauled the logs out to the beach. It did, however, lead to the considerable destruction of the forests, as exports of this wood climbed rapidly, attaining a value of 50,000 ducats by 1506. But exploitation dropped sharply as the most accessible forests near the coast were destroyed and by the middle of the sixteenth century exports amounted to only about half that earlier figure. Nevertheless, brazilwood shipments did not cease until three centuries later when a synthetic substitute was discovered that approximated the fire-coloured dye in richness, and as late as the first half of the eighteenth century exports to London alone still amounted to between £20,000 and £100,000 per annum from the country to which that wood gave its name.*

SETTLEMENT OF THE COASTAL PLAIN

While this destructive exploitation of the coastal forests was proceeding in haphazard fashion, some of the *capitanías* were being parcelled out as large land grants to Portuguese entrepreneurs. Given Brazil's unprepossessing situation *vis-à-vis* other Portuguese overseas interests at the time, these drew only people from the lesser ranks of the nobility and commerce who, lacking financial resources of their own, turned to the merchants and bankers of their own country and in Holland for backing, a good proportion of these investors being Jews.[4] They were, perhaps, encouraged by such early descriptions as that of Pedro Vaz de Caminha, who, in 1500, wrote: 'The entire shore is very flat and very beautiful. As for the interior . . . we could see only land and forests. If one cares to profit by it, everything will grow.'[5]

Although various tropical plantation crops were established during the occupance of these grants of land, specific interest centred upon the cultivation of sugar cane. At the time, it was being grown on the Portuguese islands of Madeira and Cabo Verde, in Sicily and in the Far East, reaching Europe in small quantities and at very high prices. The crop was introduced to Brazil from Madeira during the 1530s and planted on the lowlands near Recife, Rio de Janeiro and Salvador. The latter area suffered from an early shortage of Indian labour which led to the import of Brazil's first African slaves in 1538. They did not become numerous in other parts of the coast until some thirty years later, following the decimation of the aboriginal inhabitants and the rising demand for sugar in Europe. By the middle of the sixteenth century sugar was already in the process of overtaking brazilwood in the colonial economy, as indicated by their yield of approximately 1,200 and 1,800 ducats respectively in revenue to the Crown.[6]

* The Portuguese word 'pau brasil' (brazilwood) derives from 'brasa' or live coal. The original meaning in Gothic, still retained in modern Swedish, was 'fire' (Old English 'braes') and appears in the derivation of such words as 'braise' and 'brass' (*Brazilian Bulletin*, May 1970, p. 4).

By 1570 there were some 60 plantations in Brazil exporting 2,400 metric tons of sugar valued at over £270,000. A decade later the number of plantations had doubled and exports had risen to 5,250 tons worth nearly £530,000. At this time, the non-Indian population of Brazil was only about 60,000, living almost exclusively on the coastal plain.

The rate of establishing new plantations subsequently slowed down, but the value and volume of their production increased substantially, thanks in part to the rising pace of slave imports. Thus in the year 1600, 200 plantations were exporting 18,000 metric tons of sugar worth about £2,600,000. At this time much of the Brazilian sugar commerce was in the hands of the Dutch, who, thinking to control also the source of production, captured Salvador in 1624 and Olinda/Recife in 1630; they also seized São Luís from the French, thereby extending their hegemony throughout the major producing areas in the northeastern part of the Portuguese colony. The Dutch rule was relatively brief, however, and they were ousted completely by 1654.

The economic peak of this early phase of sugar production in Brazil was reached about 1650 when 300 plantations exported 31,000 tons of sugar worth nearly 4 million pounds sterling. Although the number of sugar plantations continued to increase after the expulsion of the Dutch, to some 650 in 1710, their productivity declined and their returns even more so because of competition from the French and British possessions in the West Indies. Thus, in that year, sugar exports were down to 24,000 tons with a value of only £1,700,000, or less than their worth at the turn of the previous century.

The volume of sugar exports rose again during the latter part of the eighteenth century, and in 1822, the year Brazil declared its independence from Portugal, exceeded 70,000 metric tons. This brought a return of £2,185,000—somewhat less than was obtained by shipping one-quarter the tonnage to Europe in 1600.

Therefore, although the crop retained its viability in absolute terms within the Brazilian economy for 300 years, and in fact down to the present time when much of the coastal plain is still planted to sugar, its relative importance both in exports and in the national economy was sharply reduced. On a per capita basis this is evident when one considers that in 1822 Brazil's non-aboriginal population totalled nearly 4 million (2,813,351 free and 1,147,515 slave) as compared to perhaps 100,000 in 1600, to whom a revenue of two million pounds would obviously have been of vastly greater importance.

In the long run, however, the significance of this early sugar plantation economy extended far beyond the simple question of colonial income and the occupancy of the coastal plain. It was of fundamental importance in moulding Brazil's social and economic institutions, and in establishing the land tenure and land use patterns which have been handed down to the present day. Sugar cane has left Brazil with a legacy of large landholdings surrounded by the small properties of the peasantry. These are particularly differentiated in the coastal regions, where sugar has virtually monopolized the productive mechanisms and where structural changes have been minimal. The Figure 1 diagrams demonstrate the disparity between landholdings belonging to the two socio-economic strata, epitomized by the Pernambuco coastal zone, where the pattern of minifúndios particularly resembles those of the sugar-producing islands of the West Indies.[7] The pattern of the Recôncavo, a bay area easily accessible to the city of Salvador, is similar but has been somewhat modified by a concentration on tobacco and food crops for commercial markets.

The landholding patterns of the coastal areas of northeastern Brazil are in sharp contrast to those of the semi-subsistence farming area of the hill lands in the interior of that region. On the other hand, the substance if not the details of large versus small holdings reappears in the coffee plantation zone of the São Paulo Plateau and in the area of vast latifúndios on the Central Plateau, although the minifúndios are largely superseded by moderate-sized peasant farms as the numerically predominant type of land holding in these two regions. The effects of these occupance patterns on the agricultural economy of Brazil are considered in a subsequent chapter.

As regards the social and corollary political systems that have been handed down from these early days of colonization, according to the Brazilian sociologist Floristan Fernandez,[8] the most lasting impact has been the preservation of the system of serfdom derived from Roman Law and passed on through

Portugal to its colony by means of caste stratification. Under this concept of *servus persona non habet*, only the nobility (abolished in Brazil with the end of the Empire) and the masters—who exercised absolute power as heads of households that included

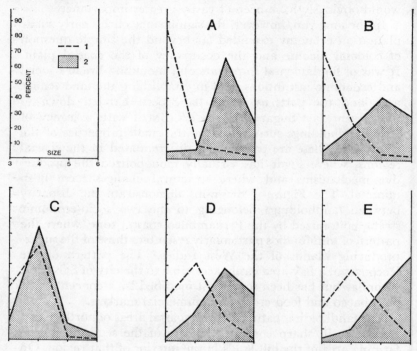

Figure 1. LANDHOLDING SIZE. Key: within diagram (1) percentage of rural holdings in each size class, (2) percentage of area in each class of rural landholding; *x*-axis indicates per cent of total holdings and area for each size class; classes are indicated along the *y*-axis by numbers, (3) less than 10 hectares, (4) 10–100 has., (5) 100–1,000 has., (6) over 1,000 has.; letters indicate locations, A. coastal zone of Pernambuco, B. zone of the Recôncavo, C. interior hill lands of the northeast, D. coffee zone of central São Paulo, E. central plateau area of Goiás. After: *Atlas Nacional do Brasil*, I.B.G.E., 1966, Plate IV–3.

family, serfs and slaves—were entitled to take stands against what the other masters did. This attitude, begun on the sugar plantations and later entrenched in the mines, the cattle ranches, the coffee plantations and the business world, was maintained not only during colonial times but later under the

Empire, the rule of the 'colonels' in the early days of the Republic, the Vargas dictatorship, and the current military regime. Only occasionally has the solidarity of the 'masters' in power been impinged upon or modified by action of the lower classes, although urban workers and the middle class have wrung a few concessions in recent decades. In Brazil, as elsewhere in Latin America, preference is still given to privilege.

This privilege can also be applied to the country's economic organization and to the distribution of profit from the means of production. What has been said about the field and factory slaves of the seventeenth century, that they were 'treated badly, victimized, and overworked',[9] is still in essence applicable to the proletariat today. There was, however, a traditional distinction between the treatment accorded the worker in the field and sugar factory and the one doing domestic or commercial chores in the urban *sobrado* or the *casa grande* of the rural areas. The well-known work of Gilberto Freyre,[10] himself one of the 'masters', therefore presents a somewhat euphoric view of the Brazilian version of institutional slavery, since it applied to those living in the most favourable conditions. This distinction is still applicable in the modern society between the urban worker, who has been granted a certain degree of social and economic recognition, and the member of the rural proletariat who is still very much a *persona non habet*.

OCCUPANCE OF THE INTERIOR

While the coastal plains were being effectively occupied by planters during the sixteenth and seventeenth centuries, the Brazilian interior was being penetrated—along the São Francisco Valley in the north and following Indian trails across and beyond the escarpment in the Santos–São Paulo area in the south—by adventurers, in groups or as individuals, as well as by a few officially-sanctioned military and ecclesiastical expeditions. The first two evolved into the *bandeirantes*, those roving backwoodsmen whose quasi-military bands, usually augmented by large numbers of Indians, scoured the interior in search of gold, precious stones, and slaves for sale to the coastal plantations.

As neither precious stones nor gold in any appreciable amounts were immediately forthcoming, it was the enslavement of ever more distant aborigines that provided the *bandeirantes* with the revenue they needed to sustain their modest habitations in the interior with meagre purchases of arms, gunpowder, salt and cloth from the coastal settlements. Whereas the eventual Jesuit, and to a lesser extent Benedictine, missions in the interior aimed at an orderly development of saleable agricultural products through the use of the labour of catechized Indians, the *bandeirante* settlements, when they were not simply grafted on to extant Indian communities, tended towards less ambitious forms of occupancy. Their individual farms were generally located near the trails along which the adventures of their more vigorous youth had led them. Settled down at last and surrounded by their half-breed families, these patriarchs grew subsistence crops of beans, rice and cassava, and raised a few head of cattle. These last were to form the basis for the herds that later constituted the basic economic activity of the interior, introducing ranching as a way of life from the Campos de Piratininga in São Paulo to the *chapadas* and Pantanal of the west, and from the northeastern *caatinga* to the *pampas* of Rio Grande do Sul.

A few hamlets evolved at strategic places in the interior as a result of these activities. One of the most important was São Paulo, the role of which as a trading centre on the route to Santos and as an outfitting place for the *bandeiras*, was enhanced after 1554 by the establishment there of a Jesuit school and mission. In 1600 discovery of placer gold in the nearby Jaraguá River led to increased activity in the São Paulo area. Settlement along the coastal plain south of Santos-São Vicente also intensified, after reaching Cananeia near the present Paraná border in the last-mentioned year. As a result, the population of what later became São Paulo State doubled by the middle of the seventeenth century from its 1600 figure of 6,000 Christians, including whites, half-breeds and Indians.[11] Nevertheless, both the interior and coastal towns of that most southerly extension of colonization were modest indeed, and population densities were far below those of the more accessible and productive areas of northeastern Brazil.

The dreams of the *bandeirantes* finally became reality when gold was discovered in the mountainous area of southeastern Minas Gerais in 1694. At the start, production was in the hands of those who reached the gold fields from São Paulo, to which all of western and southern Brazil belonged administratively, and the gold was shipped out through that city and Santos. But the *paulista* hegemony was short-lived as the Portuguese Crown, wishing to ensure a more effective tax collection system since there was much smuggling going on over the old Indian trails, in 1698 issued a Royal Order for the construction of a road linking the mining area directly to Rio de Janeiro. This was opened to mule traffic in 1705, thereby ending the isolation of that city from the interior highlands.

The *paulistas'* control of their discovery was also threatened by an influx of *bandeirantes* from the São Francisco area; and these were soon followed by plantation owners who, bringing their slaves with them, came from the coastal plains both of the northeast and of the Rio de Janeiro area. The newcomers drove the original claimants off by force and in 1720, half a dozen years after diamonds had also been discovered in the region, obtained recognition for a separate Minas Gerais Province under their domination. Thus the individual prospector, unlike his counterpart during the North American and Australian gold rushes that began a century later, played but a minor role in the development of the Brazilian mining areas. To this day he remains a rather pathetic figure, eking out a meagre living in picked-over stream beds or beyond the frontiers of settlement.

Even the *bandeirantes* were not so much individualists as the organizers of hierarchical enterprises. Those of them who became, with the ex-plantation owners, masters of the gold fields, gained control of the land and the labour, whether free or slave, and thereby the wealth, the political power and the social perquisites associated with the upper classes. Settlement nuclei were therefore not mining camps of the kind that came to characterize areas of Anglo-Saxon occupance. Instead, they evolved into colonial towns with all the architectural and personal opulence that the riches of the mines could provide, despite the most rudimentary mule train and ox-cart transport over rugged terrain and excessive distances. Outstanding examples of such extensions of the colonial ethos are Diamantina, with its lavish homes complete with patios and pools, and Ouro Prêto, the former capital of Minas Gerais, where the ecclesiastical sculptures of Aleijadinho rank with the finest of Europe. This pattern was followed, not only in the other mining centres of eastern Brazil, but also in towns of the west, such as Goiás, former capital of the province of that name, and Cuiabá, the capital of Mato Grosso. Both provinces were separated politically from São Paulo in 1748 after the discovery of gold in these remote regions.

There were several far-reaching effects of the opening up of the central Brazilian highlands during the eighteenth century. Firstly, this vast interior area was, after two centuries of virtual anarchy, brought under effective government control. Secondly, according to Furtado, 'gold production permitted the financing of great population expansion, which introduced fundamental changes into the structure of the population, so that African slaves became the minority and Europeans the majority';[12] indeed, by 1800 the non-aboriginal population of Brazil had risen to about 3 million, two-thirds of whom were free and one-third slave. Thirdly, as the population increased and as towns grew up and settlement around the mining areas intensified, systematic ranching and agriculture were established until, towards the end of the eighteenth century, exports from that region included not only gold and diamonds but also cattle and limited quantities of cheese, bacon, lard, grain, sugar, cotton, tobacco and coffee. Fourthly, the growing importance of this portion of the hinterland shifted the 'core area' of Brazil from the northeastern coast southward (Map 3).

Finally, as wealth flowed through Rio de Janeiro, the principal entrepôt for this area, that city's importance increased until in 1763 the colonial capital was transferred there from Salvador. At the close of the century an average of one ship from overseas dropped anchor there each day. Subsequently, it was to Rio de Janeiro that the Court fled after being driven out of Portugal by Napoleon. Its population at the time, 1808, was about 100,000 as compared to some 70,000 each for Salvador and Recife, and approximately 20,000 for São Luís, São Paulo and Ouro Prêto, while only a handful of other towns had more than 2,000 inhabitants. After 13 years as the temporary seat of the far-flung Portuguese Empire, Rio de Janeiro became the capital of an independent Brazil.

CONSOLIDATION OF SETTLEMENT IN THE EASTERN HIGHLANDS

The transplantation of the Portuguese Crown to Brazil, although relatively short-lived, was, according to Jaguaribe, 'one of the most significant events in the country's history, not only on account of the far-reaching changes rapidly introduced into the colony . . . but also because Brazil's entire subsequent evolution, particularly during the hundred years which followed, was conditioned by this event'.[13] In particular, he cites the importance of Dom João IV's abandonment of Portugal's traditional fiscalism, established in the late Middle Ages during the ousting of the Moors, which was a combination of mercantilism and state capitalism applied by a strong, centralized government under the direct authority of the national dynasty.

The Portuguese Crown, during its sojourn in Brazil, also endowed the country with 'a political centre of gravity, a machinery of government and administration, and an economic and social orientation'[14] at a critical stage in that country's evolution. Continuity of these institutions was assured with the subsequent transfer of the legitimate authority of the dynasty to the Brazilian Emperors, Dom Pedro I and II, thereby bringing about a stability and cohesion that was in sharp contrast to the upheavals within, and fragmentation of, the Spanish Empire in the Americas.

In the economic sphere, Dom João threw open Brazil's foreign trade to all friendly nations and lifted restrictions on manufacturing enterprises, 'thereby creating conditions for future prosperity by encouraging expansion of trade and agriculture and establishing industries'.[15] Some other progressive measures included the establishment of the Bank of Brazil, the setting up of postal services between the provinces, the construction of the first road worthy of the name over the escarpment behind Rio de Janeiro, the subsidizing of the first iron and steel foundry, on the outskirts of that city, the exemption from import duties of raw materials used by Brazilian

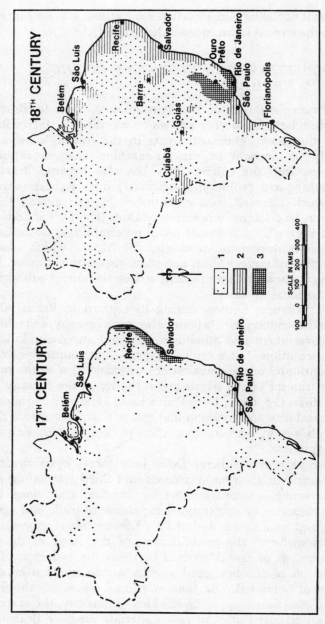

Map 3. INTENSITY OF SETTLEMENT (1) Rimlands, (2) Agricultural Periphery, (3) Heartland. After: Aroldo de Azevedo

Brasil: A Terra e o Homen, Cia. Edit. Nacional, São Paulo, 1964, p. 26.

industries, and the encouragement of organized colonization by European immigrants. Although the actual results of these measures during the time of Dom João were modest, they nevertheless furnished guidelines and established the bases for developments which were to come in the wake of the prosperity provided by the expanded revenues, increased population and intensified land occupance brought about by rising exports of coffee.

By the middle of the eighteenth century coffee was being grown for domestic consumption in northeastern Brazil, in the mining zones and on the hills around Rio de Janeiro. The exporting of coffee, which began in small quantity in 1779, increased rapidly midway during the Portuguese Crown's stay in Brazil, thanks to the lifting of trade restrictions and to the establishment of somewhat better communications with the highlands behind Rio de Janeiro.

During the Empire (1822–89) 'coffee gave rise to the last of the country's three great aristocracies: following the masters of the sugar plantations and the great mine owners, the coffee planters became the social elite of Brazil. And thereby its political leaders as well'.[16] The residential locus of this aristocracy was in the city of Rio de Janeiro, where its Barons, Dukes and Counts constituted the Imperial entourage. Its source of wealth lay, however, in the coffee producing zone which during the Empire was centred on the middle Paraíba Valley in western Rio de Janeiro Province and southeastern São Paulo. Here the plantocracy erected opulent manor houses that rivalled in magnificence their palaces in Rio de Janeiro.[17] The Paraíba Valley was linked to that city and to several ports along the coast, first by carriage roads and later by railways, both built despite incredible physical and financial obstacles.[18] Meanwhile, gangs of slaves mined the soil to exhaustion as they planted coffee trees in even rows on the steep hillsides of the valley, dooming the system to ultimate extinction even had it not been dealt its death blow by the emancipation of the slaves in 1888.

Nevertheless the growing of coffee had served to populate the hitherto nearly empty eastern highlands, a sort of no-man's-land between the coastal plantations and the mining area. It had also greatly stimulated the growth of Rio de Janeiro.

By 1890 the population of that city had risen to approximately half a million. Rio also became the birth-place of Brazil's early capitalist endeavours, to which the more enterprising members of the coffee aristocracy turned their attention around the middle of the nineteenth century. This resulted in large measure from the adoption of protectionist and industrialist policies by the government which, after 1843 when it established import tariffs, had as its objective the channelling into industry of the considerable capital that had hitherto been invested in the import of slaves. Combined with the abolition of the slave trade, these led during the decade of the 1850s to the establishment of 62 industries, 20 shipping companies, 3 urban transport companies, 2 gas companies, 17 banks and 23 insurance companies.[19]

By far the greatest Brazilian entrepreneur and financier was Irineu Evangelista de Souza, the Baron and later Viscount of Mauá. Beginning with a foundry acquired in 1845, he built up an industrial complex on Guanabara Bay that produced not only steel, steel products and machinery, but that also included a naval yard, which by the time of the Paraguayan War in 1864 had been responsible for the construction of one-third of the Brazilian Navy's steamships and a large number of its sailing vessels. By 1851 Mauá's plant was employing 1,000 workers and, from an investment worth 1,250 *contos*, had an annual production worth about 1,000 *contos*, or £350,000 at the then current rate of exchange. The importance of this enterprise can be appreciated by comparing it to Brazil's budget, which in that year amounted to 27,200 *contos*.[20] Mauá also either personally financed or organized the raising of funds for regular steamer service on the Amazon, the country's first railway (from the head of navigation on Guanabara Bay to the base of the Serra do Mar), gas lighting for the streets of Rio de Janeiro, and the submarine cable between Brazil and Europe, among other ventures.

Mauá's bankruptcy in 1875, according to Jaguaribe, brought Brazil's 'remarkable burst of industrial activity' to a virtual halt.[21] The same author states[22] that, although the industrial expansion of 1850–75 seemed to be leading to 'take-off', it did not generate a process of sustained growth similar to that of the United States for three reasons: firstly, the small size of the internal market;[23] secondly, the privileged position of export agriculture, notably coffee, the large profits from which diminished the attractiveness of other forms of investment; and thirdly, a social structure which lacked an entrepreneurial bourgeoisie, an urban middle class, and a rural stratum of yeoman farmers. These constraints to development continued to apply to a certain degree throughout the period of the Republic until the stresses of the Great Depression and the dislocations of World War II, spanning the time of the Vargas dictatorship,[24] initiated a process of economic and institutional change which laid the foundation for the emergence of the dynamic, modernizing nation of the present day, although the process has as yet by no means been completed.

DEVELOPMENT OF THE SOUTHERN PLATEAU

The changes that are today to a greater or lesser extent affecting every part of Brazil, would in all likelihood have been more difficult to initiate had it not been for the tidal wave of free immigrant labourers that washed up on to, particularly, the southern shores of that country during the last decade of the nineteenth century and the first 30 years of the twentieth. At first, they provided the labour that was needed to expand and harvest the coffee crop that was spreading across the plateau in São Paulo and northern Paraná. Later they supplied the independent yeomanry that for the first time furnished a rural base for the marketing of urban industrial production. Finally, they contributed substantially, both through their numbers and through their ambitions, to the emergence of an urban technocracy and bourgeoisie.

It can be appreciated that it was no easy matter for these groups of immigrants to the rural areas, given their bondage in tenancy in the one instance and their isolation and virtual self-sufficiency in the other, to set about forthwith to alter their lot radically. Nor was the economic and social climate propitious for such changes at first, particularly prior to World War I. They had, then, to be content to work within an economic system which at that time was overspecialized, in that capital investment was attracted almost exclusively to the expansion of coffee production or the construction of the railways associated with it. Despite these inhibitions, and because the immigrants' expectations were higher than those of the native rural proletariat within the new, albeit modest, rural economy that succeeded slavery, they did contribute significantly to the expansion of the Brazilian domestic market and eventually to the steps that were taken to satisfy it.[25]

Although Brazil continued to be organized essentially along the lines of a colonial economy until relatively recently, some modest industrial investment did take place even during the early years of the Republic. In the closing days of the Empire there were approximately 600 industrial establishments in the country. These increased to something over 1,000 by 1895, and to 3,258 in 1907.[26] In the latter year, when about 150,000 workers were employed by Brazilian industry, over half of its invested capital was in textile production, a proportion which had changed little from the end of the Imperial era. Forty per cent of Brazil's industrial production in 1907 came from in or near the city of Rio de Janeiro with the Federal District, now Guanabara, and Rio de Janeiro State being responsible for 33 and 7 per cent respectively. Sixteen per cent came from São Paulo State and 15 per cent from Rio Grande do Sul. Of São Paulo's output 40 per cent, or roughly $6\frac{1}{2}$ per cent of the national total, came from within the city itself, which thereby already surpassed all but four political units in industrial productivity, as none of the other states attained even 5 per cent of the total.

World War I brought a considerable impulse to manufacturing in Brazil, and by 1920 there were 13,336 industrial establishments in the country employing over a quarter of a million workers; of these plants, nearly 6,000 had come into being after 1914. The war also laid the foundation for the first large-scale exploitation and use of Brazil's extensive ore bodies, which are concentrated in east-central Minas Gerais. This started with the expansion of a small, 30-year-old pig-iron plant at Itabirito, which increased its production from 3,300 tons to 15,300 between 1915 and 1921. In that year the Belgo-Mineira Company opened its first blast furnace at nearby Sabará, using charcoal from the surrounding forests supplemented by small amounts of imported coking coal. These developments were instrumental in raising Brazil's iron and steel production to 71,000 tons by 1931. Of passing interest is the fact that at this time Brazil was producing an average of about 4,000 kilogrammes of gold per year, most of it from within the same mineralized zone of Minas Gerais.

Meanwhile, the war had also brought about changes in the composition of Brazilian industry, textiles being supplanted in first place by food processing, which rose from 27 per cent of total production in 1907 to 40 per cent in 1920. This was due, in part, to the cutting off of outside supplies during the war years, forcing more foodstuffs to be processed within the country. Another important factor was the demand for meat by the European belligerents, leading to the establishment and rapid expansion of a meat packing industry in Rio Grande do Sul, the principal cattle raising area of the country from the eighteenth century onward, and in São Paulo, which drew not only on its own herds but also on those of southwestern Minas Gerais, Goiás and Mato Grosso.

Commercial and industrial developments within both the state and the city of São Paulo led to their rapid growth, more particularly the latter. Between 1890 and 1920 the city's population increased from 70,000 to 600,000. Thus São Paulo City in 30 years attained a numerical increase that it had taken the city of Rio de Janeiro the entire preceding century to achieve, marking the start of a high rate of expansion which it has maintained to the present day.

During this period, in the last decade of the nineteenth and the first two decades of the twentieth centuries, and particularly in the wake of the First World War, the foundations were laid for the evolution of Brazil's economic geography into its modern form, the subject of subsequent chapters. First, however, the country had to pass through the setbacks of the depression and the dislocations and stimuli of the Second World War.

THE AMAZONIAN BACKWATER

During much of the course of occupance and development of Brazil's territory, the largest of the regions which comprise it—the Amazon—was of little more than peripheral interest and significance, despite the fact that it was among the earliest to be discovered and explored. Superficially at least, the Amazon appears to have remained virtually unchanged since the dawn of European penetration: the greater portion of its land surface is still mantled in seemingly virgin forest; no bridge or dam spans any of the major rivers that flow through it; and its present population is no greater than the 3·7 million of the pre-Columbian era.[27] Yet it has witnessed almost unprecedented human upheavals during the nearly half a millennium of the European presence.

In human terms, the apparent continuity derives from the fact that today's subsistence farmers and extractors, mostly of mixed white and Indian ancestry, are probably little better off than were their aboriginal predecessors. The underlying change is indelibly recorded by the isolated remnants of the original Amazonian peoples who, even with the addition of refugees from the drier lands to the south, now number no more than 50,000 to 100,000 and would easily be lost in either of the two major capitals, Belém and Manaus, with populations of roughly 700,000 and 320,000 respectively. But whether from the vantage point of an urban centre, an Indian village, or the remote hut of some *seringueiro*, and whether in the past or in the present, it has been the interrelationship of jungle and river that has dominated the lives of men in the Amazon.

Only in the last decade has that part of Brazil's culture from the highland core, which is land-based and interior-oriented, succeeded in penetrating this alien environment with its roads, its machinery, and its insensitive, denuding farming practices. Perhaps it will be able to demonstrate that at last man's technology has attained a level capable of taming the Amazon.[28] This approach, if not the techniques of the plateau-people, is by no means a new one, however. As Tocantins points out, the early white colonists who came to take up land in Pará, 'after having participated in the life-style of the Northeast . . . aspired to construct a society with the same norms as had already existed on the Brazilian coast for a hundred years. But greater exposure to the regional environment eventually dissuaded them.'[29] Whether the new attack launched from the south will prove better able to survive such exposure than the one which began 350 years ago from the coast remains to be seen.

The first Portuguese settlement in the Amazon was established at Belém, founded in 1615 by colonists from São Luís. The object was to block the encroachment into Portuguese territory of the English and the Dutch, who had already set up factories and sugar mills on the Xingú. Although the planters succeeded in establishing their sugar cane culture at the mouth of the Amazon and in driving out the other European interlopers, more widespread occupancy of the basin rested mainly on the activities of two different groups: the individual traders who circulated along the waterways in pursuit of spices and the Jesuits who induced the Indians to settle in their missions and produce tropical crops. Both depended upon the native to obtain for them, more or less voluntarily, the cocoa, vanilla, cinnamon, cloves, indigo, aromatic resins and cabinet woods which were exported from the Amazon region to Europe in significant quantities during the succeeding century.[30]

The banishment of the Jesuits in 1759 paved the way for predatory expeditions against the Indians on behalf of the plantation owners of Maranhão and the Belém area, whose sugar, rice, cotton, and coffee crops were endangered by the high mortality rate among their African slaves as a result of mistreatment and disease. The 100,000 or so mission Indians were particularly vulnerable, but the others fared little better and those who were not captured or killed by the raiders fell victim to epidemics of smallpox, measles and other diseases carried by Europeans.

The Amazonian nadir was probably reached in the first half of the nineteenth century. By this time the population of the Brazilian part of the basin may have dropped to as low as 40,000; commercial export agriculture had collapsed as a result of being unable to compete with the coastal plantations, so that most of the population was reduced to shifting cultivation and the gathering of native forest products; and strife had broken out between the Portuguese, supported by a military garrison, and the native Brazilians whose forces included Indians and mulattos. Bates writes that, as a result of all this, the population of Belém decreased from 24,500 in 1819 to 15,000 in 1848 and that, 'the Portuguese merchants and tradesmen would not trust themselves to live at their beautiful country-houses . . . second-growth forest had grown over the once cultivated grounds, and now reached the end of all the suburban streets. The place had the aspect of one which had seen better days; the public buildings all seemed constructed on a scale of grandeur far beyond the present requirements of the city. Streets . . . were in a neglected condition, weeds and flourishing young trees growing from large cracks in the masonry. The public squares were overgrown with weeds, and impassable on account of the swampy places which occupied portions of their area.'[31]

He points out, however, that by 1853, when most of the Indian tribes along the main river were 'extinct' and 'forgotten', commerce through the mouth of the Amazon was beginning to revive.[32] This reflected to some extent the more settled conditions that had by then prevailed for about a dozen years; but it was also directly related to the discovery of the process of vulcanization in 1839. This initiated a spiralling world demand for rubber, for which the Amazonian *selva* was an almost unique source. Whereas this region had shipped out less than 50 tons of rubber in an average year during the 1820s, in the 1850s it was exporting almost 2,000 tons annually, at prices which had risen from £45 to £180 per ton. This was, however, just the beginning, and before World War I the Amazon was exporting 35,000 tons of rubber per annum at prices of over £500 per ton.

Of all the so-called Brazilian 'booms', that of Amazonian rubber is perhaps most worthy of the name. This is not only because of the meteoric speed with which it developed, the astonishing revenues which it engendered, and the relatively short span of its existence, but also because its sudden and almost total collapse left the region as destitute as it had been at the beginning. Deflation of the boom became total during the 1920s as the Southeast Asian plantations of *Hevea brasiliensis*, established from seeds smuggled out of Brazil, not only took over the world market but caused the price of rubber to drop to a fraction of its pre-war levels. Many years were to pass before the first signs of recuperation appeared to alleviate the subsequent Amazonian depression.

It would be gratuitous to attempt a summary of that well-chronicled phase of Brazil's economic history. At one extreme there was the frivolous expenditure of vast sums to build an opera house in Manaus and bring to it the finest performers of Europe; at the other were the heroic efforts that went into constructing the Madeira–Mamoré Railway, for which 15,000 labourers had to be hired annually in order to maintain a work force of 1,000 men (after a hospital was built this ratio dropped to 3,150 per 1,000) and where American engineers 'like men fearing leprosy poked the flesh of their legs to test for beri-beri due to malnutrition'.[33] The human foundations upon which these and all other developments rested, however, were the numberless immigrants who spread out through the forest to tap the wild rubber trees. These *seringueiros* came almost exclusively from northeastern Brazil, impelled by a recurrence of severe drought conditions and attracted by the recruiting agents' offers of free passage and promises of wealth.

By 1872 their numbers had swollen the population of the Amazon to over 300,000. The 1890 census recorded 476,000 inhabitants, and 1910 estimates placed the number at about 900,000. In 1920 the census counted 1,432,956 in the political units that comprise the Amazon region, but the economic decline that followed was paralleled by one in population which had still not been made up in 1940, when that year's census put the total number of inhabitants at 1,402,420. But these numbers tell only a part of the story of this *Volkerwanderung*. The net increase, which on the one hand adds those who were born in the Amazon, on the other hand fails to account for the many who lost their lives to malnutrition, disease, and accidents in the unfamiliar forest. Whatever the figure of those who perished as against the greater number who managed to survive, the life of the *seringueiro* was a hapless one. Indebted to the landowner for his passage upon arrival, only rarely was he able to escape from economic bondage as his rubber was sold and his equipment and food were bought (there was little time or energy left for food production) at prices established unilaterally by the owner through whom all transactions had exclusively to take place.

When the bubble burst, the Amazon fell back into its earlier torpor as most of those who were able to departed, leaving behind very little in the way of tangible benefit to the region and even less hope for those who were forced to remain behind. One of the authors recalls visiting Manaus in 1940 when many of Bates's observations about Belém almost a century earlier were applicable to that city despite its population of nearly 70,000. Among the earliest of Brazil's state capitals to install electric lighting and a streetcar system, Manaus' ancient blue lights now glowed fitfully along unkempt streets and a tram line, which ran to a somnolent country club at the end of the line, passed through what must once have been a handsome suburb but was then in the process of reverting to jungle.

BACKGROUND TO MODERNITY

The Manaus country club represented, perhaps as well as anything, a land that was in the throes of shaking off the depression of the 1930s. But some parts of Brazil had, in fact, already begun the struggle to reconcile outmoded institutions and relic ways of life with a new dynamism and developmental philosophy as the country entered the war on the side of the Allies. Now it was forced once again, as in 1914 but on a much larger scale, to harness essentially untapped resources for the use of manufacturers attempting to supply internal markets that could no longer be met by imports.

Following the war, a backlog of funds combined with pent-up demands gave even greater impetus to industrial growth,[34] with its adjunct of urbanization and transport expansion. Whereas the political scene was often in a turmoil, guided alternately by philosophies that ranged from the state capitalism of Vargas and his successors, through the quasi-socialism of Quadros and Goulart to the regulated free enterprise of the current military regime, the economic affairs of the country have somehow managed to take care of themselves.

Most authorities would probably now agree that Brazil has, indeed, 'taken off'. Yet it is a diverse and complex country and its many legacies from past patterns of regional evolution are not easily set aside. These factors have contributed to striking economic-geographic disparities that still differentiate the various parts of this nation, an analysis of which is the subject of the following chapters.

REFERENCES

1. The *Brazilian Bulletin*, June 1968, p. 7 (also reported in *Time* magazine May 24, 1968, p. 33), states that shards found at the mouth of the Amazon

have been identified as of Phoenician origin, and that the 'Paraíba Stone', found in northeastern Brazil in 1872, describes the landing of a party of 12 men and 3 women from a ship that during a storm became separated from a fleet of ten trading vessels en route to the Red Sea in the 19th year of King Hiram. Gordon, Cyrus H., in *Before Columbus: Links between the Old World and Ancient America*, Crown Publishers, New York, 1971, places the date at 531 B.C. and presents an interesting theory (pp. 122–124) that this stone may have been found in the Paraíba Valley, beyond the Serra do Mar, although the authors tend not to agree with this view because of the distances involved and the topographic and human barriers along the routes in contrast to the easily accessible shores of what is now Paraíba State.

2. Davies, Arthur. 'The First Discovery and Exploration of the Amazon in 1498–99', *Transactions and Papers, 1956*, The Institute of British Geographers, pp. 87–96. Evidence of explorations to Brazil earlier in the fifteenth century is summarized in Prestage, Edgar, *The Portuguese Pioneers*, Adam and Charles Black, London, 1966 (reprinted from the 1933 edition), pp. 227–236.

3. *Cabral*, No. 2 in the series *Grandes Personagens da Nossa História*, Victor Vicita ed., Abril Cultura Ltda., São Paulo, 1969, p. 44.

4. Prado, Caio, Júnior. *História Econômica do Brasil*, 14th edition, Editora Brasiliense Ltda., São Paulo, 1956, p. 32.

5. Reichmann, Felix. *Sugar, Gold and Coffee*, Cornell University Library, Ithaca, 1959, p. 20.

6. Jaguaribe, Helio. *Economic and Political Development*, Harvard University Press, Cambridge (Mass.), 1968, pp. 100–101.

7. See, for instance, Henshall, J.D. 'The Development of Peasant Agriculture', Chapter 3, in *The Geography of Land Use and Population in the Carribean*, unpublished Ph.D. thesis, University of London, 1969.

8. Fernandez, Floristan. 'The Negro in Brazilian Society', lecture delivered at the University of Calgary (Canada), October 30, 1970.

9. *Ibid.*

10. Freyre, Gilberto. *Casa Grande e Senzala*, Schmidt-Editora, Rio de Janeiro, 1936.

11. For a more complete description of the settlement of this region and the coastal plain of the Rio de Janeiro area through the seventeenth century see Momsen, *Routes over the Serra do Mar, op. cit.* (Ch. 2), pp. 17–25.

12. Furtado, Celso. *The Economic Growth of Brazil*, University of California Press, Berkeley, 1963, p. 37.

13. Jaguaribe, *op. cit.*, p. 113.

14. *Ibid.*, p. 114.

15. *Ibid.*, p. 117.

16. Prado, *op. cit.*, p. 171.

17. For an exhaustive, illustrated description of the life style in the Paraíba Valley in those times see the section, 'Os Barões do Cafe', pp. 301–397 in Lamego, Alberto Ribeiro. *O Homem e a Serra*, Conselho Nacional de Geografia, I.B.G.E., Rio de Janeiro, 1963.

18. For further details see Momsen, *op. cit.*, pp. 39–84.

19. Prado, *op. cit.*, p. 197.

20. Jaguaribe, *op. cit.*, p. 134.

21. *Ibid.*, p. 135.

22. *Ibid.*, pp. 136–138.

23. Brazil's population in 1850 was 8 million, of which 2·5 million were slaves. In 1872 it was still only about 10 million with 1·5 million slaves. Of the 'free' population most had an extremely low purchasing power either because of low earnings or because they were tied to the economy of the estates.

24. An outline of the political and, in summary fashion, main social and economic events of the Vargas dictatorship will be found in Chapter 33, 'The Era of Getúlio Vargas', by Bello, José Maria, *A History of Modern Brazil 1889–1964* (James L. Taylor, trans.), Stanford University Press, California, 1966, pp. 279–308.

25. A survey of the role played by immigrants in the growth of trading and manufacturing enterprises in São Paulo from the early days of the Republic will be found in Dean, Warren, *The Industrialization of São Paulo*, University of Texas Press, Austin, 1969, specifically Chapter 4, 'Social Origins: The Immigrant Bourgeoisie', pp. 49–66.

26. These and subsequent figures on industrialization to 1920 are from Prado, *op. cit.*, pp. 265–267.

27. Pre-Columbian estimate from Denevan, W. M. personal communication of July 1970. The population of the political units (Pará, Amazonas, Acre, Rondônia, Roraima, and Amapá) that include most of the area and almost all of the people in Brazilian 'Amazonia' was 3,650,750 at the time of the 1970 census.

28. It is possible that the ultimate step in this process has been reached, as reported in the following item which is quoted *in toto* from the *Calgary Herald* (Canada) of February 9, 1971: 'RIO DE JANEIRO (AP)— Indians and others working on the 3,000-mile Trans-Amazon Highway will get their paycheques from a computer brought into the jungle especially for that purpose'.

29. Tocantins, Leandro. *Amazônia—Natureza, Homen e Tempo*, Conquista, Rio de Janeiro, 1960, p. 60. This book is a detailed and, although rather hyperbolical, highly readable account of the Amazonian environment and man's historical and ecological relationships to it. There is considerable emphasis on the aborigine and on events in colonial and Imperial times, profusely and aptly illustrated with photographs and drawings.

30. It is impossible to determine the volume or value of this traffic as the Jesuits kept no books, nor did they pay any taxes. Later information, dating from 1755 and ending in 1914 when the company was liquidated, is detailed in the voluminous records (nearly 400 volumes and packages of correspondence, inventories, bills of lading, trade figures, and documents) of the Companhia Geral de Comércio e Navegação do Grão Pará e Maranhão, located in Lisbon's Arquivo Historico do Ministerio de Financas, further information on which will be found in Rau, Virginia, *Arquivos de Portugal: Lisboa*, Comissão Cultural Luso-Americana, Lisbon, 1961 (mimeographed), p. 10.

31. Bates, Henry Walter. *The Naturalist on the River Amazons*, University of California Press, Berkeley, 1962, p. 18.

32. *Ibid.*, p. 19. 1853 was also the year in which the province, now state, of Amazonas was separated from Pará within which it had previously been a *capitanía*.

33. Gauld, Charles A. *The Last Titan*, Stanford University, California, 1964, p. 153. Chapter IX, 'Amazon Railway: the Madeira-Mamoré', of this biography of the engineer and financier, Percival Farquhar, contains a thoroughly documented account of the entrepreneurial and other difficulties encountered while building this railway; it is illustrated with excellent contemporary photographs of the project and other aspects of life in the Upper Amazon.

34. For an extended analysis of this process in the post-war period see Bergsman, Joel, *Brazil: Industrialization and Trade Policies*, Oxford University Press, London, 1970.

CHAPTER 4

Economic Regions of Brazil

Ordem e progresso. Brazilian national motto

An appreciation of the diversity of Brazil is essential to an understanding of the modern economic patterns of the country. One of the first parts of the New World to be colonized by Europeans, Brazil's development history and vast size make it necessary to consider the country on a regional scale. The ordering and grouping of the various parts of Brazil will hopefully make it possible to analyse the economic progress of the nation.

The colonial export economy produced a spatial organization of Brazil based on semi-independent trade basins oriented towards external markets. Coffee production gave rise to the largest of these demographic groupings providing the preconditions for the development of industry. The postwar concentration of industry and modernization in the triangle São Paulo–Rio de Janeiro–Belo Horizonte and improvements in the transport network led to greater spatial integration and the development of a classical core-periphery structure.[1]

The concentration of growth in the core region has exacerbated regional disparities. Within the immediate periphery rural-urban differences are being eliminated and agricultural specialization related to local resource endowments is developing.[2] In the traditional societies of the distant periphery, that is the North and Northeast, the trickle down process is hindered by high population growth rates and considerable rural migration leading to polarization of growth and stagnation, a widening gap between city and countryside and the maintenance of a 'dual economy'.

The traditional economic dominance of the coastal areas, however, is still evident. Notwithstanding the progress towards the interior, as idealized by the building of Brasília, 90 per cent of Brazil's population still lives within 600 kilometres of the sea on less than two-fifths of the nation's territory. At the same time the overwhelming concentration of economic power in the core area may be weakening as government policy channels development funds into the distant peripheral areas, the spread of power and communications out from the metropolitan zones reduces the differences in locational attractiveness between the core and periphery and rapid urban growth leads to diseconomies of size in the biggest cities.

REGIONS

This spatial dynamism has led to a variety of approaches towards regional subdivisions by geographers, regional planners and economists. The most long-standing regional division has recognized the dichotomy of the *sertão*, or virtually uninhabited back country, and the oecumene, or inhabited and economically-integrated coastal part of the country.[3] The boundary between these two major regions has shifted northwards and westwards as the country has been settled.

'Standard' regions for Brazil, aiming at a more rational and stable division, were drawn up by the *Conselho Nacional de Geografia* in 1941,[4] with some modification in 1945. These regions were based on physical characteristics of the country, since they were primarily designed as a framework for the collection of statistics and it was felt that regions based on economic criteria would be too unstable from one census period to the next. Five major regions were set up with a hierarchy of 30 regions, 79 sub-regions and 228 zones, the boundaries of these smallest regional units following those of the smallest political units, the *muncipios*.

More recently the need for a regional division which specifically reflects the differences in levels of economic development within Brazil has been felt. The *Conselho Nacional de Economia* has developed its own regional system, in which the state of Maranhão is included within the Northern region rather than the Northeast as in the 'standard' division, and the states of

Minas Gerais, Espírito Santo, Rio de Janeiro, Guanabara and São Paulo constitute a Central Eastern region. The *Banco Nacional do Desenvolvimento Economico* also utilizes its own particular regional division of Brazil, with Maranhão and Bahia States included within a Northeastern region and with a Southeastern region having the same boundaries as the Central Eastern region of the *Conselho Nacional de Economia*. The *Conselho Nacional de Geografia* has itself recently recognized the existence of a Southeastern region and of a Mid-North region made up of the states of Maranhão and Piauí, although these changes do not constitute an official regional division of Brazil.[5]

Individual geographers have drawn up other regional divisions of Brazil which take into account economic differences. Pokshishevskiy provided a Marxian interpretation recognizing four major economic regions of Brazil: a capitalistic South and Southeast; a former slave-holding Northeast; an inner Western colonization belt; and a zone only slightly touched by colonization.[6] He based this division on an analysis of 36 different indices covering various aspects of population, industry and agriculture, the sole reference to infra-structure being a variable concerning the length of railway track. Geiger, with a more traditional approach, further reduced the number of major regions of Brazil to three: the Southern Centre, the Northeast and Amazonia.[7] Each of these macro-regions was subdivided by Geiger on the basis of major industrial activity and agricultural land use.

The regional boundaries most difficult to define have been those between the South and the East and between the North and the Northeast. In both these cases rapid development in the last two decades has produced anomalies in the 'standard' regional system for Brazil. In response to these economic differences, planning agencies such as SUDENE, SPVEA and most recently SUFRONTE[8] have been assigned large sections of the country over which to preside (Map 4), in an attempt to bring the less-developed parts of Brazil up to the high socio-economic levels of the richer southeastern portion of the nation.[9] Most recently, in recognition of the changes in Brazil's spatial structure, the Brazilian Institute of Geography has reconsidered the regionalization of the country. The natural regions of the 1940s have been replaced by 361 functional micro-regions grouped into five major regions which are now the major units for official data gathering.[10]

NEW REGIONAL DIVISION

Previous regional divisions of Brazil have generally been designed to fulfil specific needs. Thus none fully reflects the modern reality of the spatial structure of Brazil's economy.

Map 4. BRAZIL: STANDARD AND PLANNING REGIONS

The authors have therefore designed a regional division of Brazil, using modern statistical techniques, which recognizes the spatial variation of the characteristics of economic development across the country. This division provides the framework for the study of the economic geography of Brazil.

The underlying dimensions of a set of 37 socio-economic variables for the 25 states and territories of Brazil plus the Federal District were identified, using principal components analysis and then a grouping algorithm was used to group the political units according to their scores on these dimensions, or factors.[11] The input variables were selected as being indicative of inter-regional disparities in economic development in Brazil, and covered aspects of population, agriculture, industry, communications, services, income and trade for the mid-1960s. The analysis of the data matrix revealed eight meaningful basic dimensions after orthogonal rotation, the first four of which accounted for two-thirds of the total variance. These dimensions can be identified by examination of the loadings of each of the variables on the factors.

The first factor is characterized by high loadings for the variables concerned with the density and urban proportion of the population, the percentage of small farms, trade, and per capita levels of income, communications, and power consumption. It identifies national heartland—hinterland contrasts and extracts 31 per cent of the total variance. Guanabara and São Paulo States have the highest positive scores on this dimension followed by the Federal District, reflecting the concentration of Brazil's wealth in these three areas. Guanabara has a very high score, stressing the overtowering dominance of the 'marvellous city' of Rio de Janeiro within this tiny state and the country as whole. Since São Paulo City is included within the much larger São Paulo State, the score is considerably lower than that for Guanabara, although still well above that for any other state. In fact these two states of Guanabara and São Paulo provide over 70 per cent of Federal taxes and have between them 55 per cent of the nation's industrial workers, nearly three-quarters of Brazil's industrial production by value, two-thirds of the telephones, three-quarters of the mail receipts, and nearly half of the country's motor vehicles. The highest negative scores are found in the states to the north and south of São Paulo and Guanabara, where a fairly dense population puts pressure on moderate levels of communications facilities, and in those states and territories fringing the Amazon with both low per capita and low absolute levels of communications, trade and income. Thus this factor not only recognizes the basic heartland-hinterland regional division but also identifies an urban-rural spatial pattern and picks out the major metropolitan axis of the nation.

The second dimension is one characterized by per capita services, mainly banks, cinemas and medical services, and tractors per hectare of cultivated land. This factor extracted 14 per cent of the total variance. States with high scores on this dimension, that is those with the greatest availability of tractors, hospital beds, doctors and banks, fall into two groups, firstly, Mato Grosso, Rondônia and Roraima, and to a lesser extent Acre and Amapá, where low population densities enhance the effectiveness of agricultural improvements and existing, federally-provided services, and, secondly, states such as Rio de Janeiro and Rio Grande do Sul, where moderate population densities are well-served by heavy investments in agriculture and services. The development of Rio de Janeiro has been influenced by the spread effect of the economic growth of neighbouring Guanabara, whilst increased demand on the domestic market for subtropical agricultural products such as wheat, tobacco and wine have led to rapid agricultural development in Rio Grande do Sul and the transformation of the regional capital of Pôrto Alegre into a modern metropolis. The states with negative loadings are those with a traditional, unmechanized agriculture and a low level of socio-economic structures, stretching from Espírito Santo through the North-east to Maranhão and across the two giant states of Pará and Amazonas, where great difficulties exist in serving adequately a widely dispersed population. The highest negative score occurs for the state of Maranhão where provision of services has not been able to keep pace with recent immigration and the equatorial forest environment makes mechanization of agriculture difficult.

The third factor accounts for 13 per cent of the total variance and is characterized by high loadings for population size, number of educational establishments and, to a lesser degree, by the availability of roads and electric power. It differentiates between the thinly populated states of the North and West and the more densely peopled coastal regions.

The fourth factor is characterized by levels of mortality and wages, and accounts for only 8 per cent of the total variance.

Those states with the lowest ranking, denoting high infant and total mortality rates and low minimum salaries in the state capitals, are found in the traditional Northeastern region. This suggests that despite some thirty years of Federally-supported programmes for improving the lot of the 'Nordestino', this area is still unified by living standards markedly lower than those found elsewhere in the country. This situation may offer some explanation for the continual social unrest in this part of the nation, aggravated by natural climate-related catastrophes. It may be noted that there is no significant correlation between the overall death rate and the per capita availability of doctors and hospital beds, whilst there is a fairly high negative correlation between income and mortality, especially infant mortality. High ranking scores on this fourth dimension are found among the rich states of the southeastern part of the country (São Paulo, Paraná and Rio de Janeiro). The lower score for Guanabara reflects the poor living conditions of the *favelados* of the City of Rio de Janeiro. Scores are high, surprisingly, in Goiás and Rondônia, perhaps because of the influx of healthy young adults to these pioneer fringe areas, compared to an overall loss of this segment of the population from the Northeast.

The final four factors extract the remaining 34 per cent of the total variance. They identify further aspects of the heartland-hinterland pattern such as cost of living differentials, intensity of agriculture, the size of industrial firms and road density.

The principal components solution recognizes several spatial patterns basic to the structure of the Brazilian economy. Most outstanding is the dominance of the two major metropolitan centres, the twin primate cities of Rio de Janeiro and São Paulo, within the nation's economic life. Related to this is the existence of some degree of distance-decay away from these two centres on almost every factor. The analysis also identifies contrasts between the dynamic states on the margins of the *sertão* such as Goiás, Mato Grosso, Maranhão and Amapá, where development is taking place, and the stagnating states forming the core of the *sertão*, such as Acre, Amazonas, Roraima and Pará, barely yet touched by twentieth-century technology. The peculiar problems of the Northeast, which have made this region a long-term recipient of development aid from the Federal government, are recognized. A final dimension revealed by the analysis is that of rural-urban contrasts, especially in the east. These spatial patterns form a basis for the grouping of the political units of Brazil into economic regions.

LINKAGES & REGIONAL GROUPINGS

The second part of the technique used to obtain an economic regionalization involved the problem of generalizing these eight dimensions into regional types. This process required the grouping together of the states and territories on the basis of their factor scores in a series of 25 steps, each step linking the most similar political units, until in the final step the country would appear as a unified whole. As the grouping proceeded, with increasing differences between the units, the regional pattern revealed at step 17 was most meaningful and is shown on Map 5.

Each of the five major regions identified is typified by a particular stage and type of economic development. These divide the country into a core region surrounded by two traditional and two innovative peripheral regions.[12]

1. THE NORTH. This is basically a resource frontier region yet to be integrated into the economic life of the nation. It includes the political units Amazonas, Pará, Roraima, Rondônia and Acre containing a mere 3·74 per cent of the country's population and occupying some 40 per cent of the area. Only 0·1 per cent of the land is cultivated and there are on average no more than two kilometres of road per 1,000 square kilometres. The spatial integration and development of this region is now beginning with colonization taking place along the new roads.

2. THE NORTHEAST. The states of Sergipe, Alagoas, Paraíba, Bahia, Pernambuco, Ceará and Rio Grande do Norte once formed the economically dominant part of the nation but as the importance of traditional plantation agriculture has declined the region has become increasingly poorer in relation to other parts of Brazil. Thus it constitutes a vast 'downward transitional area' in Friedmann's typology.[13] The Northeast

has high levels of emigration and infant mortality. Yet because
of its long history of settlement it still has 25 per cent of the
people of Brazil living on 11 per cent of the nation's land, and
35 per cent of the agricultural workers.

3. THE EASTERN HEARTLAND. This region, consisting of the
two large industrial states of São Paulo and Minas Gerais
and the two city states of Guanabara and the Federal District,

North
Northeast
Eastern Heartland
Eastern Periphery
Rimland

0   200 400 600 800 Kms
0   250   500 Miles

Map 5. ECONOMIC REGIONS OF BRAZIL

contains 37 per cent of the population of Brazil on one-tenth
of the area. The inhabitants of this core region have an average
per capita income half as much again as that for the nation as
a whole. The gross product of Guanabara alone exceeds that
of the whole Northeast. Within the region are concentrated

three-quarters of the nation's telephones, 59 per cent of the motor vehicles and over half the bank branches. Eastern industry employs 67 per cent of Brazil's industrial workers and consumes more than three-quarters of the national steel production. Agriculture in this region is relatively scientific and modern, utilizing over half the total number of tractors in Brazil.

4. THE EASTERN PERIPHERY. This region may be sub-divided into a southern sub-tropical portion made up of the states of Santa Catarina and Paraná and a tropical periphery of Rio de Janeiro and Espírito Santo States.[14] The subtropical plateau areas are characterized by small family farms, craftsmanship and small-scale industries. This is the most dynamic and innovative part of the periphery. The tropical periphery was, for a long time, an isolated depressed area with limited natural resources and inefficient agriculture. This sub-region lies within the sphere of influence of the city of Rio which is a less dynamic growth pole than São Paulo City, whose influence dominates the subtropical part of the region. New transport routes, however, particularly the Rio–Bahia highway and the Coastal road, are providing channels for contact with other growth poles, such as Belo Horizonte and Salvador. The longstanding demographic vacuum in this area, forming a barrier between the northeast and the south, is disappearing and the sub-region is developing as an inter-metropolitan periphery. The region as a whole contains 17 per cent of Brazil's population but only 4·5 per cent of its area.

5. THE RIMLAND. Bordering the Heartland and the Northeast, and forming a transition zone between them and the North, this is a frontier region in the process of up-grading a traditional ranching economy. It stretches in a crescent-shaped curve from Rio Grande do Sul in the south, through Mato Grosso and Goiás to Piauí. In the north are the two equatorial states of Amapá and Maranhão characterized by recent colonization in an equatorial forest environment. This dynamic region comprises 34 per cent of the area of Brazil and contains 17 per cent of the population with 47 per cent of Brazil's cattle. Roads are rapidly being built giving a relatively high level

of road mileage per capita. Following the roads and in some cases railways, and the opening-up of resources such as the manganese mines of Amapá, the forests of Goiás or the *pampas* of Rio Grande do Sul, has come expansion of the commercial cultivation of such crops as wheat, rice, coffee and black pepper for export or to feed the urban markets of the Heartland.

Some of the problems of allocating political units to specific regions result from the often marked internal heterogeneity of many of these units. For example, the industrialized part of the state of Rio de Janeiro along the middle Paraíba valley should probably be included within the eastern Heartland, and the more densely-settled area of medium-sized farms on the lava plateau of northern Rio Grande do Sul as well as parts of northeastern São Paulo and southern Minas Gerais might be considered as part of the Eastern Periphery, whilst the western frontier areas of subtropical, broadleaf forests in Santa Catarina and Paraná might more appropriately be included in the Rimland. Unfortunately, most statistics were not available at the micro-level necessary to achieve a more refined regional division.

The regions identified by the above analysis differ significantly in some places from those of the standard Brazilian regional division. The East has been divided into an industrial core segment and an agricultural peripheral segment made up of Espírito Santo and Rio de Janeiro. This latter portion is linked to Paraná and Santa Catarina, formerly considered part of a separate South, whilst the southernmost state of the country, Rio Grande do Sul, has joined the western Rimland. These new groupings suggest that recent processes of economic development have been more successful in changing the character of the West, the South and the East than they have been in altering the nature of the North and Northeast which remain nearly as defined three decades ago by the *Conselho Nacional de Geografia*. As mentioned earlier, however, the non-conformity of the states of Maranhão and Piauí to the Northeastern mould was recognized by the *Conselho* a decade ago, when it established a separate region known as the Mid-North. In a broad sense, the regional groupings identified by the analysis parallel those of the divisions presently in use by Brazil's Federal planning agencies SUFRONTE, SUDENE and SUDAM, as might be expected if these are based on economic criteria.

REFERENCES

1. Friedmann, John. *A general theory of polarized development*, Santiago, 1967, Mimeo.
2. Nicholls, William. 'Agriculture and Economic Development', in J. Saunders Ed., *Modern Brazil*, Gainesville, 1971, pp. 245–246.
3. Azevedo, Aroldo de. *Op. cit.*, p. 12.
4. Guimaraes, Fabio M.S. 'Divisão regional do Brasil', *Revista Brasileria de Geografia*, Ano III (2), 1941, pp. 318–342.
5. Bernardes, Nilo. 'A Divisão Regional', in *Atlas do Brasil*, Instituto Brasileira de Geografia e Estatística, Rio de Janeiro, 1966. Accompanying Map 1–4.
6. Pokshishevskiy, V.V. 'The Major Economic Regions of Brazil', *Izvestiya Akademii Nauk SSSR, Seriya geograficheskaya*, No. 4, 1958, pp. 42–56.
7. Geiger, Pedro Pinchas. 'Organização Regional do Brasil', *Revista Geografica*, Vol. 33, 1964, pp. 25–57.
8. SUDENE is responsible for the economic development of the Northeast, SPVEA for the Amazon region until 1966 when it was replaced by SUDAM and other agencies (see pp. 256–258), and SUFRONTE for the southwestern frontier areas. The full names of these Federal government planning agencies are as follows: SUDENE—Superintendency of the Development of the Northeast; SPVEA—Superintendency of the Plan for the Economic Valorization of the Amazon Region; SUFRONTE—Superintendency of the Plan for the Economic Development of the South-Western Frontier.
9. For an early example of regional boundary delimitation for planning purposes see Soares, Lucio de Castro, 'Delimitacão de Amazônia para fins de planejamento econômico', *Revista Brasileira de Geografia* Ano X (2), 1948, pp. 163–210.
10. See Instituto Brasiliero de Geografia, *Divisão de Brasil em microregiões homogêneas, 1968*, Rio de Janeiro, 1970. Although other government agencies were consulted in setting up this new official regional framework, it has come under criticism, especially from local planning groups such as SUDEC, when they have attempted to use it as a basis for applied analysis. According to the *Brazilian Bulletin* of March 1973, and several popular Brazilian weekly magazines of about the same date, another plan for the division of Brazil purportedly on demographic grounds is being studied by the Ministry of Justice. Developed by a technical adviser to the BNDE in Rio, Severino Monteiro, it proposes that the country be divided into 22 provinces (instead of states), the Federal District, and 15 territories which will 'fill the empty demographic spaces' (*ibid.*, p. 6). In fact, it leaves the states of the eastern seaboard intact and merely carves up the interior into smaller, and therefore even less populous and viable bits. Neither the 'demographic' nor the 'homogenous' (essentially economic) regions are particularly useful for planning purposes, nor are they valid geographically, and both

reflect their origins in the bureaucracy of Rio de Janeiro and the cavalier treatment accorded the more distant reaches of the country.

11. A preliminary version of this analysis of Brazil's regions was presented by the authors at the 21st Congress of the International Geographical Union, New Delhi, 1968. For a discussion of this analytic technique see Berry, B. J. L., 'A method for deriving Multi-Factor Uniform Regions', *Przeglad Geograficzny*, Vol. 33, 1961, pp. 263–279.

12. Friedmann, John. 'The Future of Urbanization in Latin America: Some observations on the role of the Periphery', *Papers of the Regional Science Association*, Vol. 23, 1969, p. 166.

13. Friedmann, John. *Regional Development Policy: A Case Study of Venezuela*, M.I.T. Press, Cambridge, Mass., 1966.

14. Bernardes also recognizes this subdivision of the region. Bernardes, Nilo, 'The State of Espírito Santo in the Brazilian Macroregional Background', in N. Bernardes, Ed., *A Case of Regional Inequality of Development. Espírito Santo, Brazil*, Vol. 1, Rio de Janeiro, 1971. It is probable that a new state created by the fusion of Guanabara and Rio de Janeiro would produce a unit that would be statistically more akin to those of the Heartland than the Periphery, adding the weight of Rio de Janeiro City to that of the industrial centres satellite to it in Rio de Janeiro State, across the bay around Niterói and in the Paraíba Valley. This merger, which has been proposed unenthusiastically ever since the Federal capital moved to Brasília, was activated by President Ernesto Geisel almost immediately after he took office in March 1974, maybe because of the euphoria that followed the opening of the spectacular Rio–Niterói bridge on March 5, or perhaps because Guanabara had the only state government controlled by the opposition to the official ARENA party. Although the merger would make sense geographically and constitutionally (the original separation of the city from the province of Rio de Janeiro as a Federal District was supposedly only a temporary measure), various problems including such fiscal ones as the erosion of Guanabara's tax base and the fact that civil servants' salaries there are twice those prevailing in Rio de Janeiro, will require careful planning and long-term Federal intervention and assistance.

CHAPTER 5

The Modernization of Agriculture

Plantando dá, mas quem planta? Popular saying

Agriculture occupies almost half the labour force and earns two-thirds of Brazil's foreign exchange, yet it has long been the neglected sector of the economy. The traditional exploitative approach to farming based on the laissez-faire attitude that one can reap without sowing and that virgin land will always be available to take the place of over-worked farmland, is still widespread. Brazilian agriculture is both backward and dynamic, and recognition of this apparent paradox has been the stimulus for much recent research.[1]

Rural field studies have stressed the primitive technology, the extravagant use of resources resulting in forest destruction, soil erosion and loss of fertility, the 'hollow' frontier land use pattern, the weak attachment to particular localities that accompanies the prevalent shifting cultivation, the concentration of land ownership, and the inefficient marketing system.[2] The inadequacies of agriculture have been generally blamed on its institutional structure.[3] Revisionist criticism points out that, to a large extent, agrarian structures are the effect rather than the cause of primitive production techniques and low capital input.[4] Despite some traditional attitudes Brazilian farmers have shown themselves ready to adopt new crops in response to changing consumption patterns.[5] Agricultural production has managed to keep pace with population growth and increases in demand resulting from rising incomes, although productivity has remained low.[6] Nicholls has shown that Brazilian farms are more fully commercialized than previously believed and that they make efficient use of the resources available to them.[7] Some have held that the doctrine of the frontier has impeded agricultural development, but Mandell, in his study of the growth of the Brazilian rice industry, indicates that frontier farming displays a significant degree of dynamism, flexibility and technological and organizational innovation in its performance.[8]

The military government, however, saw agriculture as a brake on the overall development of the country and therefore in 1964 set in motion a plan, under which agriculture was to be given priority over industry for the first time. This plan had the following objectives: to supply the food basis indispensable to greater urban and industrial growth; to contribute to further diversification of exportable commodities so as to help finance imports essential to general economic development; to bring about a balance in rural-urban migration patterns both by providing greater employment opportunities in the cities and by expanding the agricultural frontier; and finally by thus raising the standard of living in the rural sector, to increase the domestic market and so absorb the increased industrial production.[9] This policy for rural development was instrumental in doubling the annual growth rate of agricultural production between 1964 and 1970. By the end of this latter year the Brazilian Minister of Finance was able to say that such satisfactory progress had been made in farming that from 1971 onwards the government would give equal encouragement to both the industrial and the agricultural sectors of the economy;[10] yet in 1974 agriculture still lagged behind.

Brazil's agricultural potential can be suggested by what was achieved with relatively primitive methods. In the mid-sixties Brazil was first in the world in the production of coffee, bananas, edible beans, castor beans and cassava and the leading producer of rice in the Occident. It occupied second place as a producer of sisal and oranges, third in cocoa, jute, soyabeans, black pepper and maize, and owned the third largest herds of cattle and pigs in the world. The inefficiencies of Brazilian farming, however, are reflected in the country's long record of seeing its position in world markets as a leading producer of a particular crop lost to stronger competitors.

AGRICULTURAL METHODS

To the early European settlers the area of Brazil seemed limitless and the fertility of the tropical forest soils inexhaustible. They quickly adopted the slash and burn, or *derrubada e queimada* as it is called in Brazil, shifting cultivation techniques of the Indians. This method involves the clearing of a patch of forest with axe and cutlass, followed by the burning of the cut vegetation. The crop is planted with a digging stick or hoe in the soft soil and wood ashes amongst the charred stumps and logs, and requires little cultivation since the growth of weeds has been almost eliminated by the fire. The clearing can be used for only two or three years before declining yields and the invasion of weeds and secondary forest growth forces the *roceiro* to move to another location and start the whole process over again.

This method of land rotation was well suited to a country in which land was in excess and labour limited, and it is still widely used throughout Brazil. It is popular with large land-owners since it is an inexpensive way of enlarging the usable part of their estates. In the cattle areas the *roceiro* is allowed to clear patches of land and to plant his subsistence crops of maize, beans, rice and cassava—of which the landlord gets a share—in return for sowing the area to pasture grasses before he moves on to a new *roça*.[11] *Parceiros*, or sharecroppers, are particularly numerous in the Northeast especially in the states of Paraíba and Rio Grande do Norte.[12] The coffee plantations of São Paulo and Paraná were established by *roceiros* clearing patches of land and planting coffee seedlings amongst their subsistence crops. The *colono* in effect leased his services, albeit on an areal basis, to the *fazendeiro* who retained the responsibility for administration, processing and marketing for the *fazenda* as a whole. The income of the *colono* is directly related to the productivity and size of his piece of the coffee plantation and to the number of able-bodied family members he can muster at harvest time. Thus this system of tenancy provides an important economic incentive for the siring of a large number of children in the rural areas. The *colono* and his family may stay on the land as much as seven years gathering and selling the first small crops of coffee beans before moving on to new areas on the coffee frontier. In this way over the last four centuries cultivation has moved out from the major coastal population centres into the interior, exacerbating problems of marketing and communication.

About 30,000 square kilometres of forested land are devastated each year with the felling of some 300 million trees,[13] largely by itinerant farmers, although some of the timber is used commercially, especially in the pine forest areas of Paraná, Santa Catarina and Rio Grande do Sul. As population density increases, the area available for *roça* cultivation becomes more restricted. A growing appreciation of the need to conserve Brazil's forest resources has led many states to seek to control indiscriminate burning,[14] and to the founding of the Brazilian Institute for Forest Development in 1967. This Institute uses tax incentives to encourage business concerns to invest in replanting of formerly forested areas, and by the end of 1970 some 400 million trees had been planted.[15]

Methods of farming associated with permanent settlement in Brazil vary in degree of sophistication from the traditional system of river-bank cultivation to modern, highly-mechanized commercial agriculture.[16] The cultivation of riverine silts supported the development of large settlements of forest Indians[17] and is still found along many of the waterways of the Amazon drainage system today (Map 6). This type of cultivation makes full use of intimate knowledge of the flood regime of the river, with houses and permanent crops located just above permanent flood level (approximately 11 metres above low water in the settlement depicted in Map 6) on a broad part of the levee. The soil on this levee is only rarely renewed by floods and is beginning to show early signs of laterization. The smaller lower levee on the opposite bank of the river from the village is covered by floodwaters for some two weeks each year and this annual deposition of fresh silt maintains a high level of fertility. Consequently this bank is used for those annual crops which are grown for sale to itinerant traders in launches during the high water period when the trading boats reach thus far up the river. Variations on this type of agriculture, such as the *vazante* agriculture of the North-

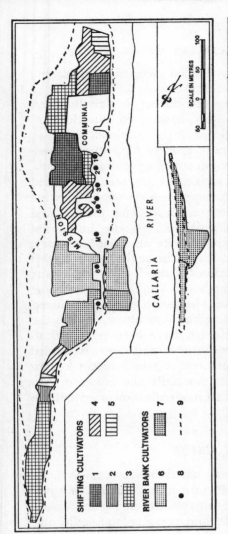
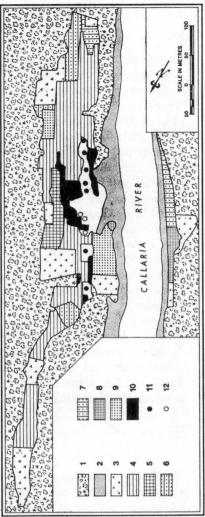

Map 6. TYPES OF AGRICULTURE IN THE UPPPER AMAZON

A—LAND OCCUPANCE. (1) man, woman; (2) man, woman; (3) two men, one woman, two children; (4) two men, two women; (5) man, three women; (6) man, two women, two children; (7) two men, two women; (8) home (hut or house); (9) 10 metre contour above low water. M = mission.

B—LAND USE. (1) forest; (2) grass; (3) clearing; (4) bananas; (5) cassava and bananas; (6) maize and bananas; (7) maize and cassava; (8) maize and watermelons; (9) maize; (10) mixed vegetables and tree crops—predominantly squash, pineapples, green vegetables, sugar cane, cotton, papaya and pipayo palm; (11) Indian hut; (12) mission building. Source: *Fieldwork* by R. P. Momsen Jr, 1961.

east associated with seasonally flooded rivers and reservoirs, are found in several parts of Brazil.[18]

In areas colonized by immigrants during the last hundred years new methods of agriculture have been introduced.[19] These colonists were not burdened with traditional Brazilian attitudes to the land and generally brought with them knowledge of the techniques of fairly advanced agricultural systems. The cultivation of new crops such as grapes was introduced by Italian settlers whilst black pepper was brought into the Amazon region by a Japanese colonist. The plough first came into common use in Brazil amongst the immigrant settlers of Rio Grande do Sul in the late nineteenth century, and even in 1950, when some four-fifths of the farms in this state had ploughs, the proportion for Brazil as a whole was only one-quarter. Intensive methods of agriculture such as crop rotation, fertilizer use and irrigation were introduced into the extensive pattern of Brazilian agriculture, and in the last two decades Japanese colonists have even managed to develop intensive horticulture in the vast and backward Northern region.[20] It is in those areas in which recent foreign colonization has been greatest, especially the States of São Paulo and Rio Grande do Sul, that modernization of agriculture is advancing most rapidly.

FARM SIZE, TENURE & LABOUR

The number of farms in Brazil has risen very rapidly from just over half a million in 1920 to nearly 5 million in 1970. Of the 1·6 million new holdings established during the 'sixties 38 per cent were in the North and the Rimland, reflecting expansion at the frontier, and most of the remainder resulted from the subdivision of existing units in the older settled parts of the country. Some 51 per cent of farms are less than ten hectares in size and occupy only 3·1 per cent of the total farmland, whilst 39 per cent of the land in farms is included in the 0·8 per cent of properties that are larger than 1,000 hectares. Regional differences in farm size are marked. The city state of Guanabara has 30 per cent of its farmland in farms of less than ten hectares whilst this category of farms occupies only 0·2 per cent of farmland in the under-populated northern territory of Rondônia. The Northeast has the highest regional average proportion of farmland in small farms, whilst the states of the North and the Rimland have the greatest proportion of extensively farmed land. Most of the new farms established since 1950 have been of less than ten hectares and the average farm size fell from 112 hectares in 1950 to 59 hectares in 1970. In Acre, Roraima and Amapá, however, there was an increase of over nine million hectares of farm land in the 'fifties, most of this held in properties in excess of 1,000 hectares, suggesting land speculation in this region.

This institutional framework dominated by large estates and extensive agriculture presents an effective barrier to technological and social change. Many of the large holdings are held as an investment and a protection against inflation by absentee owners who have little interest in agriculture *per se*. The small farmer is often a sharecropper or tenant with financial and institutional ties to the landlord. In these tenure conditions innovations are inhibited.

Land reform has long been held as the answer to many of these problems[21] and Cline has estimated that an across-the-board redistribution of land would increase Brazilian farm output by about 20 per cent.[22] The Federal Government adopted an agrarian reform programme in 1964.[23] The basis of this reform was the reclassification of Brazil's farms into four types: minifúndio, 'emprêsa rural', latifúndio-by-size and latifúndio-by-use.[24] The minifúndio is defined as a property which may be adequate for a family's subsistence but not for its social and economic improvement, whilst a latifúndio-by-size is a holding that is too large to contribute effectively to the accomplishment of Brazil's social and economic goals. Both these types of farms may be expropriated. The other two classes are distinguished on the basis of performance, the latifúndio-by-use being a large holding which is being economically exploited whilst the emprêsa rural is the ideal economically-efficient holding. Central to the system of classification is the concept of the 'módulo'. A módulo is that quantity of land which is capable of absorbing all the labour of four working adults and of supporting them at a standard of living which is consistent with the overall goals of economic progress and social justice.[25] It recognizes that two holdings of equal size may have different productive capacities due to differences in the physical qualities of the land and in relation to distance to the market. Thus the módulo is a measurement unit that varies from place to place but always has the same economic meaning, allowing the size of a specific property to be stated in terms of módulos once its productive capacity is known. Because of the impracticability of establishing the individual productive capacity of every holding in Brazil, this capacity is inferred from the present land use and the regional market potential.

Properties of less than one módulo are by definition classified as minifúndios and subdivision is not allowed below this size. A latifúndio is classified as a property consisting of 601 módulos or more.[26] The remaining properties of between one and 600 módulos are divided on the basis of four economic criteria and one social criterion.[27] To be classed as an emprêsa rural a holding has to satisfy all five of these criteria. A holding is defined as a latifúndio-by-use if it fails to meet any one of these standards.

The coefficient of social conditions serves to organize information on land tenure and labour conditions, with the highest value placed on owner-operated farms. Wage labour is most important in São Paulo and Paraná, whilst states such as Minas Gerais and those of the Northeast region have the highest seasonal fluctuations in labour needs. Twelve per cent of Brazil's farms have sharecroppers or tenants and together they work 14 per cent of the total farmland.[28] Sharecropper and tenant densities vary widely from place to place, sharecropping being most important in the North and feudal Northeast regions, whilst the European family-farm tradition of Santa Catarina and Rio Grande do Sul discourages sharecropping. The number of hectares per sharecropper or tenant (Table 1) tends to be above the national average in the large, sparsely-populated states of the North, whilst the more densely settled areas of the Northeast and East provide below average amounts of land for their sharecroppers and tenants. The latter usually work larger areas of land than do the sharecroppers.

The Land Law established 3 year terms for tenancy contracts and a maximum rent of 15 per cent of the land value. Sharecropping is controlled, with limits on the owner's share from 10 to 50 per cent depending on the facilities provided.

By 1969 76 per cent of Brazil's farms occupying 12 per cent of the farmland had been classified as minifúndios, whilst only 335 properties or 0·001 per cent of the total holdings had been classified as latifúndios-by-size. A mere 2 per cent of the properties, occupying 4 per cent of the farmland, were classified as emprêsas rurais whilst the remaining 22 per cent of the farms, including 77 per cent of the total land in farms, were identified as latifúndio-by-use.[29]

The 1964 Statute gave IBRA power to expropriate all or part of a property declared a latifúndio-by-size or a latifúndio-by-use, or a minifúndio. It was hoped that the mere threat of expropriation would be sufficient to encourage the owners of such holdings to make decisions about the social organization and economic use of their properties that would enable them to be reclassified as emprêsas rurais. In addition a differential land tax was applied to all holdings of more than 20 hectares, which was designed to provide an incentive for improvements.[30] To take possession of a property IBRA has to pay no more than the unimproved value as declared by the land-owner for taxes plus the value of the improvements, and payment can be in government bonds. Expropriated lands are made available to newly-formed co-operatives and to government for afforestation or for agricultural research stations. Land is redistributed to individuals, priority going to the former owner and his family, squatters, sharecroppers or tenants on the land, operators of minifúndios and those who have special skills in farming, with heads of large families taking precedence in all groups.

Priority areas in which the land situation was most acute were identified. In 1965 three areas were given priority. A northeastern one covered part of Pernambuco and Paraíba. This area included the dry interior of these states and thus the eroded sisal plantations of Paraíba as well as the humid litorals dominated by sugar cane latifúndios, heavy rural population pressure and low labour and land productivity. Associated with this priority area is the comprehensive agrarian reform plan for the sugar areas of Paraíba, Pernambuco and Alagoas, aimed at modernizing the sugar industry, providing land for subsistence farms for the workers and retraining workers displaced by mechanization.[31] Another priority area covers all

TABLE I

Distribution by Political Unit of Hectares
per Sharecropper and Tenant

Political unit	Hectares per sharecropper	Hectares per tenant
Acre	565·0	2,080·0
Amazonas	471·0	160·0
Roraima	462·0	—
Pará	109·0	190·0
Amapá	50·0	66·0
Rondônia	47·0	4,100·0
Mato Grosso	30·0	117·0
Goiás	23·0	39·0
Rio Grande do Sul	16·6	123·0
Ceará	16·5	26·0
Piauí	15·7	27·0
São Paulo	13·0	33·0
Paraíba	12·5	6·0
Rio Grande do Norte	12·2	19·5
Paraná	12·0	18·1
Santa Catarina	10·0	19·3
Espírito Santo	9·0	44·0
Pernambuco	8·8	14·4
Bahia	8·3	9·0
Maranhão	8·2	12·6
Minas Gerais	7·2	48·5
Distrito Federal	7·1	—
Alagoas	3·1	9·5
Sergipe	3·1	12·0
Guanabara	3·0	5·0
Rio de Janeiro	2·7	35·2
BRAZIL	12·6	44·6

Source: Ludwig and Taylor, op. cit., p. 55.

the states of Rio de Janeiro and Guanabara and the neighbouring parts of Minas Gerais and São Paulo. It includes Brazil's
most important food-producing region, running between the
two major cities and focusing on the Paraíba valley with its
heavily eroded and exhausted soils. The third area established

at the beginning of the reform programme was that of the Federal District. Here the level but infertile plateau area surrounding Brasília, which had traditionally been a cattle ranching area and where half the farmers in the District were squatters, was expected to provide food crops for the nation's new capital.[32] In 1966 the entire state of Rio Grande do Sul was given priority on the basis of the extreme development of very small farms amongst the Italian, German and Polish settlers, largely through fragmentation due to inheritance, and the growing importance of large extensive holdings in the southern grasslands. Even later a fifth priority area, the drought-devastated state of Ceará, was added.

Although the Federal Government still expresses interest in the aims of land reform[33] very little has actually been achieved and emphasis is now being placed on the politically-easier approach of colonization, especially in the North, to the problems of the rural sector. The Land Law, combined with the 1964 and 1973 implementations of a Rural Worker's Law which provides the farm labourer with a minimum wage and certain social security benefits formerly the exclusive privilege of the urban worker, has, however, brought about changes. Farm owners have reacted to both these laws by reducing the number of workers in agriculture through introducing both machinery and crops needing less labour. Preference is being given to the system of *volantes*, in which the displaced rural worker lives in a town and his labour is contracted for by jobbers who deliver him to the farm in the morning and return him to the town at night. These changes increase production per worker but often decrease gross income per unit of land. The large number of displaced workers causes social disruption in the countryside and contributes to the decline of many small urban centres.[34]

LAND USE

Traditionally increases in agricultural production in Brazil have been brought about by expanding the area of land in farms rather than by changes in agricultural systems or by the application of new agronomic practices. There has been a steady increase in the proportion of land in farms in

TABLE 2

Farmland 1940, 1950 & 1960

	1940	*1950*	*1960*
Percentage of total land area in farms	23·3	27·4	32·1
Number of holdings (thousands)	1,905	2,064	3,349
Area of holdings (thousand hectares)	197,720	232,211	265,451
Crops	18,835	19,095	29,760
Woods, unutilized	90,743	105,568	107,891
Pastures	88,142	107,548	127,800

Source: Censo Agrícola de 1940 and 1950 and Censo Agrícola Preliminar, 1960.

Brazil (Table 2) and in the number of holdings. Intensity of use has also increased slightly, with cropland occupying 12 per cent of farmland in 1970 as compared to 9 per cent in 1940. The proportion of farmland cultivated varies from 0·35 per cent in Roraima to 18 per cent in Espírito Santo and 32 per cent in Paraná (Map 7). On the other hand the percentage increases in cultivated land between 1960 and 1970 were highest in the pioneer zones of the North and Rimland and least in the Heartland, with Rondônia increasing its cultivated acreage 274 per cent whilst Guanabara declined by 54 per cent.

According to the 1967 cadaster a quarter of the land holdings comprising half the farmland was dedicated to the raising of livestock of '*grande porte*', predominantly cattle, whilst 8 per cent of farms and land were involved in the production of small livestock. The gathering of wild vegetable products from the forest was the main occupation on 13 per cent of the holdings, occupying 22 per cent of the land in farms. Only one-fifth of the farmland was used for crop production although this area included nearly half the number of farms in the country. Annual crops were the main product of 12 per cent of the land, permanent crops such as coffee and cocoa occupied 6·5 per cent of the land and 18 per cent of the farms, whilst a mere 5 per cent of farms practised horticulture on 0·5 per cent of the farmland. Over half the ranchlands were found

Map 7. INTENSITY OF CULTIVATION. (1) micro-regions with between 5 and 29 per cent of their farmland in cultivation; (2) micro-regions with more than 30 per cent of their farmland in cultivation. Compiled from *Divisão do Brasil em micro-regiões homogêneas, 1968*. Instituto Brasileiro de Geografia. Rio de Janeiro, 1970.

in the Rimland states whilst one-third of the acreage in annual crops and one-fifth of the perennial cropland was located in the Heartland.

Brazil is a major world producer of most tropical crops, and the only staple agricultural commodity that has to be imported is wheat. The basic components of the ordinary Brazilian's diet, rice, beans, cassava and maize, are grown throughout the country, whilst certain areas with peculiar environmental or marketing advantages specialize in the commercial production of particular crops (Map 8). Jute is grown on the seasonally-flooded riparian lands of the North, the *várzea*, where the flood regime of the Amazon offers exceptional conditions for harvesting at the appropriate time of year

Map 8. MAIN COMMERCIAL CROP REGIONS. (1) cocoa; (2) sugar cane and coconuts; (3) sugar cane and bananas; (4) jute and black pepper; (5) cotton, sisal, castor beans and sugar cane; (6) coffee, cotton, sugar cane, groundnuts; (7) wheat, soyabeans, grapes, tobacco. Compiled from *Divisão do Brasil em micro-regiões homogêneas, 1968*. Instituto Brasileiro de Geografia, Rio de Janeiro, 1970.

and sometimes allows two crops per year.[35] In the interior of the Northeast tree cotton, now cultivated largely for cattle feed, and sisal are grown. Sisal was introduced into this area in the 1930s, and because of high war-time demand the state of Bahia offered incentives to farmers who would plant sisal as a cash crop. Many small farmers gave up subsistence cultivation for this new 'green-gold', only to find themselves impoverished and hungry when world sisal prices fell in 1952 and African producers expanded exports.[36] In the East coffee, sugar and cotton are produced on the rich _terra roxa_ soils, whilst many other crops are grown to feed the large urban population. Crops needing seasonal variation in temperature, such as wheat and grapes, are found in the extreme south of Brazil, especially in Rio Grande do Sul. The coastal zone has generally higher rainfall than the interior and so has developed its own peculiar land use patterns. Sugar cane is a major crop throughout the coastal area from Paraíba southwards. In the northern part of this zone the soil is sandy and coconut palms are grown in association with sugar cane; around Ilhéus in Bahia cocoa becomes the dominant crop on the _massapé_ soils formed where crystalline rocks reach the coast; and to the south of the cocoa area, heavier alluvial soils become predominant and bananas are important in the crop mix.

Some two-thirds of agricultural output comes from crops, one-quarter from livestock products and the remaining 8 per cent comes from extractive forest production. The relative importance of these three components of Brazilian agriculture varies from region to region. Extensive livestock ranching is most important in the pioneer zone of the Rimland. Stock are driven from the _sertão_ along traditional routes to feed lots and abattoirs just inland of the coast of the Northeast, the Heartland and Rio Grande do Sul (Map 9). The dairy industry is more strongly localized, with just over half the milk production in 1969 coming from two states of the Heartland, Minas Gerais and São Paulo,[37] close to the country's two largest urban markets, Rio de Janeiro and São Paulo. In the interior of the Northeast goats as well as cattle are raised, largely for their skins, whilst sheep farming is concentrated in Rio Grande do Sul.

Extractive industries are of great importance in the North, where over much of the region the value of rubber and Brazil nuts gathered from the forest exceeds the value of cultivated crops (Map 10). The gathering of wild palm products is especially important in the Northeast. Maranhão produces 80 per cent of the Brazilian output of babassu oil and production doubled between 1950 and 1965.[38] The leaves of the carnaúba palm provide a wax which is used in the manufacture

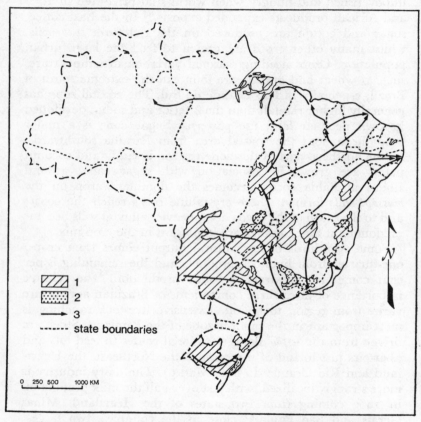

Map 9. MAIN CATTLE REGIONS. (1) micro-regions with more than 500,000 head of cattle; (2) micro-regions producing more than 100 million litres of milk per year; (3) major stock routes. Compiled from *Divisão do Brasil em micro-regiões, op. cit.*, and *Atlas do Brasil, op. cit.*, Map IV-9.

of records, films and polishes, and 90 per cent of production comes from the states of Maranhão, Piauí, Ceará and Rio Grande do Norte. Oiticica oil is used in the paint industry and Ceará produces 75 per cent of this palm oil. This state also produces 68 per cent of Brazil's cashew nuts.[39] Two wild plants, piassava and caroá, found in the eastern part of the region, provide fibres which are used for the local manufacture

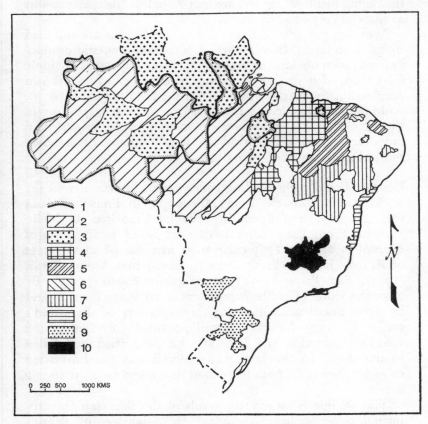

Map 10. MAIN REGIONS OF GATHERING VEGETABLE PRODUCTS. (1) area within which wild forest products are more valuable than cultivated crops; (2) rubber; (3) Brazil nuts; (4) babassu; (5) carnaúba; (6) oiticica; (7) caroá; (8) piassava; (9) mate; (10) charcoal. Compiled from *Divisão do Brasil em micro-regiões, op. cit.*

of hammocks. Bahia state is the main producer of piassava whilst Pernambuco produces most of the caroá fibre. Charcoal is a traditional forest product of central Minas Gerais, largely as a raw material for small mills producing high quality steel.

In the interior of Paraná, Santa Catarina and Rio Grande do Sul and in a small area of Mato Grosso, mate, used to make green tea, is harvested. Attempts to develop commercial plantations of many of these wild plants have not been very successful and this component of agriculture has failed to increase as fast as those of crops and livestock.

About 95 per cent of Brazil's home food needs are supplied by her own farms. Even for wheat increased domestic production may soon obviate the necessity for large imports. The staple food crops of maize, rice, beans and cassava have all shown considerable increases in output over the last decade (Table 3), with the first two crops mentioned becoming important in the export market. Brazilians eat more fruit per capita than any other nation in the world and fruit production has shown marked increases since 1960.

COFFEE. Brazil is the leading coffee producing country in the world. Coffee brought from Martinique to French Guiana was smuggled into Brazil in 1727 by Francisco de Mello Palheta. From Pará coffee seeds were taken to the state of Maranhão and by 1774 cultivation had started in the state of Rio de Janeiro. From there it spread into Minas Gerais (1775), São Paulo (1800) and Espírito Santo (1815). By 1825 the value of coffee exports exceeded that of sugar, and by 1900 Brazil accounted for three-quarters of the world's coffee. By 1959, however, Brazil provided only half of the world's production and by 1965 this proportion had fallen to one-third. In the late 'sixties Brazil was not harvesting enough coffee to fill both her export quota and satisfy domestic needs.

This decline is largely the result of the Brazilian Government's coffee policy. Nowadays three-quarters of Brazil's coffee comes from the states of São Paulo and Paraná, the latter state becoming the leading producer in the early 1960s. Coffee is grown on many different soils, although the rich *terra roxa* soil of Minas Gerais, São Paulo and Paraná is best suited to it. Coffee is grown at altitudes ranging from sea level to 1,700 metres and in rainfall conditions varying from 800 mm per year as in Bahia to 1,800 mm a year as in Santa Catarina. Most of the coffee produced in Brazil is of the *Robusta* type

TABLE 3

Principal Crops of Brazil, 1960, 1965 & 1969

Crops	Volume (1,000 metric tons)			Value (Cr$1,000)
	1960	1965	1969	1969
Coffee	4,170	3,664	2,567	2,039,314
Maize	8,672	12,112	12,693	1,730,110
Rice	4,795	7,520	6,394	1,690,888
Sugar cane	56,613	75,853	75,247	1,241,677
Cassava	17,613	24,993	30,073	1,136,209
Black beans	1,731	2,290	2,200	1,060,195
Cotton	1,609	1,986	2,111	1,048,687
Wheat	713	585	1,374	599,649
Bananas*	229	349	463	565,245
Cocoa	163	161	211	437,601
Oranges†	8,360	11,428	14,484	344,780
Irish potatoes	1,113	1,246	1,507	317,938
Groundnuts	408	743	754	267,191
Soyabeans	206	523	1,057	265,213
Tomatoes	397	580	700	254,544
Tobacco	161	248	250	249,523
Sweet potatoes	1,283	1,721	2,175	141,671
Grapes	427	551	483	127,684
Castor beans	225	355	378	114,117
Coconuts†	436	529	656	112,749
Onions	210	225	275	105,904
Sisal	164	242	311	78,016
Pineapples†	178	195	260	69,079
Mangoes†	1,824	2,019	2,210	57,573
Tangerines†	1,495	1,991	2,293	51,843
Black pepper	4	9	14	30,002
Alfalfa	227	196	180	29,892
Jute	39	62	49	25,407
Peaches†	516	946	974	22,406
Flaxseed	30	42	31	11,723
Tea	3	6	5	11,642
Barley	36	27	31	10,604

* Million stems. † Million fruits.
Source: *Anuário Estatístico do Brasil*, Rio de Janeiro, I.B.G.E., 1962, 1966 and 1970.

with a recently introduced variety, *Novo Mundo*, giving higher yields and quicker maturing trees. The life expectancy of the average coffee tree is 30 years and the average yield is 2 lbs of milled coffee per tree. There are in Brazil some half a million coffee farms with about half the production coming from medium-sized properties of 8 to 65 hectares. The coffee tree is particularly susceptible to fluctuations in production, a bumper harvest usually being followed by a couple of years with poor crops. These fluctuations combined with the major variations in harvests brought about by the occasional incidence of drought and frost forced the Brazilian Government to control the volume of coffee exports so as to keep gluts and shortages on the world market and the consequent low and high prices to a minimum.

The number of trees trebled and production more than doubled between 1890 and 1900 and thus, given the relative inelasticity of demand, prices fell sharply. In 1902 the government of São Paulo State prohibited all new plantings for five years. Trees planted immediately before the ban continued to expand output and in 1906 there was a bumper harvest bringing world prices to less than half those ruling a decade earlier. The state government bought up almost one-third of the crop and stored it to be released in subsequent seasons when the production was low. This state valorization of the coffee was so successful that it was repeated in 1917 and in the early 'twenties, to be followed by the introduction of a permanent control scheme in 1924 when the Federal Government participated.[40] Some 500 million new coffee trees were planted between 1922 and 1930 and coffee monoculture became as dangerously dominant as it had been thirty years earlier. Brazilian control of exports kept world prices at a profitable level, encouraging other countries to expand their production whilst Brazil carried the burden of maintaining those prices. The increased planting in Brazil led to the breakdown of export control and political revolution in 1930. Between 1931 and 1944 over 78 million bags of coffee, the equivalent of three years' world supply, were either burned or dumped in the sea. In the post-war years coffee planting continued with the coffee frontier moving south and west of São Paulo, so that between 1940 and 1960 Paraná's share of Brazilian coffee production increased from 7 per cent to 52 per cent. The number of trees planted in Paraná increased from 55 million in 1939 to 695 million in 1954 and reached 1,316 million by 1963,[41] representing an investment of US$370 million.[42] This increase in new plantings, combined with the growing contributions of African coffee producers, led once again to lower world prices.

In 1957 first attempts were made by the producing countries to control exports jointly and in 1962 an International Coffee Agreement was drawn up between 41 producing and 21 consuming nations and ratified by the United States in 1964. The success of this pact is dependent on agreement between the main producing country, Brazil, and the main consuming country, the United States of America. In 1967 a dispute broke out between these two countries. The Brazilians were worried by declining world prices and the Brazilian Minister of Industry and Commerce pointed out that in 1950 a Brazilian farmer had to sell only 18 bags of coffee in order to buy a lorry but in 1967 the lorry cost the equivalent of 49 bags of coffee. In the mid-sixties Brazil began to manufacture instant coffee. Most of this was exported to the United States and used as a blender with American-made soluble coffees which were based on cheaper but bitter-tasting African coffees. For the Brazilians this was a method of earning foreign exchange from their poorest grade of coffee beans that the Brazilian Government would not allow to be exported, and also an important step in economic development. The American manufacturers complained that they did not have access to this cheap source of beans and accused Brazil of dumping soluble coffee on the United States market, although the price of Brazilian soluble coffee was higher than that of other countries and Brazil supplied only 14 per cent of the instant coffee consumed in America in 1967. In order to preserve the International Coffee Agreement which was renewed in 1968, Brazil bowed to United States pressure and in May 1969 agreed to place a Brazilian Government tax of 13 US cents per pound on soluble coffee exports to the United States.

The impact of currency realignments on producers' earnings led the four major producing countries of Brazil, Colombia, Angola and Ivory Coast to impose export limitations and set up an international company to sell coffee. The Coffee

Agreement, however, after three years of dispute as producers and consumers failed to agree over the use of the export quota system, was eventually renewed for six years from October 1976.

At the same time as the coffee dispute has been worsening the United States share of Brazilian coffee exports has been going down steadily since the crop year of 1965/66. In that year it was more than 43 per cent, in 1966/67 it was 39 per cent and in 1968/69 it was 36 per cent,[43] whilst in 1970 United States imports of Brazilian coffee declined a further 11·2 per cent and their imports of African coffees increased some 21·4 per cent.[44] Because of the importance of coffee amongst Brazil's exports any reorientation of her coffee trade is followed by an associated change in the direction of flow of her overall trade pattern.

The Brazilian price support programme, involving buying up the excess production of the coffee growers and storing it, was expensive and contributed to the nation's rapid inflation. Considerable international pressure was put on Brazil to reduce her stocks of coffee, 60 million bags in 1963, and to diversify out of coffee. In 1962 a massive coffee-eradication programme was initiated under which about half the nation's coffee trees were to be destroyed at a cost of US$100 million.

Most of the coffee eradicated was in the low-grade areas of Espírito Santo[45] and Minas Gerais and the medium-grade coffee areas of Paraná. Over a million hectares were taken out of coffee and put into new crops. The vast proportion of this land-use revolution was achieved in five months between September 1962, and February 1963. Farmers were paid indemnities ranging from 11 to 22 cents for each tree they uprooted, depending on the quality of the coffee in their areas and how many trees they eliminated. One-third was paid when the trees were levelled, one third when the land had been cultivated and seeded with a new crop, and the final third some 60 days thereafter.[46] A farmer who agreed to eradicate his trees not only received the indemnity but was also given expert advice on the type of new crop best suited to his soil, such as rice, beans, maize, soyabeans, groundnuts, sunflowers, citrus fruits, ramie, avocado, mango, pecan, banana and other tropical fruits or pasture for beef cattle. Special loans were made available to the farmer to help him buy new farm tools and seeds. Aid was also given in marketing, with minimum prices guaranteed by the Brazilian Coffee Institute.[47] Many of these new crops have proved more profitable than all but the best coffee;[48] however, the rate of labour absorption by the diversified crops is less than 30 per cent of the total formerly employed.[49]

The restructured coffee industry of Brazil was seriously threatened in January 1970, when two varieties of a devastating plant disease, coffee rust, borne by a fungus called *Hemileia vastatrix*, were discovered on coffee plantations in Bahia. This disease attacked the coffee trees of Ceylon in the second half of the nineteenth century and within twenty years had virtually destroyed what had been the centre of the world's coffee industry. The coffee rust attacks the leaves of the tree, gradually weakening the tree until it is unable to produce a coffee crop.

Measures to combat the disease have added considerably to production costs. The programme has two main lines of attack: firstly, the use of fungicides with an associated change in planting patterns, replacing tight clusters of four to six bushes with wider-spaced individual plants which are easier to dust with fungicides; and, secondly, the planting of new disease-resistant varieties of coffee trees.[50] Extensive replanting was undertaken in 1970 and 1971 with the aid of government loans, in an attempt to maintain a sufficient volume of coffee production to meet both home and export demands. Coffee is still the biggest single earner of foreign exchange and the largest industry, employing six million people. Output, however, has declined considerably since the late 'sixties, following the heavy frosts and rains of 1969, 1972 and 1975 and the impact of the coffee rust. The three-year programme launched in 1972 to increase production had little effect and exports are not expected to return to normal levels until 1979.[51]

COTTON. This has traditionally been Brazil's second most important export crop and production increased considerably during the nineteen-sixties, largely through an expansion of acreage from 2·75 million hectares in 1959 to 4·2 million hectares in 1969. The greatest increases were in the states of Ceará in the Northeast and Paraná in the Periphery, whilst the cotton acreage of São Paulo state decreased by one-third mainly because of the profitability of alternative crops. Although cotton is produced in most parts of Brazil there are two main cotton zones: a northern one made up largely of the states of Ceará, Rio Grande do Norte, Pernambuco and Paraíba and a southern zone comprising the states of São Paulo, Paraná and Minas Gerais. The northern zone grows three varieties of cotton. Behind the humid litoral lies the upper coastal cotton area where the short staple variety known as 'Mata' is grown. Further west lies a second region of lower rainfall where both annual and perennial cotton is found. Still further inland, where rainfall is usually insufficient for annual cotton, tree cotton, with a life span of 30 years and with roots which can penetrate the soil to a depth of 5 metres in search of water, dominates cotton production. The northern cotton is generally of medium to long staple, includes some 'Sea-Island' cotton and is mostly consumed within Brazil. Cotton productivity in this region has declined because of degeneration of the planting stock caused by accidental crossings between varieties.[52] In the southern zone, which produces some two-thirds of Brazil's cotton, the cotton is mostly of short or medium staples and is comparable with the United States 'Upland' cotton.

SUGAR CANE. This was the first major commercial crop of Brazil and is still important in many parts of the country today. In weight it is by far the main harvest and it ranked fourth in value both in total production and in exports in 1969. Sugar production is the dominant economic activity of some of the Northeastern states, especially Pernambuco and Alagoas, but since the 1940s the major producing centres have lain further south, with the state of São Paulo producing approximately one-third of the nation's total in 1969. Sugar production has increased considerably over the last ten years, both in response to increased domestic consumption, which rose from 33 kilogrammes per capita in 1959 to 40 in 1965[53] and to higher United States quotas and world prices. In 1966 there were some 350 sugar mills in eighteen states processing sugar cane. Incentives for mergers and modernization of sugar mills led to a reduction in their number, only 261 mills operating in 1971.

The Sugar and Alcohol Institute, founded by the Federal Government in 1933 to assure the orderly growth of the sugar industry, imposes restrictions on production and on the operation of sugar mills, regulates the flow of surplus sugar to external markets and channels excess cane to the manufacture of alcohol for blending with petrol. Improvements in the quality of Brazilian sugar, a revision of production quotas to mills and states and the development of facilities such as the bulk loading terminal at Recife led to Brazil becoming, in 1972, once again the largest producer of sugar on the world market.

COCOA. Brazil is the leading Western Hemisphere producer of cocoa, providing about 10 per cent of world output. In 1969 exports of cocoa products were exceeded in value only by those of coffee and cotton. Brazilian cocoa commands lower prices on the world market than African cocoa because in the southern part of the cocoa zone the beans are dried over fires which give the cocoa a smoky flavour. Although only 3 per cent of the beans are originally contaminated they are mixed with other beans so that 20 per cent of the exports are finally affected. Some 95 per cent of Brazil's cocoa is grown in Bahia, centred on the town of Ilhéus. Mean yields per hectare have declined from 654 kilogrammes in 1939 to 315 in 1968, and absentee landlords and traditional atttitudes are hampering the replanting of the 60 per cent of plantations that are over fifty years of age. The research, technical assistance and financial aid provided by CEPLAC (Plan for the Economic Recovery of Cocoa Cultivation) established in 1957 is, however, bringing about changes slowly. Replanting was started in 1967 and it is hoped to replant 150,000 hectares by 1980 using a hybrid variety which gives on average farm yields of 1,200 kilogrammes per hectare. By 1971, 150,000 hectares of cocoa had been rehabilitated by reducing the number of shade trees per hectare, increasing fertilizer application and improving general cultivation practices.[54] The effects of these changes can be seen in the production figures: between 1962 and 1969 acreage fell by 6 per cent but output rose by 50 per cent.[55]

PRODUCTIVITY

The rate of growth of agricultural production has lagged behind that of other sectors of the economy. Table 4 shows that while industry and population increased their growth rates steadily between 1920 and 1962, agriculture fluctuated wildly. The variation in growth rates was even more marked for the various components of agriculture, the range being least for the most highly commercialized aspect, export agriculture, while the most primitive form of agriculture, the gathering of forest products, had the greatest variation in productivity over the period. By 1970 the productivity of agriculture had improved considerably, with crop output 8 per cent above that of 1969 and livestock products up 7 per cent.[56] It was thought that these gains were largely due to the government programme of credit incentives and new price minima.

Between 1940 and 1960 the value of agricultural output increased 84 per cent whilst the number of hectares cultivated increased 40 per cent and the number of agricultural workers grew by 50 per cent. In the period 1940 to 1950 much of the increase in total production was the direct result of an increase in the area cultivated (Table 5). In the following decade, however, productivity increased somewhat more. Schuh has suggested that of the 30 per cent increase in productivity per hectare some two-thirds can be accounted for by a shift in the relative value of products per hectare, that is, a change from low-value crops to high-value crops or from crops to livestock, whilst the remaining third came from an increase in productivity, most of which reflected improvements in livestock production per hectare.[57] In the period 1960 to 1970 the number of farms rose from 3·3 to 4·9 million and the number of agricultural workers in Brazil as a whole rose by 2·5 million, but there was an absolute decline in São Paulo, where the agricultural labour force fell from 1·7 to 1·5 million and the number of farms remained static. At the same time both the value of agricultural products and the area under production have increased considerably, indicating higher levels of productivity for labour in terms of both the area worked and the value of the product.

TABLE 4

Percentage Growth Rates of Agriculture, Industry
& Population, 1920 to 1962

	1920–1922 to 1930–1932	1930–1932 to 1940–1942	1940–1942 to 1950–1952	1950–1952 to 1960–1962
Industrial production	2·7	6·0	7·7	8·9
Agriculture production	2·9	6·3	1·4	4·7
Crops	3·5	1·1	2·0	4·9
Export products	2·1	0·1	2·0	2·3
Products for domestic market	5·1	−0·4	1·0	5·4
Animal products	1·4	0·6	1·0	4·2
Extractive plant products	4·8	23·1	0·5	5·9
Population	1·5	1·5	2·4	3·0

Source: Schuh, op. cit., pp. 75–77.

TABLE 5

Agricultural Productivity and Employment,
1940, 1950, & 1960

Year	Total production (NCr$)*	Hectares in production†	Persons employed (millions)	Hectares per person	Production per hectare (NCr$)	Production per person (NCr$)
1940	79·3	107·0	11·3	10·1	0·741	0·748
1950	95·2	126·7	11·0	11·2	0·751	0·842
1960	146·3	150·0	15·6	11·8	0·975	1·152

* Million NCr$, 1953. †Million hectares, including natural pastures.

Source: Schuh, op. cit., p. 183. Survey of the Brazilian Economy, op. cit., p. 40.

A characteristic of Brazilian agriculture is that crop yields tend to decline in the old traditional areas of production whilst new, higher-yielding areas are coming into production. This pattern explains much of the increase in sugar cane yields over the last two decades (Table 6) as the centre of production has shifted from Pernambuco to São Paulo. The growth of coffee yields is also probably as much due to the shift in production from the low-yielding areas of Minas Gerais and Espírito Santo to the higher-yielding soils of Paraná, as to the introduction of new, higher-yielding varieties of coffee. On the other hand the agricultural revolution of the last decade has made improved agronomic practices the main reason for higher productivity in most aspects of agriculture. This is particularly noticeable in export crops, other than sugar and coffee, and in market garden crops. The recent improvement in cocoa yields is almost entirely due to replacement of old trees and better management. The introduction of improved varieties of maize, cotton and wheat has been a major contributor to the higher yields obtained for these crops.

The overall picture is one of great diversity of yields both within and between crops, with much of the year-to-year variation reflecting weather conditions. In addition the figures for the country as a whole often mask consistent yield differences between different parts of the country. The yield of maize in Paraná, for example, is twice that of Bahia, and the yield of black beans in Rio Grande do Sul twice that in Rio Grande do Norte. Yields for most crops grown in Brazil tend to be lower than yields in other parts of the world. For example, in the early 'sixties wheat yields in Argentina, rice yields in Uruguay and sugar cane yields in Barbados were double those of Brazil. This would suggest that despite problems of climate and infertile soils in Brazil there is scope for considerable improvement in average yields for many crops.

Productivity in the livestock sector is also low. The carcass yield per animal slaughtered averaged only 164 kilogrammes in the period 1955–59 as compared to an average of 207 kilogrammes in Argentina.[58] In most beef-producing countries cattle are typically slaughtered at between two and three years of age but in Brazil the average age at slaughter varies from three years in Rio Grande do Sul to as many as six years in the Northeast. Fertility rates are low and the calf mortality rate high. Milk production per cow is low generally because of poor farm management.[59] The differences in productivity between the milk supply areas of the two major cities of Rio de Janeiro and São Paulo and those of the smaller cities of Belo Horizonte and Niterói (Table 7) probably reflect a higher level of technology in the dairy industry serving the nation's major markets. Productivity of the smaller animals is also fairly low, although wool production, 97 per cent of which comes from Rio Grande do Sul, has improved rapidly in both quantity and quality with a doubling of value between 1965 and 1969. The number of chickens increased by almost

TABLE 6

Yields of Selected Crops, 1952–54, 1960–62 &
(1953 = 100)

Product	1952–54	1960–62	
Coffee	99	127	
Maize	103	112	ꞏ5
Rice	100	112	100
Sugar cane	101	111	125
Cassava	101	104	115
Black beans	97	94	94
Cotton	108	129	114
Wheat	99	83	103
Bananas	103	104	120
Cocoa	105	81	103
Oranges	102	93	97
Irish potatoes	99	114	137
Groundnuts	103	125	111
Tomatoes	98	123	158
Tobacco	96	97	120

Source: Anuário Estatístico do Brasil, Rio de Janeiro, I.B.G.E., various years.

100 million between 1960 and 1970 and poultry production is becoming more highly commercialized, especially in São Paulo, which produces 30 per cent of the nation's eggs and 20 per cent of the chickens, and the rate of output is improving.

TECHNOLOGICAL CHANGE

During the 'sixties increased agricultural productivity came about as a direct result of the modernization of farming. The Brazilian government is stimulating the spread of new farming technology by both indirect services and by direct subsidy.

In 1960 three-quarters of Brazil's farms used only human power for agricultural activities,[60] 22 per cent used draught animals but less than 1 per cent used mechanical power. The actual number of tractors in Brazil increased from 1,706 in 1920, 3,379 in 1940 and 8,372 in 1950 to 61,345 in 1960 and 156,592 by 1970. There have been two main diffusion centres

TABLE 7

Productivity in Four Important Milk Supply Areas

	Production per cow (kilogrammes)	Period of lactation (days)	Daily average per cow (kilogrammes)
Rio de Janeiro	780	240	3·25
São Paulo	732	240	3·05
Belo Horizonte	446	190	3·35
Niterói	594	220	2·70
Average	718	235	3·05

Source: Schuh, op. cit., p. 181.

for the spread of the farm tractor (Map 11). The tractor was first adopted by the immigrant farmers of Rio Grande do Sul and in 1920 this state had 48 per cent of the nation's tractors. The progressive farmers of São Paulo were rapid acceptors of mechanization and by 1940 this state had 42 per cent of all the tractors in Brazil. It increased this proportion to 46 per cent in 1950, when Minas Gerais had some 9 per cent of the total and Rio Grande do Sul's share had fallen to 27 per cent. Between 1950 and 1960 the diffusion process entered a second stage in which tractors became familiar to most farmers in the two source states and spread into the neighbouring states, especially those of Minas Gerais and Paraná bordering the major diffusion centre of São Paulo. This greater spread is shown by the one per cent decline in the shares of the three leading states and the rise of Paraná from 3 per cent of the total in 1950 to 8 per cent in 1960. In this latter year the number of hectares of cultivated land per tractor varied from 173 in Guanabara to 28,535 in Maranhão, with the average for Brazil falling from 2,281 in 1950 to 469 in 1960.

Since 1960 the rate of growth in tractor numbers as well as the spatial diffusion has increased, although the level of mechanization in Brazil as a whole remains low. By 1970 São Paulo had 42 per cent of Brazil's tractors whilst the proportion in Rio Grande do Sul and Minas Gerais had fallen to 25 and 6 per cent respectively and that of Paraná increased to 11 per cent.[61] A third wave of mechanization had come into being with a rapid growth of tractor use along the agricultural frontier in Mato Grosso and Goiás and in the North and North-east under the stimulus of Federal aid.

Within states local patterns of mechanization are often influenced positively by the presence of paved roads, urban

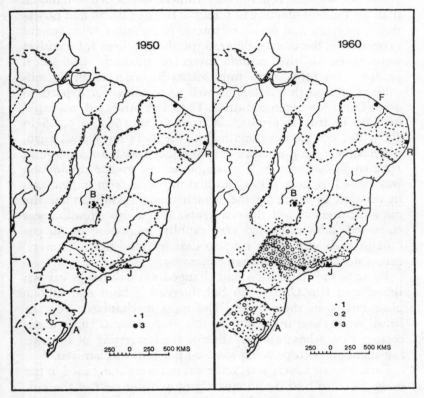

Map 11. DIFFUSION OF TRACTORS, 1950–60. (1) 100 tractors; (2) 1,000 tractors; (3) cities: L–Belém, F–Fortaleza, R–Recife, B–Brasília, J–Rio de Janeiro, P–São Paulo, A–Pôrto Alegre. *Source: Atlas do Brasil, op. cit.*, Plate IV–6.

centres, agricultural colleges or centres for tractor rental services, and negatively by the existence of areas of uncultivated latifúndios or of minifúndios too small to be mechanized.[62] Factors encouraging mechanization have been the gradual change in the agricultural economy of many areas from grazing to crop cultivation, and a growing shortage of farm labour accompanied by a rise in minimum wage levels, whilst uncertainty as to Federal agricultural policy and high prices for tractors have hindered their purchase.[63]

To make the rapid and widespread mechanization of the 1960s possible the Federal Government developed a national plan for the manufacture of tractors. In 1959 Brazil had no less than 143 types and makes of tractor of various foreign origins in operation, but in 1960 domestic production began. Incentives were given to the manufacturers of tractors, mechanical ploughs and other farm implements in order to bring self-sufficiency into this sector, as well as to allow for exports to other Latin American countries. These incentives led to a rapid increase in tractor production from 37 in 1960 to 9,908 in 1963. But production remained at the 1963 level until 1970, when some 13,205 tractors were produced with an upsurge in 1972 to 34,000 units.[64] This stagnation in tractor production was caused by high prices and high taxes on farm implements in relation to farm income, which made it difficult for the manufacturers to sell their tractors. When this situation was corrected, sales expanded very rapidly, increasing by 50 per cent in each year since 1967 so that by 1969 manufacturers' excess stocks of tractors were exhausted.

By 1970 mechanization had changed agriculture in eastern Brazil and Rio Grande do Sul, increasing land and labour productivity in these areas. The most mechanized crops in Brazil were those important in this area, such as sugar cane, cotton, rice, wheat and soyabeans, the harvesting of the two last-mentioned crops being some 60 per cent mechanized.[65]

Fertilizer use is very low, sufficient fertilizer being used in the early 1960s to fertilize adequately only 8 per cent of the cultivated land of Brazil. Of the mineral elements being taken from the soil only 12 per cent is being replaced.[66] Moreover, in general, no fertilizer is used on the pasture lands, many of which lack calcium, phosphorous and trace elements, so that deficiency diseases in livestock are widespread.

Fertilizer use did not really begin in Brazil until 1948 and its adoption was limited by high prices largely due to transport costs and heavy reliance on imports. Between 1953 and 1964 the consumption of fertilizers more than doubled, whilst between 1965 and 1968 it doubled again. Thus, as with mechanization, the rate of fertilizer use as well as the absolute amount consumed has increased rapidly in the last decade. Some 85 per cent of the fertilizer is used in the Eastern region, both the Heartland and the Periphery, and in the intensively cultivated part of Rio Grande do Sul. Much of the increase in fertilizer use in the second half of the 'sixties has been prompted by a government credit programme and an improved distribution system. Both of these stimulants, however, have concentrated their effect on the areas of highest fertilizer use, thus accentuating the disparities between the advanced East and the rest of Brazil.

Domestic production of fertilizers has also been encouraged and in 1970 Ultrafértil inaugurated its industrial complex at Cubatão in the Santos Lowland of São Paulo. The seven integrated plants of the complex are expected to produce one ton of nitrogenous and phosphatic fertilizers per minute, saving approximately US$23 million per year in fertilizer imports. Part of the production of this complex is distributed through the company's network of Agricultural Service Centres. Each centre is staffed by six or seven agronomists and equipped with fertilizer storage and mixing facilities, a railway siding, fertilizer truck spreaders and a training centre, and distributes lime, herbicides, insecticides, formicides and fungicides. By the end of 1970 the company had provided assistance to over 100,000 farmers throughout the state of São Paulo and so brought modern farming knowledge to at least one part of Brazil.[67] The use of modern inputs in Brazilian farming may be expected to diffuse outwards from São Paulo in a pattern similar to that of mechanization but so far the ripple effect has hardly begun.

Most technical assistance, however, is supplied through Federal and state government programmes. The number of technical personnel working in agricultural extension increased from 1,728 in 1966 to 2,423 in 1969, although their geographical distribution was somewhat uneven, with one-fifth working in Minas Gerais and only 18 in Acre. Over the same period the number of members of young farmers' clubs increased from 41,921 to 86,033, over one-quarter being Northeasterners.

Agricultural marketing was extremely inefficient, some 30 per cent of the nation's crops being lost between the field and the market in the early 1960s,[68] and considerable governmental assistance has been given to this aspect of the agricultural system. Feeder roads have been built and new marketing facilities set up. A programme for the construction of warehouses and cold storage plants was established.[69] In 1960 storage facilities were concentrated in Rio Grande do Sul, São Paulo, Paraná and Minas Gerais, the last-mentioned state having generally smaller capacity storage units than the other three states. Once again the leading states benefited most from development, and Rio Grande do Sul increased its storage capacity 300 per cent between 1960 and 1970. Minimum prices guaranteed to farmers for rice, beans, maize, soyabeans, groundnuts and cotton have been important in providing incentives for increases in production.

The government has invested large amounts of domestic capital and foreign aid in improving the livestock industry, providing credit for modern farm inputs, developing agro-industries and setting up agricultural colonies to open up new areas of farm land,[70] and it has also established new bodies to oversee various aspects of the nation's agriculture. The National Credit Co-ordinating Agency was established for the purpose of planning and co-ordinating the distribution of credit to rural areas, and the National Rural Refinancing Fund was created to enable the Government to build up funds from both national and international sources to finance agriculture. The Bank of Brazil, which provides 80 per cent of the loans for agriculture, increased the number of its loans for farm improvement and irrigation from 27,000 in 1966 to over 40,000 in 1968 and in this last year ranchers got a special grant of US$80 million from the Government to build up pastures and improve production of meat, dairy products, wool and hides.[71] The National Institute of Agrarian Development (INDA) started work in 1965 fostering rural extension services and the development of colonization areas, co-operatives and rural electrification. In its first year of operation INDA established 41 colonization centres in 12 states.[72] Its sponsorship of co-operatives encouraged a 30 per cent growth in the number of agricultural co-operatives between 1966 and 1968, of which two-fifths were located in São Paulo and Rio Grande do Sul. INDA has undertaken an extensive rural electrification programme mainly in the states of Espírito Santo, Piauí, Santa Catarina and São Paulo. It remains to be seen whether this proliferation of official agencies will help or hinder Brazil's agricultural development.

By 1970 modern agricultural technology had become well established in the state of São Paulo and in parts of Rio Grande do Sul, with modernizing ripples spreading outwards from these two source areas. Official policy has emphasized the dominance of the East in agricultural development in many ways. This was brought out by the announcement in July 1970, by the Federal Ministers of Finance and Agriculture, of a new campaign for the stimulation of farming, involving increased use of modern inputs with the aim of increasing the annual growth rate in the farming sector from 9·5 per cent to 12 or 15 per cent, which was to begin in this advanced agricultural area of Brazil.[73] Thus regional disparity in agricultural development appears to be becoming more acute rather than less so.

REFERENCES

1. For a review of this see Mandell, Paul I., 'The Rise and Decline of Geography in Brazilian Development Planning: Some Lessons to be Learned', in *Latin American Development Issues*, A. David Hill, Ed., C.L.A.G., East Lansing, 1973, pp. 187–196.

2. Smith, T. Lynn, in his *Brazil People and Institutions*, Louisiana State University Press, Baton Rouge, Revised edition, 1963, emphasizes this point of view.

3. Furtado, Celso, in his book *The Economic Growth of Brazil*, University of California Press, 1963, is perhaps the best known advocate of this view of Brazilian agriculture.

4. Nicholls, W. H. 'Agriculture and the Economic Development of Brazil', in *Modern Brazil: New Patterns and Development*, John Saunders, Ed,. University of Florida Press, 1971, p. 256.

5. Commercial rice production spread very rapidly in response to increased demand resulting from changing consumption patterns related to rural-urban migration amongst other things (Mandell, Paul I., *The Rise of the Modern Brazilian Rice Industry: Demand Expansion in a dynamic economy*, Food Research Institute, Stanford University, mimeo, 1971). See also Banco do Nordeste do Brasil S.A., *Arroz no Nordeste*, Fortaleza, 1969. In 1973 Brazilian consumers were faced with a shortage of a basic item in the Brazilian diet—black beans—because 'farmers throughout Brazil have given up this little profitable culture and are planting soy beans instead which fetch high prices in the world markets as an industrial raw material', *Brazil Herald*, July 12, 1973.

6. Schuh, G. Edward. *The Agricultural Development of Brazil*, Praeger Publishers, New York, 1970, p. 96.

7. Nicholls, *op. cit.*, pp. 223–231.

8. Mandell, 1973, *op. cit.*, p. 11.

9. *Survey of the Brazilian Economy, 1966.* Brazilian Embassy, Washington, D.C., 1967, p. 47.

10. Statement by Finance Minister Delfim Neto reported in the *Brazil Herald*, November 26, 1970.

11. This process is described for the Minas Gerais Triângulo region in Faissol, Speridião. 'O problema do desenvolvimento agrícola do sudeste do Planalto Central do Brasil', *Revista Brasileria de Geografia*, I (19), 1957, pp. 8–10.

12. Corrêa, R. L. 'Regime de Explotação de Terra no Nordeste, Uma Tentativa de Expressâo Cartográfica', *Revista Brasileira de Geografia*, XXV (3), 1963, pp. 57–86.

13. *Brazil Herald*, March 3, 1971.

14. Clements, H. M. Sr. *The Mechanization of Agriculture in Brazil*, Latin American Monographs—Second Series. University of Florida Press, Gainesville, 1969, p. 15.

15. *Brazil Herald*, March 3, 1971. Replanting has become so profitable that some business firms have been known to clear natural forest and replace it with eucalyptus plantations just to obtain the tax benefits.

16. For a detailed discussion of types of Brazilian agriculture see Smith, T. Lynn, *op. cit.*, pp. 357–390.

17. See Chapter 2.

18. For non-Amazon examples see Clements, *op. cit.*, p. 12, and Mario Lacerda de Melo, 18th International Geographical Union Congress, *Excursion Guidebook No. 7, Northeast.* Rio de Janeiro, 1956, p. 125.

19. See Map 15.

20. Henshall, J. 'Japanese Pioneers in Brazil', *Geographical Magazine*, Vol. XL (16), August 1968, pp. 1367–1373.

21. Agrarian reform had been discussed as early as the mid-nineteenth century even before the abolition of slavery when, in 1847, Figueiredo had said: 'Agriculture, the productive function par excellence ... is where the vital interests of our country reside; and since it is encircled by a barrier (the large landed estates), it is necessary that this barrier be torn down let it cost what it may.' Translated from Figueiredo, A. P., 'Colonisação do Brasil', *O Progresso*, Recife, II, 1847, pp. 632–637, Quoted in Smith, T. Lynn, *Agrarian Reform in Latin America*, New York, 1966, p. 69.

22. Cline, W. R. *Economic Consequences of a Land Reform in Brazil.* North-Holland Publishing Company. Amsterdam, 1970, p. 179.

23. *Estatuto da Terra: Lei No. 4504 de 30 de Novembro de 1964*, Rio de Janeiro: Departamento de Imprensa Nacional, 1965.

24. Much of this section is based on Ludwig, A. K. and Taylor, H. W., *Brazil's New Agrarian Reform: An evaluation of its property classification and tax systems*, Praeger Publishers, New York, 1969, 186 pp.

25. A módulo is defined as being able to provide an income equal to or greater than the official minimum wage level for the region for each of the four adult workers. A módulo must also generate an additional 40 per cent of the combined wages of the four adult workers to cover social services such as housing and education for the farm family, plus a 15 per cent return on land and capital.

26. Ludwig and Taylor, *op. cit.*, pp. 20–21, suggest that this large size may have been established because of political pressures from large landowners.

27. The five factors are as follows: a combined utilization factor based on the extent to which the usable land is actually used and an agricultural yields factor based on a comparison between actual yields and standard yields set up by IBRA; an economic yields factor, which is a measure of the degree to which the actual annual gross income compares with potential income as established by IBRA; an investment factor, which defines the level of capitalization of the property; and a book-keeping factor as to whether or not the farmer keeps records of his expenditures and receipts. The coefficient of social conditions is made up of an administrative factor, a habitation and sanitation factor and an education factor.

28. Ludwig and Taylor, *op. cit.*, p. 50. By 1970 there were 704,000 families of sharecroppers, tenants and landless labourers in the Northeast and only 2,510 families had been settled on new land. See Manuel Correia de Andrade, 'A Modernização da Agricultura no Nordeste do Brasil'. Paper read at CLAG Meeting, Calgary, June 1973, p. 7.

29. *Anuário Estatístico, 1970*, p. 113.

30. Ludwig and Taylor, *op. cit.*, suggest (pp. 79 & 91) that this is too low to be effective in encouraging change.

31. *New York Times*, October 16, 1966.

32. Pastore, J. *et al.* 'A agricultura e o homem do Distrito Federal, Brasil: relatório preliminar de uma investigação sociológica', research paper 28P, *University of Wisconsin Land Tenure Centre*, 1968, 46pp.

33. In early 1971 the President was still stressing his determination to tackle agrarian reform with all possible urgency. *Brazil Herald*: January 28, 1971. Quoted from *Jornal do Brasil*. Actual settlement took place in only three instances between 1964 and 1968 and involved less than 10,000 hectares of land. In 1972 large landowners were given one year to formulate plans for the voluntary redistribution of portions of their estates to peasants.

34. Strachan, Lloyd W. 'A Survey of Recent Agricultural Trends in North-western Paraná', *Land Tenure Centre Newsletter*, No. 40, 1973, pp. 19–29, for a review of these effects in one particular region of Brazil.

35. Henshall, 1968, *op. cit.*

36. See Banco do Nordeste do Brasil S.A. *Sisal-Problemas Econômicos*, Vol. 1, Ceará, 1957. Many farmers could not afford to uproot their sisal.

37. *Anuário Estatístico do Brasil, 1970*, I.B.G.E., Rio de Janeiro, 1970, p. 134.

38. The babassu palm provides the basic necessities of daily life in the region: the trunk provides wood for building; the leaves form roofing

material and can be woven into hats; the fibres can be used for rope; the young sprout for food; the rotted bunch stalks for manure; the hard shell for fuel; the residual press cake for cattle feed; and the smoke from the green nuts is used as a coagulant for primitive rubber production. The commercial product, the oil, is used in the manufacture of soap and margarine and as a lubricant and a fuel. The babassu palm can live for 200 years and it has been suggested that with careful plant selection and thinning a babassu plantation could be as productive of vegetable oil as an oil palm plantation. See Werkhoven, J. and Ohler, J. G., Babassu, *Tropical Abstracts*, 23 (12), 1968, pp. 745–749.

39. SUDEC. *Ampliação e Implantação da Cultura do Cajueiro no Ceará*, Fortaleza, 1971. Also 'A grande fonte de divisas', *Sudene Informa*, Vol. 10 (7–8), July–August 1972, pp. 11–12.

40. For an analysis of the effect of these valorization schemes on the world coffee trade see Greenhill, Robert G., *British Export Houses, The Brazilian Coffee Trade and the Question of Control, 1850–1914*. University of Cambridge, Centre of Latin American Studies, 1972.

41. Nicholls, W. H. 'The Agricultural Frontier in Modern Brazilian History: The State of Paraná, 1920–1965', in *Cultural Change in Brazil*, edited by Merrill Rippy. Ball State University, Muncie, Indiana, 1969, p. 63.

42. Strachan, *op. cit.*, p. 21.

43. *Brazilian Bulletin*, March 1970.

44. *Brazil Herald*, February 12, 1971.

45. The areas most hard hit by the coffee eradication programme were those dependent on low-grade coffee production. In the state of Espírito Santo the Brazilian Coffee Institute ordered some 180,000 coffee trees to be pulled up in 1967. But these trees represented 45 per cent of the state's annual income. Bold efforts to industrialize the state using a broad programme of tax incentives, were successful and within two years new industries had turned Espírito Santo from a poor coffee-producing state to a rapidly growing area attracting industry from other parts of the country. See *Brazil Herald*, March 3, 1971, p. 2B.

46. *New York Times*, February 26, 1967.

47. *Brazilian Bulletin*, February 1967.

48. Arak, M. 'The price responsiveness of São Paulo coffee growers', *Food Research Institute Studies in Agricultural Economics, Trade and Development*, 8 (3), 1968, pp. 211–223.

49. In Paraná 250 million coffee trees were eradicated under the programme releasing an area of over 307,000 hectares. It is estimated that voluntary eradication affected a similar number of trees freeing a total of 560,000 hectares for crop diversification. A total of 200,000 rural residents, or 15 per cent of the total 1960 rural population, was displaced. Strachan, *op. cit.*, pp. 24–26.

50. See Chaves, G. M., Filho, J. Cruz, *et. al.*, 'A Ferrugem do Cafeeiro', *Seiva*, December 1970; and Instituto Brasileiro do Cafe, *Ferrugem do Cafeeiro—Providências para controle*, April 1971.

51. The manager of the National Coffee Growers Association as reported

in the *Brazil Herald*, October 19, 1972, stated that he expected Brazilian coffee production to decline by 65 per cent over the next few years.

52. Boulanger, J. 'Rapport au gouvernement du Brésil sur les problèmes de recherche cotonnière dans le nord-est du Brésil', *Progr. Nations Unies pour Dévelopement, FAO. AT2317*, Rome, 1968, pp. 1–260. SUDENE is encouraging the production of tree cotton under irrigation. See 'Algodão a Luta pelo Equilibrio', *Sudene Informa*, Vol. 10 (11–12), November–December 1972, pp. 4–5.

53. *Survey of the Brazilian Economy, op. cit.*, p. 79.

54. The area under cocoa trees which was fertilized increased from 200 hectares in 1965 to 71,447 hectares in 1970. *Ceplac: Instrumento de progresso da região cacaueira*, Itabuna, 1971.

55. *Sinopse Estatística do Brasil, 1972.* I.B.G.E., Rio de Janeiro, 1973, p. 88.

56. *Brazilian Bulletin*, January 1971.

57. Schuh, *op. cit.*, pp. 183–184.

58. Schuh, *op. cit.*, p. 178.

59. See Moura, L. M. de and Woods, T. D., 'Impactos das mundanças de tecnologia, na produção nas rendas do gado leitero em Viçosa, Minas Gerais', *Experientiae*, 8 (2), 1968, pp. 25–89.

60. The percentage of farms using only human power actually increased from 73 per cent in 1950 to 76 per cent in 1960 but this may well be a reflection of the inadequacies of the census data rather than any real increase.

61. *Sinopse Estatística do Brasil, 1972*, I.B.G.E., Rio, 1972, p. 85.

62. Clements, *op. cit.*, pp. 56–61.

63. A tractor costing US$4,300 in the United States costs US$4,790 in São Paulo.

64. *Bolsa Review*, Vol. 7 (76), April 1973, p. 154.

65. *Brazilian Bulletin*, August 1969.

66. Schuh, *op. cit.*, p. 169.

67. *Brazil Herald*, December 25/26, 1970.

68. *Brasil '66*. Special edition of *Direção*, São Paulo, 1966, p. 94.

69. Schuh, *op. cit.*, p. 306, feels that expansion of storage facilities during the 1950s had largely satisfied the needs of the 'sixties.

70. *Brazilian Bulletin*, May 1970.

71. *Brazilian Bulletin*, October 1968.

72. *Survey of the Brazilian Economy, op. cit.*, p. 50.

73. *Brazil Herald*, July 23, 1970.

CHAPTER 6

Mineral Resources Development

Riches there are: some may be easily mobilized; others must await an opportune time or even remain unused for many years to come. D.N.P.M., 1943

Brazil is excellently endowed with subsoil resources, but over the course of settlement and development these have been yielded up only grudgingly. In contrast to the Spaniards, who had vast treasures laid practically at their feet and a large indigenous population to mine those that were not, the Luso-Brazilians had to search far and wide for their El Dorados for two centuries—and then work hard when they found them. Yet the rewards have been great, and future prospects appear even brighter.

In quantity, quality and variety of mineral resources, Brazil stands among the world leaders. Unlike the others, particularly the Soviet Union and Canada with analogous mineralized formations, Brazil has no frozen wastes that lock up access in a perennial seasonal battle with the elements. Furthermore, her most diverse and important mining zone lies within easy reach for her industrial heartland, and her deposits in the distant north, albeit far from the oecumene, are nevertheless served by the magnificent inland waterway of Amazonia, posing no problem for bulk shipments. Even the least accessible ores in the western part of the country could, if the market warranted it, be tied in to the northern inland waterway or the southeastern transport network with relative ease across the level surface of the Central Plateau.

In the past, Brazil lagged in the development of a large-scale mining industry, primarily through lack of knowledge and incentives, but the recent modernization of technical, managerial and financial institutions associated with the industry has brought profound changes. During the past quarter of a century, and particularly over the last decade, both the knowledge about, and exploitation of, Brazil's mineral resources have taken an astonishing leap forward. On the other hand, a considerable legacy from the past remains, with the *garimpeiro* working literally side by side with some of the world's largest and most modern conglomerate operations. While the independent prospector, like the *bandeirante* of old, myopically searches the earth and the stream beds for promising outcrops and ore-bearing gravels, magnetometer-equipped aeroplanes, helicopter-borne seismographic crews and, most recently, Skylab 'earth resources' satellites on photographic missions cross the heavens above him mapping out buried mineral bodies.

THE GEOLOGICAL SETTING

Map 12, showing the location of Brazil's more important mineral deposits, brings out that the main mineralized zones follow the trends of five major geanticlinal systems and their associated placer deposits. Here uplift has exposed extensive areas of pre-Cambrian rocks within which the Algonquian (Proterozoic) crystalline formations comprise about four per cent of the national territory. It is these formations which contain the deposits of metallic minerals and gemstones that are of greatest economic importance.

The most productive of these geanticlines has been the one which roughly parallels the coast in eastern Minas Gerais (where it includes the Serra do Espinhaço) and central Bahia. Northwards it merges into the radial anticlinal pattern of Northeastern Brazil, where recent studies have linked certain geological formations with those of western Africa.

Further inland, but converging on the first in the mineral-rich Iron Quadrilateral of southern Minas Gerais (insert, Map 12), a second geanticline trends in a northerly direction through the length of Goiás State and into Pará. Here it abuts against a third which follows the course of the Amazon to the south of that river. This geanticline and a fourth, which parallels

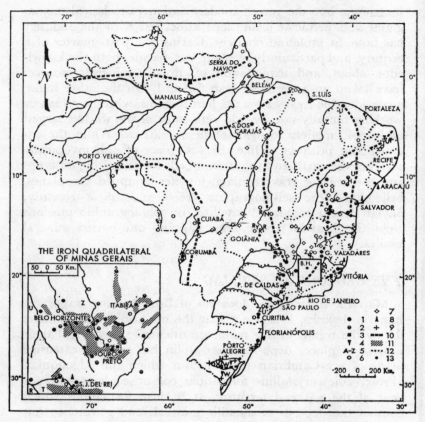

Map 12. MINERAL DEPOSITS. (1) iron; (2) manganese; (3) bauxite; (4) tin; (5) A=silver, B=niobium, H=chromium, N=nickel, P=platinum, R=rutile, S=monazite sands, T=tungsten, U=copper, W=wolfram, Y=beryllium, Z=lead and zinc; (6) gold; (7) diamonds; (8) petroleum; (9) coal; (10) anticlinal structure; (11) Pre-Cambrian Minas Series; (12) state boundary; (13) city.

the Amazon River to the north, have until recently been the most inaccessible and least known of Brazil's major mineralized zones, even though scattered prospectors (*garimpeiros*) have carried out small-scale gold and diamond operations in the placer deposits along their margins for centuries. Although the resources of these Amazonian formations are still largely untapped, recent discoveries have begun to yield promise of geological riches beyond all reasonable previous expectations.

Similarly, the most westerly of the geanticlines, which follows a northerly direction along the Paraguay River and thence trends northwestward into Rondônia, has remained undeveloped except for gold and diamond placers and the manganese deposits that out-crop near Corumbá, until the recent extension of the road network into the upper Madeira region opened up its abundant tin ores.

Finally, there are two lesser anticlinal arcs of pre-Cambrian formations: one is in Espírito Santo and is part of a fault system embracing the Serra do Mar and Serra da Mantiqueira; the other is in Rio Grande do Sul, parallel to the Serra Geral and abutting on to the coastal fault system which extends along the Lagoa dos Patos. North of that, in Rio Grande do Sul, Santa Catarina, and Paraná, and overlying the eastern margins of a crystalline complex of granites and gneisses, are Permo-Carboniferous coal deposits which have been disturbed by faulting, minor folding and the intrusion of diabase dikes.[1] Minor coal reserves elsewhere in the country are unsuited for production in the modern, industrialized sense.

THE MINING INDUSTRY

Mining is, or in the recent past has been, a part of the economy of every one of Brazil's political units,[2] albeit very unevenly distributed whether in value of production or in number of workers employed. Table 8 shows Minas Gerais leading the list by a wide margin, accounting for over half the value of Brazil's mineral production and over one-fourth of the number of workers thus employed. The bulk of this production comes from the Iron Quadrilateral, although this name does not do justice to the variety of economically significant minerals that occur in that district.

Space does not permit discussion of mineral production for each political unit, but the six principal states fall into one of two basic types. Minas Gerais, São Paulo, and Rio Grande do Sul support a diversified mining industry based primarily upon supplying raw materials to nearby manufacturing complexes, although in Minas Gerais this fact may be submerged, statistically, by the recent phenomenal growth of its iron ore exports. In contrast, the three other states—Santa Catarina,

TABLE 8

Mining & Mineral Extraction
(Rank by value of 1969 production)

Rank	Political unit	Value of prod. Cr$1,000	Number of workers	Value added per worker Cr$1,000	Aver. no. of workers per firm
1	Minas Gerais	673,798	13,558	43	36
2	Santa Catarina	99,558	8,163	10	302
3	Amapá	98,645	165	585	82
4	São Paulo	72,961	4,522	13	36
5	R. G. do Norte	69,556	3,982	12	12
6	R. G. do Sul	42,680	4,522	13	36
7	Bahia	34,191	2,868	8	68
8	Rio de Janeiro	26,000	2,007	10	13
9	Paraná	25,021	2,461	8	38
10	Rondônia	19,079	425	45	54
11	Goiás	12,393	526	19	38
12	Ceará	10,593	1,558	6	19
13	Espírito Santo	5,805	907	5	31
14	Pernambuco	5,451	621	7	39
15	Mato Grosso	4,295	583	6	28
16	Maranhão	3,882	1,979	2	19
17	Alagoas	1,189	115	5	23
18	Sergipe	1,102	355	2	2
19	Piauí	1,065	371	3	17
20	Paraíba	551	42	10	14
21	Guanabara	208	14	6	14
22	Pará	47	6	7	6
	BRAZIL	1,208,070	49,818	21	27

Source: Fundação I.B.G.E., 'Mineração e Extração de Produtos Minerais',
  Sinopse Estatística do Brasil 1971, Instituto Brasileiro de Estatística,
  Rio de Janeiro, 1971, pp. 140–141.

Amapá, and Rio Grande do Norte—have attained promi-
nence through special, if not entirely exclusive, emphasis on
a single product, coal, manganese and salt, respectively.

Besides great differences in the values of the mineral production of the various political units, which are largely the reflection of fortuitous geological endowment, Table 8 reveals an
equally significant range in values added per worker. These
range from Cr$585,000 in the modern, export-oriented
manganese mines of Amapá, where the productivity of a handful of workers places it third in the nation by value of production, to only Cr$2,000 per annum in Maranhão and Ser-
gipe. Those states with the lowest average values added per

worker are located for the most part along the Atlantic seaboard from Espírito Santo up to and including Pará, where,
with the addition of Mato Grosso in the west, mining activities
are of long standing, usually on a small scale, and dispersed.

Although these figures on productivity are to some extent
related to the value of the product being mined, they also
highlight the fact that, if there is one characteristic on which
authors writing about Brazil's mining industry are in full
agreement, it is the dichotomy between modern, industrialized
establishments and archaic operations based upon techniques
dating back to colonial times.[3] Table 8 itself suggests that in
those regions in which the value added per worker is small and
the firms on the average employ few workers, traditional
methods predominate. On the other hand, where the value
added is high and the size of the firms relatively large, the
modern sector is the stronger.[4]

While no single region is characterized exclusively by one
form of mining operation, the modern, industrialized mining
establishments are generally found under one or other of two
conditions: either where suitable mineral deposits occur near
an industrial consumers' market, or else where remote, but
exceptionally large and exploitable, ore bodies can satisfy
the export market or perhaps a sizeable but distant national
one. Only in the Iron Quadrilateral of Minas Gerais do these
two conditions apply simultaneously. Where neither of these
factors is operative, mining methods which date back to colonial times tend to be preserved essentially in their archaic
forms.[5] No political unit, however, can be categorized as
having either an exclusively modern and industrialized
mining economy, although Amapá comes exceedingly close, or
a totally colonial one, though not a few in the lower ranges of
values added per worker approach such conditions with, at
best, only a minor element of somewhat more efficient enterprises. Not unexpectedly, the larger, and presumably more
modern and efficient, firms are found in those political units
in which the national production of a particular mineral is
concentrated. Thus, Santa Catarina, with an average of 302
workers per firm, produces about 75 per cent of the nation's
coal; Amapá (82 workers) mines 71 per cent of its manganese;
Bahia (68 workers) provides 100 per cent of Brazil's barite,

96 per cent of its magnesite, 81 per cent of its petroleum, and 73 per cent of its lead; Rondônia (54 workers) mines 91·5 per cent of its cassiterite. As the Brazilian average of 27 workers per firm is approached, other elements come into play. Some of these are a function of the type of mining operation required by a particular mineral, some result from the economic climate in which the enterprise operates. The latter is reflected in the fact that, with a few exceptions, the firms of the traditional Northeastern milieu are of less than average size, whereas those of the South and West tend to be above the average.

Over the past quarter of a century, and particularly during the last decade, Brazil has been gradually but significantly upgrading its mining industry, stimulated by a general rise in the country's industrial, technical and marketing sophistication. Large-scale, capital-intensive ventures now make it possible for Brazil to exploit its major ore bodies effectively, even where these are located in remote parts of the country. While archaicisms exist in many areas, it is foreseeable that these will be eliminated as the need arises, but for the time being they play a useful role both as employers of people and as producers of raw materials. In fact, their continued presence, as well as that of medium-technology firms, gives the Brazilian mining industry a rare flexibility which enables it to exploit its mineral resources at various levels, including that of the traditional, garimpeiro-type operation, which furnishes the cheap labour needed to utilize mineralogically or marketably marginal deposits and also provides the inexpensive but wide-ranging manpower that is invaluable for prospecting over the vast and still inadequately known interior.

The changing pattern of Brazil's mining industry is best illustrated by a comparison of production figures across a twenty-five-year time span. Table 9 shows that whereas a few items no longer appear in the official statistics,[6] both the quantity and the diversity of mineral production increased strikingly from 1943 to 1968. Additions to the list of minerals being mined in Brazil range from such basic ores as those of tin, lead, copper, aluminium and nickel to less widely disseminated ones of tungsten, niobium, titanium, zirconium and beryllium.

Significant shifts have also taken place in the relative importance of various items on the 1943 list. For example, coal,

which thirty years ago led Brazil's mine output in both value
and volume of production, has since dropped to a very poor
second in volume and to sixth by value, supplanted by the formerly much less important production of iron and manganese
ores and by cassiterite, magnesite and lead ores, which were
not even being mined in Brazil in 1943. Salt and marble,
produced essentially for national consumption, were also
formerly of some importance; but despite quadrupling the
volume of production of the first-named and nearly trebling
that of the second, both now rank well behind a long list of
minerals, many of which were not being produced in Brazil,
at least in statistically significant quantities, at the earlier
date. An entire volume would be required for a discussion
of the country's multitude of mining operations which occupy
approximately 50,000 workers employed by nearly 2,000
firms.[7] Subsequent sections of this chapter will, therefore,
summarize the characteristics of certain mining industries,
selected for their importance or as illustrative of various
aspects of that sector of the economy.

SALT. Among the least spectacular but nevertheless consistently
important items, by volume, of Brazil's mineral production,
salt is also the oldest. Dating back to early colonial times, its
extraction extended from the Trade Wind estuaries of the
Northeast to the coastal lagoons to the south, and was destined
both for human use and for the cattle raising industry. This
was based on solar evaporation of sea water by traditional
Portuguese methods, using windmills to pump the water into
the salt pans. The persistence of these archaic practices, including the labour-intensive handling of the product, has kept
salt prices high on Brazil's domestic market, aggravated by
an equally out-of-date transport system in the Northeast.

Surface transport, both by land and by sea, has been significantly improved in Brazil in recent years, but little has been
done to move the salt more efficiently from the point of extraction. It is first shovelled into small piles on the edge of the pans,
then moved by wheelbarrow into larger stockpiles, thence
again by wheelbarrow for loading into barges, which sail out
to freighters anchored offshore in shallow coastal waters. Here
the salt is once again shovelled, into large baskets which are

TABLE 9

Brazilian Mining Industry Production, 1943–70

Mineral	Volume of prod., 1943 metric tons	Value of prod., 1943 million Cr$	1968-70 Rank by value	Mineral	Value of prod., 1968 1,000 NCr$	Volume of prod., 1968, 1969 or 1970 metric tons	States with 46% or more of the national prod.
coal	2,078,256	170·4	1	iron ores	356,357	27,156,684*²	Minas Gerais
gold	5	113·5	2	manganese ores	69,404	2,010,816*	Amapá
iron ore	810,504	40·4	3	cassiterite (tin ore)	15,302	3,050*	Rondônia
manganese	255,745	26·2	4	magnesite	7,554	137,820*	Bahia
mica	995	22·1	5	lead ores	7,438	340,905*	Bahia
salt	416,121	18·7	6	coal	4,828	5,171,673**	Santa Catarina
arsenic	970	5·2	7	apatite	4,199	472,309	São Paulo
marble	17,522	3·3	8	rock quartz	4,034	1,182	Goiás, M. Gerais
silver	9	0·2	9	dolomite	3,228	706,534*	Minas Gerais
			10	scheelite (tungsten ore)	3,050	151,583	R. G. do Norte
			11	gypsum	2,773	216,798	Pernambuco
			12	talc	2,551	79,490	Paraná
			13	barite	2,326	99,980	Bahia
			14	marble	2,136	49,832*	Espírito Santo
			15	graphite	2,029	22,000	Minas Gerais
			16	copper ores	1,992	162,842	R. G. do Sul
			17	salt	1,630	1,826,172**	R. G. do Norte
			18	bauxite	1,345	313,748	Minas Gerais
			19	chrysotile (asbestos ore)	1,289	345,442	Minas Gerais
			20	niobium ore (columbium)	725	130	Alagoas
			21	chromite	677	17,032	Minas Gerais
			22	phosphorite	667	66,090	Bahia
			23	beryllium	577	744	Pernambuco
			24	garnierite (nickel ore)	230	67,744	Minas Gerais
			25	mica	187	483	Minas Gerais
			26	rutile (titanium ore)	124	284(*)	Goiás
			27	zirconium ores	17	328	Minas Gerais

Note: Asterisks, referring to the last column of figures, indicate years other than 1968, as follows: *1969, **1970, (*) 1967.
1. The new cruzeiro (NCr$) was introduced in 1967, being equal to 1,000 of the old; in 1943 there were approximately Cr$20 to the U.S. dollar, which in 1968 was worth about NCr$ 3·40 (or Cr$3,400).
2. In 1970 Brazilian iron ore exports were approximately 28 million tons (see p. 130), but the quantity consumed internally was not known at the time of writing.

Sources: I.B.G.E., *Anuário Estatístico do Brasil, 1941/1945*, Conselho Nacional de Estatística, Rio de Janeiro, 1946, pp. 52–53; Fundação I.B.G.E., *Anuário Estatístico do Brasil, 1970*, Instituto Brasileiro de Estatística, Rio de Janeiro, 1970, pp. 180–187; Fundação I.B.G.E., *Sinopse Estatística do Brasil, 1971*, Instituto Brasileiro de Estatística, Rio de Janeiro, 1971, pp. 148, 150.

hoisted aboard and dumped into the holds, a process repeated in reverse at the destination. This system, which not only requires much hand labour but also causes long delays in loading, has been modernized in Rio Grande do Norte's largest salt pan area. Here a complex, completed in 1972 after five years of planning and construction, includes the Areia Branca terminal, built on an artificial island off the Mossoró River. The terminal is served by specially designed barges, and stockpiles are accumulated on the island, from which the salt is transferred to waiting ships by conveyors at a rate of 1,500 tons an hour.

It is likely, however, that the industry will soon undergo more fundamental changes, this time at the production end, as significant rock salt deposits have recently been discovered in several localities. The one closest to coming into production is in Sergipe. Discovered in the late 1960s, its estimated reserves are 6,000 million tons of potassium and magnesium compounds, including carnallite, tachydrite, halite, sylvite and bromine, constituting collectively the largest such deposit outside the Congo. The mining rights were offered for bids in 1971, in which year rock salt was also discovered in the Amazon Basin, along the lower Xingú. Promising beds have also been found near Maceió, Alagoas, attracting Du Pont to locate a chemical plant there (see Chapter 7).

GOLD. Although gold was first found in Brazil near the present city of São Paulo during the seventeenth century, creating a minor boom, the real rush did not begin until *bandeirante* expeditions from that area discovered the rich placers of Minas Gerais in 1694. These independent prospectors were soon replaced, however, not infrequently after armed conflicts, by plantation owners from the declining coastal sugar plantations, who worked the stream beds systematically with their gangs of slaves. Subsequent exploration spread these simple mining operations across the Central Plateau and into the headwaters of the Amazon and Paraguay Rivers, where practices have continued at essentially the same technological level until the present time, although dredges have also occasionally been used.

During the eighteenth century gold production was centred

on Ouro Prêto, originally known as Vila Rica. It has been mentioned in Chapter 3 that, as in Spanish-American mining towns and even Brazil's other, less important centres which grew up on the gold and diamond fields during colonial times, Ouro Prêto's élite who controlled the mining industry sought to recreate there the amenities and graces of the coastal cities. This first capital of Minas Gerais therefore became famed for the quality and the character of its buildings, in particular those churches whose charm is enhanced by the exquisite sculptures of Aleijadinho. These are also found at Sabará, which began as a gold mining town but is now a steel centre, about 20 kilometres east of Belo Horizonte. Not far from Sabará, at Nova Lima, is the Morro Velho gold mine, which has been in continuous operation since 1834, when it was started up by the St. John d'El Rey Mining Company.[8] Since then this mine has produced over £50 million worth of gold from a maze of tunnels opening off a shaft nearly 3,000 metres deep, a depth exceeded only by one mine, located in the Union of South Africa. An indication of the continued viability of the mine despite the long span of its operation, is the fact that in July 1965 it broke all previous monthly production records with a yield of 430 kilogrammes of gold. One of the few examples of foreign-controlled large mining enterprises in Brazil, the St. John d'El Rey Company, was founded and owned by British shareholders until the U.S.-based Hanna Mining Company, of which we shall hear more later, gained a controlling interest in 1958.

There are no other firms of similar stature mining gold in Brazil, and many of the companies in this field are either small, at times ephemeral, or else family affairs employing a few hired labourers or allowing their properties to be worked on a share basis. Even so, gold production today is split about evenly between the so-called mining companies and the independent *garimpeiros*.

During the fifty years preceding the mid-1960s gold production in Brazil remained remarkably steady, averaging around 4 tons per annum from registered mining operations, virtually all of which were located in Minas Gerais. Probably about the same amount again was produced by the approximately 50,000 prospectors scattered throughout the interior, although only part of this showed up in official statistics. Then production from registered mines rose sharply with the discovery of new gold fields, particularly among the placer gravels of the Madeira River in Rondônia, into which large-scale dredging was introduced, in part financed by foreign capital. By 1968 Brazilian gold production had increased from 8 to 11 tons annually.[9]

More recent figures are not yet available; it is likely, however, that some further increase in gold production has taken place since 1968. In that year new placers were discovered in Roraima, and in 1970 another rush took place in an area that should logically have been considered thoroughly explored and exploited, the upper reaches of the São Francisco between Barra do Abaeté and Pirapora at the junction of the railway from Minas Gerais, where it crosses into Goiás, with the head of river navigation. In January 1972, too, a gold rush was underway at Altamira, beside the lower Xingú River in Pará, after nuggets were found in a well being dug beside the Trans-Amazon Highway, then under construction in the area.

Clearly, then, not only are many of the operational and organizational aspects of colonial gold mining practices still extant in Brazil, but also some of the excitement and 'boom-or-bust' attitudes as well. There can be little doubt that these will continue to exist for many years as the Trans-Amazon and other highways are extended into the as yet little known areas along the flanks of the two northernmost geanticlines.

DIAMONDS. Much of what has been said about the nature of gold mining applies also to diamond mining, which began in Minas Gerais in 1729. The focal point of diamond production was then, and still is, Diamantina, 200 kilometres north of Belo Horizonte, although it spread rapidly to other locales, particularly to the north and west. The stones come either from placers or from pockets of Tertiary, Kimberley-like, blue clays; but the quest for the mother lode in the form of pipes, such as those that have made the Union of South Africa's diamond industry so successful, remains an unfulfilled dream.[10]

In the eighteenth century diamond production amounted to some two and a half million stones, but no figures are available as to the weight these represented. Substantive modern figures on diamond production in Brazil are almost equally difficult to find, in part because smaller stones do not have to be registered with the government and also because some of the larger ones reach the market, if not always clandestinely, certainly informally.[11] Recent estimates published by the United States' Bureau of Mines place Brazil's total diamond production at 320,000 carats.[12] The imprecision of this figure, however, can be deduced from the fact that exactly the same amount is given for every year from 1967 to 1970 inclusive, divided in each case into equal parts of 160,000 carats each for gem and industrial diamonds.[13] That these amounts are questionable is supported by comparing export figures for Brazil from 1968: thus, in Table 10 United Nations statistics, presumably drawn from official and unchanged Brazilian sources, indicate total exports in that year of gem and industrial diamonds combined of 6,000 carats, whereas imports into the United States from Brazil of gem quality diamonds alone, according to the Bureau of Mines, amounted to 10,000 carats. In 1969 the disparity between official export statistics from Brazil and U.S. imports of both types of diamonds came to 16,000 carats—and this, of course, ignores shipments to other destinations.

Table 10 also indicates an important characteristic of the Brazilian diamond industry which is in contradiction to the 1967–70 estimates by the Bureau of Mines, which show unchanging production levels. In fact, yields vary greatly from year to year, reflecting both the nature of the diamond-bearing formations which are, for the most part, rapidly exhausted, and the archaic ethos of the miners themselves. They live for most of their lives at bare subsistence level, panning long-worked gravels for an occasional modest stone and hoping for the big strike that will make their fortune. Whenever one of their number is successful, a great influx of *garimpeiros* takes place to the area in question, which is of course soon worked over. Occasionally the promise is such that dredges or other more advanced types of equipment are employed, but these do little more than hasten the day when the placer is exhausted.[14] Only in some of the blue clays, mostly in Minas Gerais, which are worked by hydraulicking, is there a semblance of long-term, reasonably constant yields, and that usually because the operations are small ones. It is evident, then, that except in the last-named case, practices within the Brazilian diamond industry are not conducive to a steady and consistent production, and that the prevailing character of operations makes it difficult to monitor the fluctuating output.

The major diamond-producing zones of Brazil, allowing for their shifting fortunes, are as follows: the Coromandel district in west-central Minas Gerais, to which we shall return

TABLE 10

Brazil: International Diamond Trade

Total Exports, Gem and Industrial[1]

year	(thousand carats)
1961	142
1962	76
1963	0
1964	53
1965	31
1966	27
1967	27
1968	6
1969	25[2]

United States Imports from Brazil
(thousand carats)

Year	Gem[3]	Industrial[4]
1968	10	—
1969	30	11
1970	32	5

Sources: 1. United Nations, 1970 Statistical Yearbook, N.Y., 1971, p. 220.
2. Fundação I.B.G.E., Anuário Estatístico do Brasil 1970, Instituto Brasileiro de Estatística, Rio de Janeiro, 1970, p. 301.
3. Clarke, Robert G. 'Gem Stones', reprinted from the Bureau of Mines 1970 Minerals Yearbook, U.S. Department of the Interior, Washington, D.C., 1971, p. 3 (Table 2).
4. Clarke, Robert G., 'Abrasive Materials', reprint from the Bureau of Mines 1970 Minerals Yearbook, U.S. Department of the Interior, Washington, D.C., 1971, p. 8 (Table 10).

again shortly; northern Minas Gerais, focusing on Diamantina; the Tibagí Valley in Paraná; Central Bahia; the upper tributaries of the Araguaia River in Goiás and Mato Grosso, which were more important in the past than today; the Marabá district of Pará, at the confluence of the Tocantins and Araguaia Rivers, which experienced a diamond rush in the 1940s which disappointed expectations but for which a revival is hoped with the advent of the Trans-Amazonian Highway; and in the headwaters of the Rio Branco in Roraima Territory, an extension of the Guiana diamond fields. It is of interest to note that this last-named area was the focus of a section of a 1968 agreement between the D.N.P.M. (National Department of Mineral Production) and SUDAM (Superintendency for the Development of the Amazon) which aimed at creating incentives for developing the regional economy of Roraima: included among its objectives was the 'disciplining' and upgrading of the activities of the territory's prospectors, as well as the carrying out of an airborne survey for the identification and evaluation of new mineral deposits.

Some outstanding, albeit also characteristic, events of the Brazilian diamond industry's history have taken place in the Coromandel district, centring on the town of that name in the Upper Paranaíba valley, in west-central Minas Gerais. One of the earliest strikes of the eighteenth century was made here, and it was long known for the quality of its gems. This reputation culminated in 1938 with the discovery of Brazil's most famous diamond, the blue-white Getúlio Vargas, found in the bed of the Santo Antônio River, a tributary of the Paranaíba. Weighing 726·6 carats, it was the third-largest stone in the world at that time.[15] Thereafter, the region went into a quarter of a century decline as a diamond producer and, as the population dwindled, reverted to cattle herding and cheese making for a livelihood. Then, late in 1971, a 44-carat stone was discovered in the bed of the Paranaíba during a period of exceptionally low water, followed the next day by a 24-carat diamond near the same spot. Within a few days a tent city arose near Coromandel, the town's normal population of 8,000 had doubled and the river bed teemed with prospectors. Not long afterwards a 75-carat stone turned up in the bed of the Abaeté Riber, near the town of Tiros, in the headwaters of the São Francisco, 150 kilometres southeast of Coromandel. This area, too, attracted its share of hopeful *garimpeiros*, but they were pushed out by more affluent local entrepreneurs equipped with pumps and bulldozers. Thus, in one of the oldest mining districts of the country, yet only a short distance from some of Brazil's most modern industrial centres, the colonial aspects of diamond mining are only now starting to yield to the first stages of a more advanced technology.

OTHER GEMSTONES. Brazil supplies about 90 per cent of the world's aquamarines, topazes, tourmalines, and amethysts. Most of the quality stones are found in a belt that extends along the southeastern geanticline, with production concentrated in eastern Minas Gerais and central Bahia.[16] Amethysts are produced in largest quantity in the Southern Plateau region, but the best quality stones are found in a very few mines in Espírito Santo and southern Bahia.

Production statistics are even more unreliable for these gemstones than they are for diamonds. This is because their mining is almost entirely in the hands of the *garimpeiros* or at best of small operators, at times as an adjunct to the extraction of other minerals. Furthermore, type and quality vary very greatly, defying systematic classification; production is widely scattered through the interior; and buying and selling usually involve a large number of channels and individuals. For finished stones, several large and reputable gem dealers are found in the major cities, particularly in Rio de Janeiro, where there has been a constant tourist demand for these stones for years.

Most of Brazil's gemstones are of the semi-precious type, although the highest grade aquamarines are valued as highly as some precious stones; emeralds are also mined, primarily in Bahia. Total gemstone exports, excluding diamonds, averaged about 500 tons per annum between 1967 and 1969, including 221 kilogrammes of emeralds in the first year, 329 in the second, and 1,488 in 1969,[17] presumably following the opening of a new mine. Gemstone exports consist almost entirely of uncut stones but do not of course include those taken home by tourists or exported clandestinely, both of which are predominantly cut stones.

IRON ORE. Early developments in iron ore mining and smelting in Brazil were closely tied to the gold and diamond booms of the eighteenth century, stimulated by the location of high-grade ore bodies near the principal mining areas of Minas Gerais, the accessibility of forests for charcoal production and the high cost of transporting European-made pig iron or manufactures such as horseshoes, picks and shovels by mule train over the coastal escarpment and the Serra da Mantiqueira. From then until the middle of the twentieth century iron ore mining remained essentially internal in orientation, expanding slowly to meet the demands of national iron and, later, steel industries. Table 9 shows that as late as 1943, before the Volta Redonda steel mill came into operation, the volume of iron ore produced in Brazil was not great and its value was still, after 300 years, less than that being obtained from the long-depleted gold fields.

Since then both its production and its transport have been modernized, resulting in a thirty-five-fold increase in output. This has been absorbed not only by the country's burgeoning steel-using industries (e.g. motor vehicles and shipbuilding) but also by a rising volume of exports, so that today iron ore constitutes Brazil's leading mining industry, whether by volume or by value, as well as its largest minerals export. It is export, however, that has brought about the principal recent expansion of iron mining and re-oriented national policy regarding this mineral.[18] The principal export destinations for ore and ore concentrate are Japan and West Germany, while Argentina and the United States, in that order, are the main importers of Brazilian pig iron and ingot steel.

Brazil's iron ore reserves, variously estimated at between 20 and 32 thousand million tons, are believed to amount to one-third of total world reserves and to be surpassed only by those of U.S.S.R. Although these reserves are not confined to one part of the country (Map 12), a high proportion of them is located in the Iron Quadrilateral of Minas Gerais, which district also provides 99·6 per cent of current production. It embraces an area of about 7,000 square kilometres, in a classic, complex and disturbed pre-Cambrian geological setting of granites and three unconforming sedimentary formations. Most of this ore is high grade hematite, averaging 68 per cent iron in the principal source rock, itabirito.

Production within the Iron Quadrilateral is divided,

albeit unequally, between the mines of the Paraopeba Valley and adjacent areas, east and south of Belo Horizonte, and those of the Upper Rio Doce region, most notably the 'Iron Mountain', Cauê Peak, at Itabira, a body of hematite which is 69 per cent pure iron with a very low level of impurities (0·004 per cent phosphorus, 0·005 to 0·01 per cent sulphur, and 1 per cent of insolubles). Generally speaking, ores from the former have been used primarily for local consumption in the Industrial Heartland, while those from the latter have been destined for export; but exports from the Paraopeba district are being systematized and steel mills have arisen along the Rio Doce. In view of the significance of the Rio Doce area to the present-day mining picture in Brazil and the fact that its development is illustrative of changes in, and attitudes towards, large mining enterprises in that country, we may appropriately devote some space to the events that have taken place there since the early twentieth century.

In 1911 the Itabira Iron Ore Company was organized by a group of British bankers and steelmakers, who were shortly thereafter joined by the American financier, Percival Farquhar,[19] with the view to developing a mining-industrial-shipping complex based on their ownership of 18,000 acres of land at Itabira, embracing Cauê Peak, and control of the creaky Vitória–Minas Railway. Included in their plans was the construction of a port 40 kilometres north of Vitória, through which the ore would be shipped.

A combination of nationalism, conservatism and a fear of foreign entrepreneurs, exacerbated by the latters' attempts to deal with Brazilian officialdom as if in a 'banana republic', brought the Itabira Iron Ore Company a series of reverses and delays in their attempts to get their plans under way. The Company's best chance to have its project approved *in toto*, according to Gauld, came in 1923. It is said to have failed because, in Farquhar's dealings with the then President Bernardes' Minister of Transport, the latter 'felt that P. F. had insulted him, and that was that',[20] although the concrete reason given was Farquhar's turning down of a clause in the contract (put in for the benefit of Bernardes' political supporters in the Brazilian shipping business) which would have prevented the company from carrying return cargoes, except coal, in their ore vessels. Similar difficulties, compounded by bureaucratic buck-passing, continued to beset the Itabira Iron Ore Company through the early years of the Vargas regime, with Bernardes, a Congressional Deputy until the Estado Novo was declared in 1937, continuing to lead the opposition.

In 1940 the company was reorganized, with the participation of Brazilian capital, and renamed the Cia. Brasileira de Mineração e Siderurgica. Its terms of operation had, however, been reduced to the mining and export of iron ore and the operation of the Vitória–Minas Railway—that is, without the original concept of an integrated steel mill and shipping company. In that year the company shipped out, through the port of Vitória, its first 6,000 tons of ore—to Bethlehem Steel's Sparrows Point plant in Maryland; but that market proved ephemeral, as the U.S. company had begun developing its own ore project in Venezuela. In any case, at this stage Itabira ore had to be moved to the railhead in trucks, and stored in makeshift bunkers when it reached the port. In 1940, however, construction was begun on an extension of the railway to Itabira and on an ore dock across the bay from Vitória.

Exports during the next two years totalled 100,000 tons, going almost entirely to Britain and shipped out in a motley collection of tramp steamers. Then, in 1942, encouraged purportedly by the U.S. Government, Britain used her war powers to expropriate the holdings of Itabira's overseas investors at very low prices, subsequently turning them over to the Brazilian Government. At the same time, the latter took over most of the corporate assets of the old Itabira Iron Ore Company in Brazil, including the Cauê Peak landholding, and from these fashioned the Companhia Vale do Rio Doce, with the Brazilian Government holding over 80 per cent of the stock.

The establishment of the Companhia Vale do Rio Doce marked the initiation of the modern period of ore mining and export in Brazil. But it did not get off to an auspicious start: according to Gauld, 'the men named by Vargas to run the company were mostly either crooked, indifferent, or technically ignorant'.[21] Thus, although the export target was 1,500,000 tons of ore annually within a few years of nationalization, five years later, in 1947, it was still shipping only 250,000 tons per annum, even though this constituted a significant portion of Brazil's iron ore production of 611,000 tons in that year.[22] Part of the problem was the bottleneck caused by the poor quality of the railroad, and in the late 1940s an American company, Morrison-Knudsen, was brought in to upgrade the Vitória-Minas. Because, however, of such political meddling for the benefit of local contractors as prohibiting the company from opening its own quarries to obtain ballast, substantive improvements in the roadbed became possible only in 1951–52, when a new administrator took charge of the Cia. Vale do Rio Doce following Vargas' return to power. The efficacy of these improvements was such that by 1953 the Cia. Vale do Rio Doce was exporting 1·5 million tons of iron ore, nearly one-half of Brazil's total production of 3·6 million tons in that year, and an increase of 1·2 million tons over 1951.

During the following decade the Cia. Vale do Rio Doce contributed an ever increasing amount, totally and proportionally, to Brazil's iron ore production, and by 1963 it was exporting ore at a rate of 7 million tons out of a total national production of 10 million tons. The difference was made up of 1·5 million tons consumed within the country and an equal amount, originating in the Paraopeba Valley, which was exported through Rio de Janeiro. By this time, however, facilities at the ore docks at the ports of both Vitória and Rio de Janeiro were overtaxed and lagging behind those available to competing exporters in other countries.

Some work was begun on new ore terminals and shipping facilities at the Rio Doce's outlet in 1963, partly in response to a contract signed the previous year with a consortium of ten Japanese steel companies for the delivery of 50 million tons of ore over a fifteen-year period beginning in 1966. The political unrest of the time, however, had virtually dried up Brazil's sources of foreign development capital, which were needed to finance the expansion. It was only after the 1964 military take-over that the confidence of investors returned, and in 1965 the Cia. Vale do Rio Doce obtained the largest loan ever granted by the Inter-American Development Bank to enable it to construct a new seaport, improve its mining equipment and expand the capacity of the Vitória–Minas Railroad by installing a traffic control system and new rails and locomotives.

In 1966 the new ore terminal at Tubarão, 10 kilometres south of Vitória, was completed, with an initial capacity of some 15 million tons a year. This was increased to 30 million tons in 1969, when the company's first pelletizing plant also began operating, opening up new and higher value markets. This was followed in 1970 by the company's purchase of four bulk carriers totalling 468,000 DWT from Japan, with a view to carrying some of its ore in its own bottoms[23] and bringing crude oil to Brazil from the Persian Gulf on the return journey. By 1970 the Cia. Vale do Rio Doce was exporting 24 million tons of ore through Tubarão,[24] amounting to 85 per cent of the Brazilian total. The company exported 42 million tons of iron ore in 1973, at the end of which it had long-term contracts on hand for 656 million tons, worth 6,000 million dollars, and was projecting exports of 55 million tons for 1974. Thus, after half a century's delay, it would seem that Percival Farquar's vision of the integrated development of the Rio Doce Valley, based on its fabulous iron reserves, has at last become reality—and may, perhaps, be on the way to exceeding the expectations of even his fertile imagination.[25]

A much smaller quantity of iron ore from the Paraopeba district, 4 million tons in 1970, is exported through the port of Rio de Janeiro. In that year work was begun on a new ore terminal at Sepetiba Bay, southwest of Rio, capable of accommodating bulk carriers of up to 300,000 DWT and with an initial capacity of 12 million tons of ore per year. These facilities, completed in late 1973, could be expanded in the future to handle up to 25 million tons, should production warrant it and internal transport facilities permit it, and may also ship out industrial products. The bulk of the ore for Sepetiba will come from a modern, large-scale, open pit mine inaugurated in early 1974 with a reserve at Aguas Claras, Minas Gerais, of 250 to 300 million tons of hematite assaying between 65 and 70 per cent iron. The major problem was transport, and a US$75 million loan was provided by the World Bank and the Export-Import Bank to construct 55 kilometres of new branch lines to mine and terminal, to upgrade 640 kilometres of the E.F. Central do Brasil's existing trunk line, and to purchase 1,340 special ore cars and 80 locomotives. Interestingly, however, both the financing and the construction of the US$200 million Sepetiba terminal was not a public venture but was organized by a consortium of Brazilian mining companies under the name Minerações Brasileiras Reunidas S.A., which includes the St. John D'El Rey Mining Company, now a subsidiary of the Hanna Mining Co., and ICOMI, the Antunes-Bethlehem Steel group that operates Amapá's manganese mine, which will be discussed in the following section. The consortium itself provided US$80 million; the rest came from a group of five Japanese mining and steel companies and from banks in Japan and the United States.

These strands in the development of the Minas Gerais iron ores illustrate the main lines of modernization of the Brazilian mining industry during the last quarter of a century: upgrading of private, often long-established, operations to meet the exigencies of modern industrial and export opportunities; government intervention based on nationalism and the desire to retain Brazilian control over its natural resources; and, most recently, the admission of foreign capital on a large scale if it is tempered with Brazilian participation, usually to the proportion of 51 per cent. Only after many years did the latter formula gain grudging acceptance by foreign, especially U.S., mining corporations, which had been loath to relinquish control of their investments and operations until they realized that no better alternative could be obtained. Government and foreign capital have also combined in the organization of Amazonia Mineração S.A., a joint venture involving the United States Steel Corp. and the government-owned Cia. Vale do Rio Doce (which hold 49 and 51 per cent of the stock, respectively), aimed at developing iron ore reserves recently discovered in the Serra dos Carajás in Pará, between the Tocantins and Xingú Rivers, about 500 kilometres from Belém.

The Serra dos Carajás ore body, which lies just south of the Trans-Amazon Highway, was discovered in 1967 by geologists of an exploration subsidiary of U.S. Steel. A recent geological study[26] indicates reserves of 18,000 million tons of hematite with iron content of 66 to 67 per cent. Development began in 1975 and is to involve an investment of some 930 million dollars. Of this, US$415 million will be spent on construction of a 970-kilometre railway to the industrial centre and port of Itaqui, near São Luís, Maranhão, which will accommodate bulk carriers of up to 200,000 DWT and where a steel mill will also be built. This supersedes a plan to ship the ore out by way of the Tocantins River and Belém. Exports, on which U.S. Steel, the British Steel Corporation and six Japanese firms have options to buy up to 50 per cent for use in their own plants, are expected to begin in 1978 or 1979 with an annual output of 50 million tons.

MANGANESE. Discovery of South America's largest manganese deposit, containing about 35 million tons of 50 to 53 per cent ore, is attributed to the *garimpeiro* Mario Cruz when he was prospecting for gold in Amapá's Serra do Navio in 1944. Subsequently, its development became a model for large-scale exploitation of Brazilian minerals by her own citizens in successful partnership with foreign capital and expertise.

Among those who replied to the territorial government's advertisement for bids to develop the deposit was a mining engineer from Minas Gerais, Augusto Antunes, who is said to have defeated his competitors by promising to invest 20 per cent of the operation's net profit in development projects within Amapá. In 1950 he formed ICOMI (Indústria e Comércio de Minérios S.A.), a joint company with Bethlehem Steel Corporation of the United States, with 51 and 49 per cent of the stock, respectively. Exploratory drilling began that same year to determine whether exploitation was feasible along modern lines, and in 1951 work began on the 122-mile railway to the mine and on construction of ore docks and a port at Santana on the Amazon River near Macapá.

The first cargo of 10,000 tons of manganese left Santana in January 1957, destined for Bethlehem Steel's plant at Sparrows Point. Unlike the disappointing results following the first shipment of Itabira iron ore to the same customer, Serra do Navio manganese has flowed steadily not only to the parent company, but also to others in the United States and a dozen other countries. Exports of this mineral from Amapá have amounted to about a million tons a year since the late 1960s, or about half the national production. Another half million tons from the Serra do Navio goes to the national market. This last amount approximately equals manganese production in the rest of Brazil, most of it from Minas Gerais, although small amounts, perhaps 10,000 tons a year, are also mined near Corumbá in Mato Grosso and in Bahia. Amapá's commanding lead in manganese production may one day be challenged from the Serra dos Carajás, where some 30 million tons have been discovered only 15 kilometres from the iron ore beds. Meanwhile, completion of the world's first manganese ore pelletization plant at Santana in 1972 gave Brazil international leadership in the production of this mineral and marked the coming of age of her mining industry through the rational, up-to-date exploitation of long dormant but impressive subsoil resources.

Tin. Tin mining in Brazil was, until rather recently, a desultory and marginal affair, conducted by *garimpeiros* or small free-lance operators. In Amapá placers along the edge of the Guiana Shield yielded less than 100 tons a year; production from scattered localities in Minas Gerais has fluctuated between 200 and 500 tons per annum since the late 1940s; and Paraíba, Bahia, and Rio Grande do Sul in occasional years produced a few tons. A boom of sorts began in Goiás, in 1960, when a newly opened mine yielded 2,200 tons of ore; but production tapered off rapidly and operations ceased six years later. In 1963 there were plans to organize the Amapá producers into a co-operative, and a small primary processing plant was built at Macapá in the hope of stimulating production in that region, but the hope is still unrealized. About a decade ago, then, tin production in Brazil did not suffice to supply the country's tin metal plant at Volta Redonda, which imported most of its raw material from Bolivia, and the prospects did not seem very promising.

In 1959, however, about a dozen tons of cassiterite were produced in Rondônia as a by-product of gold extraction from placers along the Madeira River, and this was increased to 50 tons in each of the two succeeding years. These deposits attracted the attention of foreign mining interests, and in 1962, in association with local operators, they brought in dredging equipment and raised production to over 600 tons in that year. By 1965 it had increased to 2,500 tons and for the next half-dozen years this district yielded between 2,000 and

3000 tons of cassiterite per annum, which sufficed to make Brazil essentially self-sufficient in this mineral, imports of which dropped to less than 400 tons of ore yearly.[27]

Then, in the latter part of 1969, a cassiterite deposit estimated to contain reserves of the order of 5 million tons—nearly equal to total known world reserves outside China—was discovered in the interior of Rondônia, about 300 kilometres from Pôrto Velho. These estimates have probably been doubled with the discovery of new, deeper veins in 1972. Development, by Brazilian capital, proceeded rapidly. In the first stages, while a road was being built, mining equipment and supplies were flown into a small airfield which had been cleared in the jungle that surrounded what was to become the Aripuanã Mine. Production began in May 1971, and is running at a rate of 200 tons of cassiterite a month. Total production in Rondônia during 1971 was 5,800 tons of 65 per cent tin ore concentrate, providing a surplus for export, and is expected to reach 30,000 tons a year by 1977. The development of the Rondônia tin mines provides an excellent example of some of the quantitative and technical changes that have transformed the Brazilian mining industry during the past decade or so.

ALUMINIUM. Aluminium mining, like tin mining, began slowly and has only recently approached a significant level of production, in this instance almost exclusively from Minas Gerais, with a negligible amount from São Paulo. The largest bauxite deposit currently being worked is near Poços de Caldas, in southwestern Minas, with reserves of about 50 million tons having a 60 to 66 per cent Al_2O_3 content; another is at Saramenha, near Ouro Prêto, with reserves of 15 million tons. The first-named extends across the border into São Paulo State, which also has fairly extensive bauxite deposits near the coast. These coastal deposits, like those of Espírito Santo and a ten million ton ore body in coastal Maranhão, have a high phosphorous content and are not of currently marketable quality, but the Maranhão deposit may be worked to produce phosphate fertilizers.

Considerably more promising is the fact that large concentrations of high-grade bauxite are located in the more northerly parts of the country. These include some 400 million tons in a deposit in Goiás, near the Belém-Brasília Highway, and several hundreds of millions of tons more located along the Trombetas River in Pará. In January 1976, Aluminas (an Alcan subsidiary) in partnership with the Cia. Vale do Rio Doce, began construction of mining, railway and port facilities along the Trombetas to export 3·4 million tons of bauxite annually, beginning in 1979, with an eventual capacity of over 8 million tons. These prospects may pale, however, in the light of the discovery, announced in April 1974, of a bauxite deposit in the Amazon region with reserves believed to be of the order of 4,000 million tons, which would make it the largest such ore body in the world, total current reserves of which are about 10,000 million tons.

Meanwhile, the ore bodies situated in Minas Gerais are ideally located in relation to the country's principal hydro-electric systems and to its internal markets in the Industrial Heartland, but are able to supply the nation's industries with only 60 per cent of the raw material they require. Paradoxically, bauxite mining was initiated in Minas in 1937 with the export market in mind, and until 1951 the whole production from the Poços de Caldas area, ranging between 9,000 and 20,000 tons a year from 1937 until 1954, was shipped out of the country.[28] A small aluminium plant had been established in Brazil in 1945, but it discontinued operations the following year in the face of competition from imports. A more successful attempt at domestic production was initiated in 1951, when 403 tons of bauxite were consumed, and its growth was such that it was soon absorbing all the national production, and export ceased in the mid-1950s. Stimulated by increasing local consumption, bauxite production in Brazil then expanded rapidly, exceeding 20,000 tons in 1955, passing 100,000 tons in 1960 and reaching a quarter of a million tons in 1966. Thereafter it levelled off at around the current 300,000 tons per annum. In fact, production no longer kept pace with the nation's needs, and Brazil now imports about 50,000 tons of aluminium a year to meet domestic demands. This deficit far exceeds the total national bauxite output of thirty years ago at a time when exports dominated the industry. This illustrates the symbiosis between at least certain of Brazil's mining industries and her rapidly expanding manufacturing capability even though they may not always remain in phase.

Current Brazilian bauxite production is divided rather evenly among three companies: Aluminas, already mentioned as an Alcan subsidiary, with an output of 27,000 tons of aluminium in 1970; the Cia. Brasileira de Aluminio controlled by Votorantim, a national industrial group, with about 23,000 tons; and Alcominas, a joint venture of Alcoa, the Hanna Mining Co. and the Minas Gerais Development Bank, which attained an annual capacity of 25,000 tons in mid-1970 with the opening of its integrated mining, smelting and refining facilities at Poços de Caldas. Aluminas is planning a new smelter with a capacity of 11,000 tons of aluminium a year at Aratu, the industrial centre near Salvador, Bahia, but whether imported or national ores are to be used is not known. It has been estimated, however, that although Brazil will be consuming at least 150,000 tons of aluminium by 1975—that is, twice the amount produced in 1970—almost all of this should be derived from the country's own bauxite deposits, even though output will have to increase to something over 600,000 tons per year. At the refining end, plans now underway envisage an expansion of aluminium production by that date to 50,000 tons each for Alcominas and Aluminas and to 40,000 tons for the Cia. Brasileira de Aluminio.

ZINC. A very interesting example of the rapid development of a mineral resource based exclusively on native technical developments is provided by zinc. Until recently, the ores of this mineral, known primarily from occurrences in Minas Gerais, were not deemed to be of marketable quality because they are in the form of oxidised zinc carbonates and silicates, which could not be processed by existing methods. Then, in 1962, a new process for zinc extraction from these ores was developed by a Brazilian metallurgist.

This discovery led to the establishment of Brazil's first zinc processing plant in 1965, at Itaguaí in Rio de Janeiro State, with an annual capacity of 7,200 tons of zinc, thereby saving US$2 million in foreign exchange on a raw material the demand for which had previously been met entirely by imports. This, however, was only a small proportion of the 52,000 tons consumed by Brazil in that year, a figure which rose to 70,000 tons by 1968. In that year a second plant, located in Minas Gerais, was built with an annual capacity of 18,000 tons. By this time, reserves of about 150 million tons of useable ore, with an average zinc content of over 17 per cent, had been proven, and exploration was underway to prove out other ore bodies not only in Minas Gerais, but also in Pará and elsewhere.

Now that the technical difficulties of processing Brazilian zinc ores have been overcome, financial problems still remain to be solved as the cost of building the appropriate plants is heavy—about US$540 per ton of annual capacity. The Federal Government, however, provides financial incentives for the development of the industry in view of the fact that considerable sums must be spent annually on zinc imports. This will undoubtedly stimulate the expansion of zinc mining, which as yet has not attained sufficient volume or value to appear in national statistical publications.

OTHER DEVELOPMENTS

There is, as can be partially noted from Map 12, a wide variety of other minerals in Brazil, either being mined or forming potentially mineable reserves. It must also be assumed that ore bodies exist in that country which are as yet unknown, but whose discovery may lead to changes in the mining industry that would be as far-reaching as those that have taken place during the past decade or so.

Eventual changes are, of course, impossible to foresee. Nevertheless, some hints as to likely developments can perhaps be drawn from an overview of recent events that have affected production of minerals, other than the principal ones already discussed, which are important either for Brazil's internal needs or for the export market. Their further development is, or will be, related to one of the five categories of change, or combinations thereof, that have already been operative in the country's progress in this field to date: new forms of organization, new markets, new means of access, new discoveries and new technical developments. As this is not a mineralogical treatise, speculations on the last-named are beyond our present scope. In view of the promising results of Brazilian research in the field of zinc production, however, it is certainly to be expected that as the country's research capability expands, enabling it to deal with mineralogical problems in terms of its own conditions and needs, rather than rely solely on imported technology, new or better uses of existing ores will emerge.

ORGANIZATION. The effects of change on the organizational structure of certain segments of Brazilian mining and ancillary industries have already been noted, in iron, manganese and tin production. Another interesting example is afforded by the monazite beach sands from the central coastal area. These sands, with those of ilmenite and zirconium, derive from the natural concentration and re-concentration of heavy minerals which are thinly diffused through granitic formations, a process which has been identified only in Brazil and India.

Monazite sands, source of the so-called rare earths, were first used by the British in the manufacture of gas mantles. Tradition has it that their ships discharged cargoes at Salvador, sailed to a beach at Cumuxatiba, near Ilhéus, loaded the valuable sands ostensibly as ballast and thence returned with their clandestine shipments to Britain. This traffic died out with the advent of electric lighting and the discovery of the practice by the authorities. But interest in the monazite sands from the Brazilian formations revived during the 1940s, particularly as it was believed that one of its constituents, thorium, might be used in atomic fission, research into which was then in its infancy. This interest was heightened by closure of the Indian beaches to foreign exploitation and by subsequent efforts of the Americans, the Russians and the French to obtain stockpiles of this material.

At this time, the largest producer of monazite sands in Brazil was a subsidiary of a Chicago-based chemical company, but other foreign interests were also involved, fronted by a company registered in São Paulo. The activities of both centred on the most accessible beaches, south of Vitória at Guaraparí and Anchieta.[29] Mining, by shovel brigades, took place amidst a Wild-West scenario of suits, counter-suits and armed claim-jumping, until the Brazilian Atomic Energy Commission tightened its export permit requirements. Pressure was also put on the exporters to build a primary refining works in Brazil. As the time was not ripe for such an expensive investment, the U.S. company withdrew, preferring to develop the extremely low-content, but politically more secure, rare earth deposits available at home. At the same time, interest in the atomic energy applications of thorium died down and the field was left to the São Paulo corporation, which reopened the beach at Cumuxatiba and industrialized the production of derivatives not only of monazite, but also of zirconite and amblygonite. This firm eventually ran foul of the law for other reasons, and in 1965 it was taken over by the Federal Government, thereby ending one of the more colourful episodes in Brazilian mining history.

MARKETS. Along the same stretch of coast, but more extensively distributed, is an abundance of ilmenite sands, to which in the 1940s and 50s DuPont staked out a number of claims and surveyed them in preliminary fashion. Again, attempts were made to get the foreign company to establish a processing plant as the price for proceeding with mining operations. But lack of enthusiasm and of suitable markets inhibited developments, although feasibility studies continued into the mid-1960s; and Brazil continued to import titanium dioxide. This is used as a white pigment in the paint, dye, textile and rubber industries. Finally, in April 1972, self-sufficiency in titanium dioxide, the demand for which had attained 22,000 tons a year, was accomplished in one step with the inauguration of a plant at Camaçari, just north of Salvador, with the assistance of Farbenfabriken Bayer A.G., the world's largest producer. The company, Titânio do Brasil S.A., expects to be producing 45,000 tons by 1975, when it hopes to have tapped markets in the other Latin American countries, all of which import their titanium.

In other cases, of course, the consumer is primarily, if not exclusively, the foreign market, over which Brazil has no control. The diversity of organizational structures that characterizes the country's mining industry, however, gives it a useful advantage in competing for these markets, whether they be large and stable or small and perhaps volatile. One such market of recent origin is for niobium, a rather rare metal of the vanadium family, formerly known as columbium, which has recently come into demand as an alloy in high-quality steels produced in the U.S.A., Germany and Japan. Niobium ore is found principally near Araxá, Minas Gerais, where some two-thirds of all known deposits are located and from which comes 60 per cent of current world production. A company was set up in 1971 by the state of Minas with 49·5 per cent U.S. corporate participation to develop these mines, but with actual mining operations under the overall charge of the Cia. Vale do Rio Doce, which is organizing production along modern lines. Table 9 shows that the quantity of niobium produced is not high, but its value makes this a profitable undertaking and significant expansion is expected, aided by the marketing expertise of the Cia. Vale do Rio Doce and its contacts among steel manufacturers.

Near the opposite end of the scale of production technology is the mining of beryllium, in which Brazil's reserves are second only to those of the U.S.S.R. This mineral (to which the gem varieties emerald, aquamarine, and the striking but little known golden beryl belong) is found principally in the granitic pegmatites of eastern Minas Gerais and southernmost Bahia, although lesser ore bodies are also known in Brazil's northeastern bulge and in Goiás. The mining of these pegmatites for gemstones and mica, which was used instead of glass for window panes, dates back to colonial times, and current practices are little different because of the limited size of the ore bodies themselves and the hand sorting involved in separating out the beryllium oxide crystals. In fact, as late as World War II, beryllium was still considered only as part of the gangue associated with the extraction of mica, which, as Table 9 indicates, then ranked fifth in value among the products of the Brazilian mining industry. In the late 1940s the first shipment of beryllium from Brazil was made by the Chicago chemical firm that was exporting monazite sand—and that only because it chanced to acquire an old mica property as part of a purchase of mining rights on the coast. Subsequently the Cold War interrupted U.S. beryllium imports from the Soviet Union, while at the same time demand for the mineral increased greatly, notably by the aerospace industry, for which it is an important alloy in the manufacture of nose cones for re-entry vehicles. As a result, the current value of Brazil's production of the once useless beryllium is nearly double that of mica, and the country has become one of the world's leading suppliers of the mineral, even though it remains a relatively modest item within the overall picture of the mining industry.

ACCESS. There are, of course, numerous instances in which access to a mineral deposit has been opened or improved once the viability of its extraction was established as, for example, a road and ship channel markers at Cumuxatiba, ore docks and a railway to the Serra do Navio and the air-strip and road to the Aripuanã mine. But in not a few cases mining, or even the discovery of new ore bodies in Brazil, had to await the advent of roads built for other purposes because of the country's vast extent and its general paucity of surface communications. Promising new discoveries, ranging from gold to iron ore, following the building of the Trans-Amazon Highway and that from the West into Rondônia, have been mentioned above; but other road building programmes in seemingly already developed parts of the country have had an impact nearly as great.

A case in point is the expected development of ore bodies along the Rio–Bahia Highway and its extension into the heart of the Northeast, particularly in the stagnant and backward mineralized zone between Teofilo Otoni and the São Francisco River. This area has long been a source of gemstones, but is also known to contain such minerals as manganese, uranium, vermiculite (although what is said to be the world's largest deposit of this mineral, estimated at 65 million tons, was discovered in Piauí in 1975), scheelite, wolframite and chromium, as well as tantalite and beryllium north of the river. The principal obstacle to their exploitation now is an organizational one and the region's paucity of capital, technical and operational resources. Nevertheless development has begun of copper deposits, discovered in the late 1960s by SUDENE geologists at Riacho Sêco in a desolate area 100 kilometres south of the São Francisco, which are significantly larger than the reserves currently being worked in Rio Grande do Sul. Both operations are controlled by the Pignatari group of São Paulo, but whereas production from Rio Grande do Sul amounts to only 12,000 tons a year, including new processing facilities installed at Caçapava do Sul in 1971, that from Bahia is expected to yield 35,000 tons, making Brazil self-sufficient in copper by 1975. The Japanese press[30] has also reported that investment interests in Japan are seeking to develop production and exports of chromium ore in this part of Bahia to the amount of 150,000 tons annually, or nearly ten times the present level of production.

One development in the Brazilian mining industry, which inaccessibility has frustrated for over a quarter of a century, involves the vast nickel reserves at Niquelândia, in central Goiás, which are believed to surpass those of either New Caledonia or Canada's Sudbury area. Recent improvements in transport within the region related to the development of Brasília have, however, made exploitation feasible. Beginning in 1971, SUDECO and others have undertaken to attract investments sufficient to develop nickel production to a level of 3,500 tons a year.

Studies are also underway in Goiás, partly supported by French mining interests, to open an asbestos mine near Uruaçú, 75 kilometres due west of Niquelândia, which is supposed to double Brazil's production of that mineral. More important, it is expected to yield a higher quality asbestos than that of the Northeast, which has been limited in use to such products as asbestos, cement, roofing, and tubing. Again, development of the Uruaçú asbestos reserves had to await improvements in the regional road network; but it was also held up for lack of an adequate source of power, which is now available from new hydroelectric installations on the Paraná River through extensions of the power grid into southern Goiás. Thanks to the general opening up of this region, deposits of apatite and corundum have been discovered which are expected to make Brazil self-sufficient in these minerals, in 1975 new uraniferous ore finds at Amorinópolis and Campo Belos doubled the country's known uranium reserves, and significant reserves of chrysolite, cobalt, and rutile have also been found, although lesser deposits of these have been known in Goiás for many decades.

New Discoveries: the Amazon. Considering the number of new ore body discoveries in even the seemingly well-known parts of Brazil, and the rising pace and technical level of minerals exploitation within the country in recent years, the excitement with which prospectors and mining companies are viewing the future seems not ill-founded. This is particularly true of the little-known Amazonian region, especially in the light of developments already under way along the peripheries of the geanticlinal formations in Amapá, Pará, and Rondônia. The general spirit of optimism has been captured by Ronaldo Moreira da Rocha, President of the Federal Minerals Research and Resources Company (Companhía de Pesquisas e Recursos Minerais, CPRM), who said he expects 'a minerals boom reminiscent of the nineteenth century gold rushes'.[31] Brazil's Minister of the Interior, Costa Cavalcanti, believes that the 'resources of the Amazon will within a short time constitute one of the principal sources of income for the country thanks to mineral exports', despite the fact that 'mineral exploration in the region is embryonic'.[32]

Few of these embryonic resources have as yet been sufficiently well pin-pointed by those reporting on their discovery to have their locations included with any degree of accuracy on the accompanying map. Some of the newly-discovered Amazonian ore bodies have already been mentioned. Others in the eastern Amazon include: diamond-bearing earths along the Tocantins River; copper, lead, silver, and zinc ores by the Xingú and Tapajós; and placer gold and tin on the lower Tapajós, near where the Trans-Amazon Highway intersects the Santarém–Cuiabá road. Outcrops of tantalite, magnesium, chromite and molybdenum ores have also been noted in these general areas by CPRM and SUDAM (Superintendency for the Development of the Amazon) technicians. To the west, in the state of Amazonas, penetration is still insufficient to permit even an educated guess as to the mineral resources potential. It would indeed be surprising, however, if the geological formations of that area, which link up with those to the east, west, and south, did not yield a considerable storehouse of exploitable ore bodies, even though the presumed westward extension of the geanticline that lies south of the Amazon River is overlain here by Tertiary formations.

THE MINERALS RESEARCH & RESOURCES COMPANY

In order to prospect for and develop Brazil's Amazonian mineral potential most effectively, both SUDAM and the

CPRM are actively encouraging the development of that region. CPRM, under the jurisdiction of the Ministry of Mines and Energy, was organized in 1969 as a joint-capital enterprise to stimulate and intensify research into, and use of, Brazil's mineral resources. It is financed primarily through a special tax on mineral sales, which in June 1970 was set at 15 per cent, with the exception of salt, which was not to reach that level until 1974. By a decree in November 1971 the company acquired an additional source of revenue, namely 80 per cent of the dividends the government receives from its shares in the Cia. Vale do Rio Doce (the other 20 per cent goes to the Fundo Nacional de Mineração, which is to study and develop the process of mine finance).

The CPRM is empowered not only to undertake and to finance studies relating to mineral discovery and development, including estimating reserves and overseeing bids, but also to invest risk capital in new ventures up to 80 per cent of the total amount needed. This latter role of the CPRM has drawn criticism: it is feared that it may be used as a vehicle for nationalization of the mining industry, or at least that it will hinder free enterprise through its sales tax and its favourable competitive position for obtaining contracts with large foreign corporations. On the other hand, free enterprise is encouraged in that prospecting and mining firms were recently granted generous tax exemptions and depletion allowances (up to 40 and 20 per cent respectively), and the government claims that it has no intention of limiting the freedom of prospecting or of mineral development by private enterprise—but it is not unknown for government policies or governments themselves to change. Thus far, the participation of Brazilian government in mining has proved salutary and the CPRM has an obviously useful role to play, when the extent of the investigations yet to be made is considered.

Shortly after its inception President Garrastazu Médici said that the CPRM 'is a fundamental undertaking for progress by means of which we have to reveal in the forthcoming years, below our feet, the real dimension of a new Brazil'.[33] Towards this goal, by the end of 1970 it had already embarked upon twenty-eight exploration, research, and mapping projects which engaged 130 geologists and mining engineers. In 1973 it had a staff of 546 geologists working on over 100 prospecting and research projects. The CPRM, jointly with NASA and the U.S. Geological Survey, is also involved in the EROS (Earth Resources Observatory Satellites) geological survey of Brazil and other Latin American countries.

Although Moreira da Rocha has pointed out[34] that Brazil uses only 4·5 dollars worth of minerals per capita, whereas 'no country can be considered as developed if it uses less than 18 to 20 dollars worth', and that it must still import some 200 different raw, half-processed or fully processed minerals, there is nevertheless little doubt that Brazil must now be reckoned among the world's leading mining countries, both in quantities produced and in the sophistication of its production processes. It has attained this position through a unique combination of private enterprise, both large and small, government participation and foreign investment, maintained in harmonious balance. It may nevertheless be conjectured that at this particular moment in time the industry is in delicate balance between the new and the old, from which it will soon be irreversibly torn. The signs are already there as large-scale exploitation of new ore bodies supersedes that of small, isolated deposits, as development funds leave old, established areas to seek opportunities on the fringes of colonization, as modern organizational forms take over from those dating back in some instances to colonial times, and as observations from aircraft and satellites replace the gropings of hordes of prospectors.

The *garimpeiro*'s days are almost over, while at the other end of the spectrum the fear of foreign domination of the Brazilian mining industry can be equally laid to rest. It remains only to be seen whether the future will belong to private corporate enterprise, to government ownership or to a workmanlike balance between the two. It is unlikely that, whichever of these directions Brazil may take, the current momentum of its mining industry will slacken in the foreseeable future. Rather, given the significant accomplishments of particularly the last decade, it may be expected to increase its rate of growth for some years to come; but it will be interesting to observe the manner in which this is accomplished.

REFERENCES

1. The geology of these coal-bearing formations is discussed in Good, John E., Abreu, Alvaro, and Fraser, Thomas, *The Coal Industry of Brazil—Part II: Technology of Mining and Preparation*, United States Department of the Interior, Technical Paper 713, Washington, D.C., 1951, p. 14.

2. Roraima and Amazonas had 106 and 13 employed in mining respectively in 1950, but there are none today. The Federal District (Brasília) was not a separate statistical unit until very recently, but at least some small-scale quartz crystal extraction took place within its present boundaries, probably during the 1940s.

3. See, for example, Departamento Nacional da Produção Mineral, *Brasil 1942: Recursos Minerais*, Boletim No. 56, Ministério da Agricultura, Rio de Janeiro, 1943, p. 23; Azevedo, Aroldo de, *Brasil: A Terra e o Homem*, Vol. II, Cia. Editora Nacional, São Paulo, 1970, p. 15; or Mesquita, Olinda Vianna, 'Extrativismo Mineral', *Atlas Nacional do Brasil*, Conselho Nacional de Geografia, I.B.G.E., Rio de Janeiro, 1966, back of Plate IV–1.

4. Santa Catarina is a unique departure from this axiom, with an exceedingly high average number of workers per firm but low on the scale of value added. This represents a special characteristic of the coal mining industry, exacerbated here by a national policy of supporting an operation that is relatively inefficient both in mining methods and in the nature of the coal seams that must be worked.

5. Since the source for Table 8 provides figures by 'establishments, persons employed, and salaries' it is assumed, although not explicitly stated, that these data do not include the self-employed prospector. The sector using archaic techniques is therefore undoubtedly under-represented, although many firms still operate with hand labour employing the pan, the pick or the shovel, a fact reflected in the statistics of Table 8.

6. The absence of these items—gold, silver, and arsenic—is not readily explainable, although it may be due to a recognition of the unreliability of the relevant statistics, at least in the case of gold and diamonds, as will be shown later.

7. Fundação I.B.G.E., 'Mineração e Extração de Produtos Minerais', *Sinopse Estatística do Brasil 1971*, Instituto Brasileiro de Estatística, Rio de Janeiro, 1971, p. 140. Additionally there are probably 50,000 *garimpeiros*, giving a total approaching 100,000.

8. Not to be confused with the Minas Gerais town of São João Del Rei, 150 kilometres south of Morro Velho.

9. *Brazilian Bulletin*, Brazilian Government Trade Bureau, New York City, October 1968, p. 3. Ashley, Burton E. and Koelling, Gordon W., 'The Mineral Industry of Brazil', Bureau of Mines, *1969 Minerals Yearbook*, U.S. Department of the Interior, Washington, D.C., 1970, give a figure of about 5.5 tons for 1968, but add that 'Much placer gold produced eludes statistical coverage'.

10. Clarke, Robert G. in 'Gem Stones', Bureau of Mines, *1970 Minerals*

Yearbook, U.S. Department of the Interior, Washington, D.C., 1971, indicates, however, that such a pipe may recently have been discovered in Piauí.

11. Stern, Hans. 'The World of Gems and Jewels', *Brazil Herald*, December 7, 1969, cites an instance which led to convictions in the courts in 1965.

12. Clarke, *op. cit.*, p. 5.

13. Figures for the years 1968, 1969, and 1970 are in Clarke, *ibid.*, p. 5; those for 1967 are from Ashley and Koelling, *op. cit.*, p. 2.

14. Used dredges change hands many times in transactions along the rivers of the Brazilian interior. For instance, diamond production on the Jequitinhonha River in northeasternmost Minas Gerais increased by 50 per cent when a dredge was transferred there in 1970 from working a gold placer in another river system. Its true origins and ultimate destination cannot even be surmised.

15. The world's largest stone is the Cullinan diamond, which weighed 971 carats. Other famous Brazilian stones have been the Darcy Vargas (460 carats), the Coromandel (430 carats), the Estrela do Sul (262 carats), and the Star of Minas (179 carats), all from the state of Minas Gerais. For an account of the discovery and marketing of the Getúlio Vargas diamond, and the vicissitudes in the life of the prospector who found it, see *Manchete*, Vol. 17, No. 910, September 27, 1969, pp. 108 & 109.

16. The geanticlinal formation in these two states is, in fact, defined with some precision by a string of apt place names like Cristalândia and Brejinho das Ametistas in Bahia, or Rubilita, Berílio and Turmalina in Minas Gerais. This legacy of place names left by prospectors in Brazil is discussed in Momsen, R. P. Jr., 'Similarities in Settlement Names of Brazil and the United States', *Boletim do Centro de Estudos Geográficos* (Coimbra University), Vol. III, No. 19 (1962), pp. 41–54.

17. Based on figures for emeralds imported into the United States, the quality of the Brazilian stones is in the lower price range, averaging approximately $18 a carat, versus $13 for Indian stones and $86 for the Colombian. From Clarke, *op. cit.*, p. 2.

18. Mesquita, *op. cit.*, back of Plate IV–1.

19. For an account of Farquhar's career, involving many successful schemes for opening up untapped Latin American resources, see Gauld, Charles A., *The Last Titan: Percival Farquhar, an American Entrepreneur in Latin America*, Institute of Hispanic American and Luso-Brazilian Studies, Stanford University, 1964.

20. *Ibid.*, p. 287. On the other hand, Farquhar is said to have complained once that, 'It was no use . . . to argue with Bernardes. If we refuted one set of his feudal ideas, he shifted to another absurdly uneconomic position.'

21. *Ibid.*, p. 337.

22. *Cf.* the 1943 figure of 810,504 tons in Table 9. Iron ore production in Brazil dropped sharply in the immediate post-war period.

23. The Cia. Vale do Rio Doce has also stimulated the long quiescent Brazilian shipbuilding industry. Its 53,500 DWT *Doceangra* from Rio

de Janeiro's Verolme Shipyard, delivered in 1972, is the largest vessel built in Latin America (see also Ch. 7).

24. Not all the ore exported by the Cia. Vale do Rio Doce originates from its own mine; shipments are also handled for two privately owned companies, FERTECO and SAMITRI. The latter (S.A. Mineração de Trinidade) produced 4 million tons in the late 1960s from its Morro Agudo mine in the headwaters of the Rio Doce.

25. Following the reorganization of the Itabira Iron Ore Company in 1940, Farquhar still pursued, with Brazilian partners, that part of the original project aimed at constructing a steel mill in the Rio Doce Valley. This project was realized in 1949 when the Acesita (Aços Especiais Itabira) high-quality steel mill began operations 100 kms. from Governador Valadares; both the plant and that city have benefited greatly from improvements to the railway.

26. *Brazilian Bulletin*, August 1972. Other promising iron ore deposits of the unfolding Amazonian region are said to exist in the Amapá highlands, north of the Amazon River in central Pará and on the border between Rondônia and Mato Grosso, all of them associated with geanticlinal formations.

27. Imports of tin from 1967 to 1969 fluctuated between 1 and 390 tons.

28. Figures on bauxite production do not appear in Brazilian statistical publications until 1950, although the I.B.G.E., *Anuario Estatístico do Brasil, 1952*, Conselho Nacional de Estatística, Rio de Janeiro, 1953, gives a figure of 9,017 tons for 1939. On the other hand, the Department of Information and Statistics of the Ministry of Foreign Affairs in *Brazil: Resources, Possibilities*, Rio de Janeiro, 1946, shows exports of 100,000 tons in 1943; but this probably indicates stockpiling during the earlier years of World War II: bauxite exports in 1940, for example, were only 82 tons.

29. The radioactivity of these sands has long been known, and their therapeutic value attracted people to the beaches, particularly to those near Vitória. The publicity attendant on their exploitation by foreign interests twenty-five years ago, combined with improvements in transport, created a sizeable tourist boom among those seeking a health cure by burying themselves in the sand. This centred on Guaraparí, advertised as the 'City of Health', which now has numerous new tourist hotels. Tourism has replaced mining as the principal source of the city's income, and renovation of the centre with new, modern buildings gives it a well-planned urban look where previously it had been an unremarkable, even run-down village. Two other towns in the area with similar beaches are Anchieta and Marataizes; they are, however, less accessible and therefore still await tourist development, as does the even more distant beach at Cumuxatiba, located in an idyllic tropical setting complete with offshore coral reef and tranquil lagoon.

30. Through *The Brazilian Bulletin* of November 1971.

31. *The Journal of Commerce* (New York), December 21, 1970.

32. *Brazil Herald*, August 21, 1971.

33. Rocha, Rolando Moreira. 'Prospects for Brazil's Mineral Wealth', *Brazil Herald*, September 6, 1970.

34. *Ibid.*

CHAPTER 7

Industrialization

Brazil progresses at night while the politicians sleep.
Popular saying

Economic analysis of the industrial development of Brazil is currently in a state of flux. The structuralist interpretation that has been dominant for the last two decades[1] stresses the uneven, lurching process of industrialization under the impact of exogenous events such as two world wars and a world depression, during which the disruption of world trade encouraged the domestic production of industrial goods. Revisionism, on the contrary, stresses the early beginning to Brazilian industrial development with its foundation in the coffee economy and its continuity of growth, and belittles the role of import difficulties during wartime or the depression.[2] 'On the whole, Brazilian industrialization seems to have taken place under conditions similar to those of other regions of recent settlement: in conjunction with rapid expansion of foreign trade and with strong government support in the form of tariff protection.'[3]

Current research also throws doubt on the role of the government policies of exchange control and import substitution, which are thought by the structuralists to be critical in encouraging industrial development.[4] Baer holds that the substantial inflation of the 1950s had positive effects on Brazil's industrial growth by acting as a mechanism for the transfer of savings into industrial investment,[5] but Huddle feels that inflation, even in the 'fifties, had some negative effects and that when it got out of control in the early 'sixties it contributed to the industrial stagnation of the period 1962–65.[6] Even the policy of import substitution undertaken after the Second World

War, 'a decision of basic importance to the intensification of the country's process of industrialization',[7] has been criticized for being costly and inefficient,[8] and leading to large scale structural disequilibrium.[9] Finally, the stagnation of domestic agriculture, seen by the structuralists as the essential concomitant of industrial development, has been denied by several recent writers.[10] Bergsman states that 'Brazil would seem to have managed the agriculture-industry balance problem fairly well—as regards output. Many less developed countries have not done so well'.[11]

THE GROWTH OF INDUSTRY

INDUSTRIAL BEGINNINGS DURING THE EMPIRE. Until the independence of Brazil in 1822 Portuguese mercantilist policies prohibited any type of industry in the colony. British and Portuguese manufacturers controlled the Brazilian market and the former group kept these privileges until 1844.[12] Free trade dominated the commercial policy of the Brazilian Empire, 1822–89, and so the development of domestic manufacturing was inhibited. The free trade policy was supported by the sugar, coffee and cocoa planters because European manufactured goods were cheaper and of better quality than the domestic products, and in addition the growth of Brazilian industries threatened the agricultural labour supply, which was not entirely protected by the existence of slavery. Some small industries did, however, develop in those areas of the country least influenced by colonial economic structures. By 1830 Minas Gerais State was producing six million yards of cotton cloth annually on hand looms. In Rio Grande do Sul the first wave of German immigration, 1815–30, had by 1829 led to the development of seven small leather works, eight flour mills, a soap factory, rope works, gold workshops and other establishments for clothing, cloth, iron and steel, and cabinet-making in Novo Hamburgo.[13]

In the second half of the nineteenth century the industrial revolution began to take hold in Brazil, with expansion of the traditional textile and foodstuffs industries. The number of textile mills grew from two in 1850 to forty-four in 1881.[14] Many of these developments were assisted by favourable terms of trade and the occasional tariff protection, and were associated with the ventures of the Barão de Mauá, Brazil's first great banker-entrepreneur.[15]

THE REPUBLIC & INDUSTRIAL GROWTH, 1889–1930. An impetus to industrial development was provided by the abolition of slavery in 1888, which disrupted the traditional agrarian system and led to considerable migration from the rural areas to the cities.[16] The establishment of the Republic in 1889 was accompanied by nationalist sentiment desiring to complement political independence by encouraging the industrialization of Brazil and so ending economic colonialism. This was a period of financial speculation, 'bubbles', swindles and many bankruptcies, but industry continued to grow because of tariff protection and government assistance. The number of industrial establishments in Brazil increased from 636 in 1889 to 1,088 in 1895;[17] but of the total number of industrial firms founded before 1900 and still existing in 1920 over one-third were processing foodstuffs.

The state having the largest number of establishments founded before 1890 was Guanabara, then the Federal District, reflecting the attractive power of the political and financial centre of the city of Rio de Janeiro. During this period, however, the export of coffee increased rapidly, bringing prosperity to the state of São Paulo, which in turn attracted European immigrants, who not only brought knowledge and experience of manufacturing with them but also provided a substantial market for locally produced goods. Industries catering to the coffee industry, food processing and textile industries were set up. This led a contemporary writer, Amaro Cavalcanti, to say, 'What São Paulo is today, from this point of view, is what all Brazil will be.'[18]

In the first decade of the twentieth century Brazil tried to speed up her economic development by adding industrial production to the traditional agricultural output. Under the presidency of Afonso Pena (1906–9) the country's policy was one of 'peopling the land, developing industrial centres and reforming the monetary system.'[19] The increased rate of railway construction and immigration, the development of electric power, protective tariffs and a conversion fund which permitted greater exchange balance all gave the incipient domestic industries encouragement. The national exposition of 1908 in Rio de Janeiro at which 11,000 exhibitors displayed the nation's new manufactured products to a million visitors was a revelation to most Brazilians.[20] Both economic change and social change were taking place, with the new urban-industrial entrepeneurs trying to replace the sugar and coffee barons who had dominated the nineteenth century.

By 1907 there were some 3,250 manufacturing establishments in Brazil, employing 151,000 workers.[21] Twelve years later production of manufactures had quadrupled in value, and the number of establishments had increased to 13,336, occupying 285,512 workers.[22] Industrial development was stimulated by improved communications, a higher proportion of urban dwellers in the population and a substantial inflow of foreign capital.

Electricity production increased rapidly from 12,185 kilowatts of installed capacity in 1900 to 159,860 in 1910 and 357,203 in 1920.[23] Even in 1920, however, only half the industrial establishments had any sort of motive power and only half the power used was supplied by electricity. The first thermal electricity plant was installed in 1883 to light the city of Campos in the state of Rio de Janeiro, and in 1889 the first hydroelectric plant, at Juiz de Fora, Minas Gerais, was opened by the Brazilian industrialist, Bernardo Mascarenhas, to provide power for his cloth mill. Large scale power supply networks had to await Canadian capital and enterprise, which exploited the hydroelectric potential of the Serra do Mar in the Rio–São Paulo area. The São Paulo Railway, Light and Power Company completed its first installation in 1900 and the Rio Light in 1908.[24] In 1920 São Paulo had almost one-third of the total installed electric power used in industry and Guanabara one-fifth; together they had over three-quarters of the total Brazilian installed capacity for electricity supplied from a source other than companies' own generators.[25] Thus the locational advantages of the Rio–São Paulo industrial axis were reinforced.

Infrastructural improvements allowed many young Brazilian industries to exploit the opportunities offered by the trade difficulties brought about by the war of 1914–18. Between 1915 and 1919, 5,936 new manufacturing establishments were set up, employing 63,950 additional workers,[26] and the value of industrial production increased about 150 per cent in real terms.[27]

The industrial census of 1920 revealed that the rapid growth of the previous two decades had done little to alter the structure of Brazilian industry. Over one-third (35 per cent) of the industrial workers and 42 per cent of total industrial capital were employed in the textile industry, which accounted for the largest proportion of value added in manufacturing. The food processing industry ranked second in both the number of workers (12 per cent) and the proportion of value added, but showed the most substantial growth over the period 1907–19, increasing from 27 per cent to 41 per cent of the total value of industrial output.[28]

Before the First World War Guanabara had more manufacturing establishments than any other state, with São Paulo second and Rio Grande do Sul third. By 1919 these positions had been reversed, São Paulo having 31 per cent of the manufacturing firms, Rio Grande do Sul 13 per cent, Guanabara 12 per cent and Minas Gerais 9 per cent.

GOVERNMENT INTERVENTION & STRUCTURAL CHANGE, 1930–64. It has been said that Brazil had industrial growth without industrialization until the 1930s.[29] Growth was slow and limited to a few branches of industry, mainly food processing and textiles. Why did industry not develop more rapidly in Brazil? The urban industrial class grew slowly, and policy-making remained in the hands of agricultural and commercial interests. A series of profitable opportunities for investment in agriculture and mining for export helped to perpetuate the power of the land-owning class and to reduce the amount of capital available for industrial financing. Brazil's role as a supplier of raw materials to the industrial nations of the world was inimical to the development of a strong industrial base. Throughout this early period industry was a marginal activity dependent on export agriculture.

With the collapse of the world coffee market in 1929 industry escaped from this dependence. The value of all Brazil's exports fell by 60 per cent between 1929 and 1932, making it necessary to restrict imports, although domestic demand was maintained by government support of the incomes of the coffee sector. Investment in manufacturing to replace scarce imports now began to look more profitable than investment in coffee. The low financial capacity to import in the 'thirties was followed by the trade disruption of the Second World War. For this fifteen-year period industrial production grew fairly uniformly by 5 per cent per annum between 1930 and 1940 and about 5·5 per cent annually from 1940 to 1945.[30]

According to Baer this industrial growth largely reflected increased utilization of existing capacity, thereby improving profitability, which in turn made funds available for further industrial development.[31] Political changes also aided manufacturing. Getúlio Vargas was elected to the Presidency in 1930 on a platform promising economic development for the nation.[32] Under his regime new roads, railways and major hydroelectric power stations improved the country's infrastructure. Modern labour legislation was enacted, although only slowly implemented. Oil was discovered in 1939, coal in Santa Catarina was mined 'properly and methodically'[33] and with the iron ore and limestone from Minas Gerais provided raw material for Brazil's first modern steel works.[34]

In the interwar years the value of industrial production doubled and productivity increased. Table 11 reveals some change in the structure of the industrial sector of the Brazilian economy. In value added in manufacturing the proportion contributed by the traditional industries such as textiles and textile products, hides and skins, lumber and furniture declined, while, for the first time, the 1940 census noted that the metallurgical, chemical, pharmaceutical and machinery industries made a significant contribution to the total.

The trend towards regional concentration of industry, apparent at the end of the First World War, became more accentuated. The proportion of the nation's industrial work force employed in São Paulo State increased from 29 per cent in 1920 to 37 per cent in 1940, while Guanabara's share fell from 20 per cent to 14 per cent and no other state had more than 10 per cent. In the Northeast, Pernambuco, whose industrial sector had equalled that of Bahia in 1920, doubled the size of its firms and the number of its workers in manufacturing, so that by 1940 it had become the regional industrial centre, with growth particularly noticeable in the textile and chemical industries based on local raw materials.

The nation's industrial growth was accompanied by population movement from the rural areas into the cities of the Heartland. Between 1940 and 1950 the industrial labour force

TABLE 11

Value added in Manufacturing by Industry, Per Cent

Industry	1919	1939	1949	1959	1969
Non-metallic minerals	4·7	5·3	7·1	6·7	5·8
Metallurgy	4·3	7·6	9·3	11·9	11·4
Machinery	2·0	4·0	2·1	3·5	6·0
Electrical and communications equipment	0·0	0·9	1·6	3·9	6·3
Transportation equipment	0·0	0·6	2·2	7·6	8·6
Lumber	{7·8	3·4	4·2	3·3	2·6
Furniture		2·0	2·2	2·2	1·6
Paper and cardboard	1·5	1·5	2·2	3·1	2·7
Rubber	0·2	0·6	1·9	2·3	2·1
Hides and skins	2·4	1·7	1·3	1·1	0·6
Chemicals and pharmaceutical products	6·0	8·4	8·1	11·2	14·2
Soaps, perfumes, cleaners, toilet goods	0·0	2·3	1·6	1·4	1·6
Plastic products	0·0	0·0	0·3	0·8	1·8
Textiles	28·6	22·0	19·6	12·1	10·1
Wearing apparel, footwear and textile products	8·6	4·8	4·3	3·6	2·8
Foodstuffs	22·2	23·5	20·4	16·6	12·9
Beverages	5·9	4·3	4·5	2·9	2·7
Tobacco	3·9	2·3	1·4	1·3	1·5
Printing and publishing	0·0	3·6	4·0	3·0	3·0
Miscellaneous	1·9	1·1	1·6	1·6	1·7

The Brazilian concept of 'transformação industrial' is used for value added: the former includes services performed by contractors. The difference does not seem to be more than 3 per cent of the value in any sector, or more than 1 per cent in any but one sector. See Bergsman, J., *Brazil Industrialization and Trade Policies*. Oxford University Press, 1970, p. 23.
Sources: Censo Industrial, 1950, *op. cit.*, *Anuário Estatístico do Brasil, 1964*, I.B.G.E., Rio, 1964. *Sinopse Estatístico do Brasil, 1971*, I.B.G.E. Rio, 1971.

increased by 71·8 per cent, the agricultural by only 7·3 per cent and services by 34·1 per cent, reducing the proportion of the active population engaged in the primary sector from 71 to 64 per cent and increasing that in manufacturing from 9 to 13 per cent and in services from 20 to 23 per cent.

Between 1947 and 1961 industry was the most dynamic sector of the economy, with an annual average growth rate of 9·7 per cent, while the volume of industrial production tripled. In 1958 Brazil displaced Argentina as the leading industrial nation of Latin America. During these years the composition of industrial output changed in favour of heavy industry. In 1939, 70 per cent of manufacturing output by value was provided by non-durable consumer goods but in 1961 more than half the country's manufactures were final and intermediate capital goods and consumer durables, by which time Brazil had become self-sufficient in home appliances such as electric stoves, refrigerators and television sets.

This was a period marked by both increasing government participation in industry and considerable foreign investment. Amongst foreign investors in 1960 the United States led with 38 per cent, followed by Western Europe, especially West Germany, with 35 per cent and Canada with 19 per cent.[35] A series of economic surveys led to the formulation of the *Plan Salte*, 1950–54, and the *Programa de Metas*, 1956–61. The former was not fully carried out but was responsible for some infrastructural development which encouraged the growth of modern industry. The *Programa de Metas* was aimed at eliminating structural bottlenecks in the economy and had a much greater significance. It covered five areas: energy, transport, food supply, basic industries and education, especially technical education. Not all the targets were met on time but by the early 'sixties Brazil had doubled its installed capacity of electric energy, trebled its mileage of paved roads, become self-sufficient in cement, increased its production of steel ingots from 1·4 million tons in 1956 to 2 million tons in 1961, and transformed its motor vehicle industry from mere assembly in 1957 to a producer of 146,000 vehicles in 1961, of which 90 per cent of the total weight was provided by Brazilian-made components. Brazilian industry was also aided by tariff protection and foreign exchange control to stimulate import substitution, emphasis on maximizing both forward and backward linkages, and special incentive programmes. These last were mostly initiated under the Kubitschek administration, 1956–60. The impetus of this and preceding periods carried through for a year or so after he left office, but with the increasingly unsettled political situation of the early 'sixties, declining opportunities for import substitution, accelerating inflation, and the growth of economic nationalism accompanied by restrictive legislation against foreign investment, the manufacturing and other sectors of the economy began to stagnate. In 1962 industrial output increased by only 7·8 per cent as compared with the 12·7 per cent average from 1957 to 1961. In 1963 the growth rate fell catastrophically to 0·2 per cent. Furtado, in analysing this crisis, said, 'The structural changes that have already taken place in the Brazilian economy indicate that the decisive phase of its industrialization process has been approached. This enormous potential is only waiting for the country to find the definitive path for its development.'[36]

THE TAKE-OFF AFTER 1964. The change to a military government in 1964 and the introduction of new economic policies reduced the rate of inflation, attracted back foreign investment (over US$10,000 million by 1976) and reformed the fiscal and monetary systems of the nation, thus providing the environment for renewed industrial growth. Industrial production was stimulated by the expansion of the domestic market through the recovery of real wages, the organisation of the credit market and government incentives to exporters of manufactured goods. By 1967 Brazil's economy was once more growing rapidly with a 9 to 10 per cent growth rate, the world's highest, in the early 'seventies and about 7 per cent in 1975.

Only three groups of industry showed lower than average increases in 1970: metallurgy, machinery, electrical and communications equipment (8·8 per cent), beverages and tobacco (8·1 per cent) and textiles and wearing apparel (3·8 per cent). The industrial groups of greatest dynamism were those transforming non-metallic minerals (25·4 per cent), rubber (22·0 per cent), chemicals (17·9 per cent), transport equipment (16·3 per cent) and paper and cardboard (11·5 per cent).[37] This rapid rate of growth led to some bottlenecks, especially in the basic industries, and as existing industrial capacity was fully utilized by 1968 further industrial growth involved the establishment of new plants, thus facilitating changes in the regional pattern of industry. In 1971 programmes were announced for the expansion of the steel, shipbuilding and petrochemical industries. The nation's infrastructure was to be strengthened by building highways and hydroelectric plants and installing a national telecommunications network. The National Development Plan, 1972–74, placed emphasis on the creation of large industrial units to enhance competitiveness and efficiency and to increase exports of manufactured goods. These steps were expected to maintain a growth rate for industrial output of around 10 per cent per year.

Within the overall pattern of Brazil's industrialization each industry has responded to a different combination of growth stimuli. Three different groups of industry may be distinguished: firstly, the traditional consumer industries, such as textiles and foodstuffs, which have received comparatively little government or foreign investment and include many small family firms; secondly, the traditional heavy industries, such as iron and steel and shipbuilding, which have been greatly subsidized by the Federal Government and have had large inputs of foreign capital; and thirdly, the new industries such as motor vehicles and petrochemicals, which were encouraged by protective legislation and are largely in the hands of subsidiaries of foreign companies.

THE TRADITIONAL CONSUMER INDUSTRIES

Industries in the first group process raw materials which are widely available but there is some concentration in the Heartland where consumption is greatest.

THE TEXTILE INDUSTRY. Brazil produces more textiles than any other Latin American country and the industry employs about 15 per cent of the nation's industrial workers. It dates back to colonial times but was abolished by Portugal in the eighteenth century, and the trading privileges granted Britain allowed Lancashire cotton goods to dominate the Brazilian market. Imports, however, could not satisfy the demand for cheap, coarse material for clothing the slaves and the rural poor, so in 1814 a textile mill was established in Brazil. In 1844 a 30 per cent import tariff gave the domestic industry the protection under which it could grow. The industry began in Bahia, where in 1866 five of Brazil's nine firms were situated.

It was based on local supplies of raw cotton, abundant water power, a servile labour force and capital freed by the decline of the sugar industry. The loss of the market in the United States for Northeastern raw cotton after the American Civil War and the decline of exports from 1874 onwards gave further stimulus to the Northeastern textile industry. Market location, however, became more important and as early as 1881 Rio de Janeiro produced two-thirds of the nation's cotton cloth, although Bahia still had twice as many cotton mills as Rio.[38] The southward migration of the industry was reinforced by the development of cotton-growing on old coffee plantations in Rio de Janeiro and São Paulo around the turn of the century and by the general population movement from the Northeast towards the Heartland. The textile industry in São Paulo grew very rapidly in the first two decades of the twentieth century and by 1920 this state had become the major producer, with one-third of the total textile workers. The textile products industry was even more concentrated, with two-thirds of the work force in the metropolitan cities of São Paulo and Rio de Janeiro. The industry continued to grow rapidly and by 1930 Brazil was virtually self-sufficient in cotton textiles. The spatial pattern of the industry has changed little since the 'twenties, 61 per cent of the value of production of textiles in 1968 and 71 per cent of textile products being in the Heartland, whilst the Northeast produced only 11 per cent and 5 per cent respectively of the total (Table 12). There is some local product specialism, jute weaving being concentrated in the North and wool in the state of Rio Grande do Sul. Santa Catarina specializes in hosiery manufacture, Rio Grande do Sul in shoes and Ceará in hammocks. Consumption has increased steadily but in the early 'sixties production failed to keep pace. By the end of the decade, however, exports of cotton cloth were considerable, with three-quarters of the total going to E.E.C. countries and the remainder to the United States. A great variety of related goods is being exported, ranging from pantyhose from Santa Catarina to Italy, shoes from Rio Grande do Sul to Canada and Northeastern hammocks to Guyana, to Paulista swimwear to the United States.

Dualism is perhaps the most striking characteristic of the textile industry. Pre-industrial techniques continue to exist side by side with the most modern and there are wide regional variations in wage rates and local differences in managerial and technical skills. Much of the production comes from traditionalist, small, family firms, and equipment is often obsolete. 'The conservatism of textile mill proprietors, their unwillingness to alter organization and administration, stems from the

TABLE 12

Regional Distribution of the Textile Industry, 1968

Areal unit	Textiles			Textile Products & Shoes		
	No. of firms	Work force	Value of production (NCr$1,000)	No. of firms	Work force	Value of production (NCr$1,000)
Amazonas	14	1,336	25,030	4	19	211
Pará	10	2,172	24,215	8	296	3,365
NORTH	24	3,508	49,245	12	315	3,576
Ceará	107	5,335	177,307	39	1,072	14,786
Rio Grande do Norte	42	1,899	56,134	16	1,125	25,347
Paraíba	61	6,446	109,383	12	186	1,162
Pernambuco	65	15,064	208,881	70	2,413	25,462
Alagoas	27	4,936	51,283	7	212	2,781
Sergipe	13	4,467	32,257	16	106	780
Bahia	84	4,734	54,748	110	1,185	8,559
NORTHEAST	399	42,881	689,993	270	6,299	78,877
Espírito Santo	5	1,026	8,474	20	343	4,582
Rio de Janeiro	76	23,193	319,921	64	1,527	20,927
Paraná	54	2,386	249,545	41	972	9,882
Santa Catarina	70	18,472	239,796	41	2,076	21,995
PERIPHERY	205	45,077	817,736	166	4,918	57,386
Minas Gerais	148	29,654	375,698	228	4,397	48,231
Guanabara	64	21,220	484,681	341	18,793	268,168
São Paulo	1,051	155,733	3,531,949	766	47,059	854,596
HEARTLAND	1,263	206,607	4,392,328	1,335	70,249	1,170,995
Rio Grande do Sul	66	8,736	157,317	458	26,944	320,016
Mato Grosso	5	65	3,318	21	108	847
Goiás	3	758	16,823	46	312	5,546
Piauí	18	181	10,338	31	125	456
Maranhão	25	532	7,223	7	119	919
RIMLAND	117	10,272	195,019	563	27,608	327,784
BRAZIL	2,008	308,425	6,144,321	2,346	109,389	1,638,618

Source: Produção Industrial, 1968. I.B.G.E. Rio. 1970. pp. 31–32.

experience of past decades when government aid supported them in times of crisis'.[39] Obsolescence is most serious in the cotton textile industry but is also a problem in the weaving of man-made fibres and flax and in the spinning and weaving of jute. Efficiency is highest in the Heartland but even there the output of the existing machinery in the cotton spinning mills in the early 'sixties was only about half the average for Latin America. Productivity was above the Brazilian mean level in about one-third of the cotton mills but most of these were located in the state of São Paulo with a few in Minas Gerais, Rio de Janeiro, Guanabara, Rio Grande do Sul and Santa Catarina.[40] In the Northeast, where the industry provided 16 per cent of the region's industrial production and employed 18 per cent of its workers, SUDENE found in 1959 that 30 per cent of the machinery was more than thirty years old whilst many pieces of equipment dated from the 1890s.[41] By 1970 the number of looms had been halved and 209,000 of the 642,000 spindles eliminated without reducing the overall level of production, and it was planned that by 1973, 26 new mills should be producing eleven types of fabric new to the region and providing 2,611 additional jobs.[42]

The textile industry has declined steadily in relation to other industries and its share of the total value added in the manufacturing sector has fallen from 29 per cent in 1919 to 10 per cent in 1969. Since 1964 the Federal Government has made funds available for re-equipping the industry and for technical training, and tariff protection has been reduced to force the industry to become more competitive on the international market. Brazilian 'haute couture' commands high prices in New York, but it remains to be seen if the industry as a whole can achieve the efficiency levels of its leaders.

FOOD PRODUCTS. This industry has grown steadily to keep pace with the population increase, although its relative importance has declined from 24 per cent of Brazil's total value added in manufacturing in 1939 to 13 per cent in 1969. Its productivity is quite high but it suffers from seasonal variations in the supply of its raw materials.[43] Improvements in transport and storage facilities are needed to overcome this. In 1968 a new programme provided US$50 million for financial assistance to increase processed food production by 8 per cent per year.[44] Dualism is again apparent but modernization is going ahead rapidly. More sophisticated products are coming on to the domestic market. Commercial mixed feed for livestock, which was not produced at all until after the Second World War, is now made by 175 mills in seventeen different states, although half of it is produced by a few large mills in São Paulo.[45] Brazil is especially advanced in the processing of coffee, putting out both instant coffee and coffee tablets with or without milk. In 1970 there were a dozen instant coffee mills, including four of the freeze-dry type, and the Soviet Union was helped to set up its first instant coffee plant.[46] Because of the large size of the food products industry and its relative efficiency, when Brazilian food processors began to expand exports in the late 'sixties they were quickly able to obtain a considerable share of the world market. For example, the export of orange juice was promoted for the first time in 1969 but by 1971 Brazil was exporting more than California and Florida combined.

CEMENT INDUSTRY. The first cement mill was established in 1888 but production did not really become significant until 1926. The post-war building boom stimulated a sevenfold increase in output between 1945 and 1965. Since 1965 production has almost trebled and Brazil is now the tenth largest producer of cement in the world, with an output higher than that of Canada, and has been self-sufficient for several years.

Growth in this industry has been achieved almost entirely by private enterprise, with little government or foreign participation. In 1966 over two-thirds of the production came from the factories of five large companies, only one of which was foreign-owned,[47] but several foreign firms are involved in the planned doubling of capacity between 1973 and 1977. Limestone is found in many parts of the country, although the purest deposits of limestone and the principal gypsum beds are in the Northeast. Over half the nation's production, however, comes from the states of Minas Gerais and São Paulo, whilst São Paulo and Guanabara together consume almost half the output. Per capita consumption of cement in 1969 was highest in Brasília at 0·34 tons per person, followed by Guanabara with 0·22 tons per person, São Paulo with 0·16 and Rio de Janeiro with 0·14, whilst in Roraima in most of the years of the past decade no cement at all was used.

TRADITIONAL HEAVY INDUSTRY

Industries in this group are generally raw materials oriented, although site factors are of considerable importance. Market orientation, however, is becoming more important.

IRON & STEEL. Government policy during the last three decades has made the iron and steel industry one of the more dynamic sectors of the Brazilian economy.[48] Steel output increased at an annual rate 50 per cent higher than that of overall industrial output, and Brazil now produces almost twice as much steel per year as its nearest Latin American rival, Mexico, although per capita consumption remains below average for the region.

The earliest iron ore deposits utilized were those of the state cf São Paulo, where in 1597 the first commercial iron works in the western hemisphere was set up near Sorocaba. Production was mainly of horseshoes and harness parts for the horses and mules brought from all over the country to be traded at the annual Sorocaba fair. There was little growth of ironworking during the seventeenth century, but the discovery, in Minas Gerais, of gold in 1694 and diamonds in 1725 created a demand for iron implements for mining. In 1785, however, the King of Portugal decreed that all domestic iron production in Brazil must stop and that economic activity should be concentrated on agriculture and mining. Policies became more liberal with the accession of a new monarch, and in 1795 the order was revoked. In 1801 the re-founding of an iron industry in the Sorocaba region was ordered.

The establishment of the Portuguese Court in Brazil in 1808 gave a new impetus to the industry by attracting foreign technicians to the country and providing capital for plant construction. The first blast furnace was completed in 1815 at Morro do Pilar in Minas Gerais. The iron industry of the early nineteenth century was not very successful because of the short-term presence of foreign metallurgists, intermittent shortages of basic material inputs, inadequate facilities for the transport of products to the major market, the city of Rio de

Janeiro, and competition from imported British goods produced by more modern methods. In 1821 there were thirty forges in Minas Gerais producing about 120 tons of iron a year and by 1860 120 furnaces produced about 1,550 tons annually.[49] In 1869 the first railway line entered Minas Gerais and in 1888 and 1893 respectively, despite the loss of labour following slave emancipation, two furnaces were built along this line. These plants became the country's main producers during the first three decades of the twentieth century.[50]

At the turn of the century production of iron in Brazil was still very small.[51] Brazil produced its first steel ingots in 1917, and eight years later the construction of a Siemens-Martin furnace by the Belgo-Mineira Company created the first integrated steel works in South America. Production of pig iron and steel ingots increased sixfold in the 'thirties making the country almost self-sufficient in these products by 1940, eighteen of the twenty-seven steel firms operating in 1939 having been founded during the decade. The iron and manganese ore deposits of the Iron Quadrilateral of Minas Gerais, close to both limestone and a source of charcoal, were a major factor in the industry's location. In 1945 Minas Gerais supplied 83 per cent of Brazil's pig iron, 57 per cent of the ingot steel and 51 per cent of the rolled steel.

While the steel industry was started with private initiative and financing, private interests could not provide the funds required for the construction of the large plants needed to support Brazil's rapid industrialization. In 1941 the National Steel Company was created and when its plant at Volta Redonda commenced production in 1946 the industry started on its major period of expansion. During the 'fifties three other projects for integrated steel plants came into being, namely those for the Mannesmann, COSIPA and USIMINAS plants, thus emphasizing the growing vertical integration of the Brazilian industry. By 1970 there were 16 integrated steel plants, 17 semi-integrated, 4 rolling mills, 62 producers of pig iron and 15 producers of alloy iron, with a joint output of 5·39 million tons of steel ingots, 4·21 million tons of pig iron and 1·89 million tons of rolled steel.[52]

All Brazil's integrated plants are located in the Heartland or Periphery. Three main facts have determined such location:

the occurrence of iron ore and limestone in Minas Gerais, the possibilities for transport of coal imported by sea, and the large markets of São Paulo and Guanabara States. At first most plants were raw materials oriented, and the development of USIMINAS in the 'fifties based on the ore deposits of the Rio Doce valley, charcoal from the nearby forests, hydro-electric power from the river and good transport involved the building of a town for the workers. Market orientation, however, is becoming more common, and plants such as COSIPA have been built close to major markets. Some, like Volta Redonda and Barra Mansa in the Paraíba Valley, have been established at points between markets and raw materials. At the end of the 'sixties slightly more than one-third of Brazil's steel production was raw materials oriented, just over one-quarter was market oriented and one-third was produced at a mid-point location, mainly at Volta Redonda. Approximately three-quarters of Brazil's apparent consumption of steel takes place in and around the cities of São Paulo and Rio de Janeiro. The construction industry absorbs 26·1 per cent of national steel production, followed by wire-drawing mills with 13·8 per cent and the automobile industry with 12·6 per cent.[53]

The technology of the Brazilian iron and steel industry is distinguished by the widespread use of charcoal instead of coke in blast furnaces. Volta Redonda was the first plant in Brazil to use coke for steel making, burning in its furnaces a mixture of Brazilian and foreign coal. In Minas Gerais supplies of charcoal are becoming exhausted, but the major companies are securing their future fuel supplies by planting extensive stands of eucalyptus trees. Many semi-integrated and specialist steel firms located close to their markets use electric furnaces charged with scrap. In the late 'fifties several small charcoal-based pig iron producers were established in response to demand from the motor vehicle industry, but by the mid-sixties they were unable to utilize their capacity to the full against competition from the large integrated mills and some closed down.

Steel output almost doubled between 1964 and 1970. This was achieved largely by expanding the capacity of existing plants to obtain adequate scale economies rather than by the establishment of new enterprises. Production is now about

8 million tons a year and the National Steel Programme is projecting 25 million tons by 1980. Capacity is to be doubled at the three major, government-owned steel mills of C.S.N. at Volta Redonda in the State of Rio de Janeiro, USIMINAS in Minas Gerais and COSIPA near Santos in São Paulo. There is to be some decentralization of the industry with the establishment of a mill in Maranhão using the Serra dos Carajás ore to produce 5 million tons of steel a year for export. This programme represents an annual rate of increase in installed capacity of over 12 per cent at an estimated cost of 1·28 thousand million dollars, of which $620 million is coming from external sources, half in loans from the World Bank and the Inter-American Development Bank and half in bilateral credits from nine major steel equipment producing countries.[54] At the beginning of the 'seventies Brazil ranked twentieth among world steel producers, but may figure among the ten largest by 1980.

The Brazilian steel industry has had a substantial growth impact through its high linkages with other industries. The development of infrastructure in transport and power supply associated with the building of steel mills and the training given to its labour force have made the developmental impact of the industry through its external economies extremely high. In Brazil the iron and steel industry has the advantage of cheap labour, plentiful supplies of high grade ore, cheap imported coal[55] and mills using the most modern techniques. Baer concludes that Brazil 'could be one of the most efficient steel producers in the world.'[56]

SHIPBUILDING. For a country with a coastline of 7,400 kilometres and 44,000 kilometres of navigable waterways shipbuilding has a vital contribution to make to national development. The recent growth of Brazilian shipyards results almost entirely from government assistance over the last fifteen years. In 1971 Brazil built seventeen ships, totalling 147,045 gross tons, equivalent to 0·59 per cent of the world total, and became Latin America's leading shipbuilder.[57]

During the Empire the Baron Mauá founded a shipyard in Rio de Janeiro and over a period of eleven years built seventy-two vessels for the Brazilian merchant marine and the Navy. Foreign competition, however, eventually destroyed the domestic industry. The modern shipbuilding industry started with the law of April 1958, which created the Merchant Marine Fund for the purchase and construction of ships, the re-equipment and expansion of shipyards and the financing of national steamship lines and shipyards, public or privately owned. Within one year six shipyards, three large and three medium-sized, had been installed, representing an initial investment of almost US$60 million. By 1966 there were twenty shipyards in operation in Brazil, an increase of four over 1965, most of them located around Guanabara Bay. Of the six major shipyards four are on Guanabara Bay, one near Angra dos Reis just south of the Bay and one in Rio Grande do Sul.

The capacity of Brazilian shipyards has grown rapidly. In October 1961 the Dutch-owned Verolme yards launched its first Brazilian-made vessel, the *Henrique Lage* (named after a former Brazilian shipping magnate), which at 10,500 tons was the largest ship built in the southern hemisphere.[58] Almost 50 per cent of the costs in 1961 were made up of imported parts; but by early 1966 imports for shipbuilding accounted for only 10 per cent of the value and 3 per cent of the weight of the hull and 40 per cent of the value of the engines. In 1964 Brazil sold four ships to Mexico and the largest, Japanese-owned, Brazilian yard won the contract to supply a floating dock to England. In 1966 the Mexican Government signed a contract ordering three ships from Brazilian builders and reserving the option on two more. The order worth US$27,450,000 was the largest single industrial export transaction ever filled by a Latin American country.[59] By the beginning of the 'seventies Brazil was building satellite-guided oil tankers for Petrobrás, refrigerated ships and bulk carriers for export to the United States,[60] and had secured orders for the export of 640,000 tons of ships by 1975.[61]

The government's reorganization of the ports, begun in 1964, and its new freight policy, started in 1967, stimulated domestic shipbuilding. The capacity of Brazil's merchant fleet in 1972 was five times that of 1964, when the military government came into power, and much of the additional tonnage came from Brazilian shipyards. Investment in shipbuilding is planned to reach US$920 million between 1970 and 1975, with 1·6 million tons dead weight being constructed

for the domestic market. The Federal Government is also financing the construction of a new slipway for the Ishikawajima
shipyards, which will enable ships of 400,000 tons to be built
in Brazil, and has been giving tax exemptions on materials
and parts used by the industry. This combination of government assistance and foreign technology has enabled the
Brazilian shipbuilding industry to reach a size and level of
sophistication (increasing employment from 1,000 in 1959 to
15,000 workers in 1970) at which it can supply most domestic
needs and some exports, in a remarkably short space of
time.

NEW INDUSTRIES

In its efforts to widen Brazil's industrial base the Federal
Government encouraged the development of industries new
to the country by such indirect methods as providing incentives
to private domestic and foreign investors and setting up co-
ordinating agencies, rather than by direct participation.

MOTOR VEHICLES. In 1971 Brazil produced over half a million
vehicles, 25 per cent more than in the previous year, and in
1972 output increased by a further 18 per cent. It is the largest
producer in Latin America, with an output greater than that
of Argentina and Mexico combined, and ranks eighth in the
world. It now exports throughout Latin America and occasionally to North America and Europe. The Brazilian Ford
plant is supplying 'Pinto' engines to Detroit and Volkswagen do
Brasil has a sports car model, the Puma, designed and manufactured in Brazil, which has been well received abroad.

Before 1955 the motor vehicle industry in Brazil was limited
exclusively to assembly-plant operations and the manufacture
of a few spare parts. In 1956 the government set up an agency
to co-ordinate the development of the industry, and companies
which accepted the Federal plan were granted many incentives,
including favourable tariffs for imported capital goods as well
as financial, fiscal and foreign exchange facilities. One of the
main features of the programme was the gradual nationalization of the various component parts of the vehicles. By 1959
locally produced parts made up nearly 70 per cent of the total

weight of a vehicle, and this increased to 90 per cent in 1961 and 99 per cent in 1966.[62]

Table 13 shows that production of vehicles has increased rapidly. Emphasis was at first on cargo-carrying vehicles in order to improve the movement of goods within Brazil, but in 1958 the first Brazilian-made passenger cars were produced and in 1960 production of tractors began. Having succeeded in establishing the motor vehicles industry, the government sold its share of productive capacity to Alfa Romeo and imposed heavy taxes on finished vehicles. This tax burden combined with lack of scale economies for most producers makes the price of a Brazilian-made car average about twice that of a similar model in North America or Western Europe. After 1960 as the whole motor vehicle fleet in use was slowly replaced sales declined, resulting in a slow down in production whose effect was felt by many Brazilian industries. Improvements in real income, easier credit facilities and the imaginative use of such techniques as the revolving credit system led to a resurgence of vehicle sales and an expansion of production towards the end of the decade. Widespread road improvement, however, has reduced the demand for jeeps. In April 1969, the two-millionth car made in Brazil came off the assembly line and by mid-1972 when the 50,000th Brazilian-made Massey-Ferguson tractor went to work along the Trans-Amazon Highway, 3·5 million vehicles had been manufactured. The growth of the industry enabled the number of people per car in Brazil to decline from 78 in 1956 to 31 in 1969.

Foreign participation in the industry has been considerable. Government incentives attracted many foreign companies and the punitive tax on imported cars gave the world's major car firms little alternative but to establish plants within Brazil. By 1960, two-thirds of the motor vehicle industry were foreign owned, as was over half of the enterprises manufacturing automobile parts.[63] The industry became too fragmented for production efficiency and there was some consolidation, Ford absorbing Willys and Volkswagen taking over Vemag. The industry is largely concentrated in Greater São Paulo. Volkswagen do Brasil is the largest German investment abroad and the biggest single foreign investment in Brazil, and the company is among the twenty largest Brazilian enterprises.[64] By

TABLE 13

Production of Motor Vehicles in Brazil, 1957–71

Type of vehicle	1957	1959	1961	1963	1965	1967	1969	1971
Heavy trucks and buses	3,372	5,031	5,147	3,478	4,060	2,973	4.453	11,899
Medium trucks	15,457	34,625	25,352	20,546	20,899	28,854	41,333	31,362
Cargo and passenger vans	2,562	26,408	42,492	50,157	46,720	52,991	63,661	124,548
Jeeps and related vehicles	9,291	18,178	17,618	13,922	10,057	8,547	5,852	6,044
Passenger cars	—	12,001	55,065	86,023	103,437	132,124	236,893	341,884
Total	30,700	96,243	145,674	174,126	185,173	225,389	352,192	515,737
Tractors			1,653	9,908	8,123	6,219	9,471	22,124

Sources: Anuário Estatístico do Brasil for the years 1962, 1964, 1970 and 1972. All published by the Brazilian Institute of Geography and Statistics, Institute of Statistics, in Rio de Janeiro.

mid-1970 one million Volkswagens had been produced in Brazil and about one-third of the vehicles in use in the country were made by this company. Volkswagen, with 56 per cent of the market in 1970 as compared to 35 per cent for Ford and General Motors combined, owes its success to its early establishment in Brazil (1953) and the cheapness and suitability of its cars to the narrow, congested streets of Brazilian cities.

In the mid-sixties the capital invested in the motor vehicle industry was greater than the entire budget revenue of each of the 26 states and territories of Brazil with the single exception of São Paulo. Brazilian interests held 37 per cent of the capital followed by those of the United States, West Germany, Switzerland, France, Japan, Sweden and Italy with 32·9 per cent, 18·1 per cent, 5·8 per cent, 2·3 per cent, 1·7 per cent, 1·5 per cent and 0·7 per cent respectively.[65] Both Volkswagen and Ford are planning major plant expansion in the 'seventies, Fiat and Toyota are building new plants and a total of US$400 million of investment by foreign motor vehicle manufacturers will boost car production to meet increasing domestic requirements appropriate to the rapid extension of the road network and provide exports to other LAFTA countries.

The setting up and growth of the motor vehicle industry stimulated Brazil's industrial development. Reserves of foreign currency were freed for investment in other fields, and demand from vehicle manufacturers caused a boom in the steel, machinery, rubber and electronics industries. The transport equipment industrial sector employs some 150,000 people at above average wages and is one of the largest tax payers.

PETROCHEMICALS & OTHER CHEMICALS. In 1972, with thirty-one plants in operation, the petrochemical industry in Brazil ranked tenth in the world and first in Latin America. The petroleum products industry was initiated about fifteen years ago by Petrobrás, the national petroleum company. Expansion did not really take place until after 1964, when a government sponsored programme providing tax incentives to the industry was set up. In 1965 the military government reversed its predecessor's policy, ordered Petrobrás to throw open its petrochemical section to private investment and encouraged foreign investors to establish plants in Brazil. At this time there were twenty-six petrochemical plants in operation in the country, and fourteen under construction, and within a year forty-nine new projects had been presented to the Chemical Industry Executive Group for its approval. Growth in the petrochemical industry accelerated at the end of the 'sixties. Some thirteen major projects started in 1965 came into production in 1969. New investment in the industry amounted to US$200 million in each of the years 1969, 1970 and 1971, with an outlay of $650 million planned for the rest of the 'seventies, thus maintaining a high growth rate stimulated in particular by strong domestic demand for plastics and fertilizers.

Most of the industry is market oriented and is concentrated in São Paulo and Rio de Janeiro, but the natural gas and oil of Bahia, the sugar alcohol of Pernambuco and the rock salt deposits of Alagoas have attracted projects to the Northeast. Synthetic rubber has been produced by a Petrobrás unit located near the Duque de Caxias refinery in Rio de Janeiro state since 1962 and now satisfies domestic demand and provides for exports to LAFTA countries. The plant, designed by the famous Brazilian architect, Oscar Niemeyer, is wholly staffed by Brazilian personnel and two-thirds of its equipment and machinery is of Brazilian manufacture. Three years later, in 1965, a second synthetic rubber factory, on a site thirty kilometres from Recife in Pernambuco, began production. Financed partly by American foreign aid funds, this project involved the dismantling of a plant in Kentucky, its shipment to Brazil and reconstruction under the supervision of a United States engineering firm with technical assistance for production from Union Carbide and Firestone. Production is based on the use of sugar alcohol, a by-product of the region's sugar industry, as raw material. As the first heavy industry to be located in the Northeast it was hailed as a major step in the development of the region. It appears, however, that pre-investment planning was inadequate and the plant, which cost US$33 million, has had difficulty marketing its product. A key reason for setting up the plant was to make use of excess sugar alcohol, but the cost of the finished product was so high that it could not compete with other sources of synthetic rubber on the Brazilian market.[66]

Fertilizer production was assigned a high priority in national planning because of its importance to the development of the agricultural sector. The petrochemical complex at Cubatão, São Paulo, near the President Bernardes Refinery, has an ammonium and fertilizer plant. Ultrafértil, recently completed with largely American financing, is the biggest privately-owned fertilizer complex in South America. Urea projects are under construction in Minas Gerais and Bahia. Super-phosphates are produced mainly in Pernambuco at Olinda, in São Paulo at Jacupiranga and Serrote and in Minas Gerais at Araxá, and Goiás plans to open nine phosphate mills in the near future.[67]

Other major chemical complexes are being developed. União, located in a suburb of São Paulo and built with some French financing and 25 per cent Brazilian government participation, is expected to supply the domestic demand of ethylene, benzine, propylene, solvents and aromatic oils. Close by, Poliolefinas S.A. is building a US$29 million poly-ethylene plant, and Prosint, a petrochemical unit associated with the Manguinhos Refinery in Rio de Janeiro inaugurated in 1971, has a capacity to produce 33,000 tons per year of methanol, which is more than domestic demand. The Petrobrás and Union Carbide plants at Cubatão produce polyethylene, vinyl chloride, benzine, acetylene, ethylene, toluene and nitric acid. In Bahia a methanol plant is under construction at Candeias, and at Aratú three plants will soon be producing ammonium sulphate, hydrogen, sodium cyanide, acrylic fibres and propylene. Amongst other major chemical projects beginning construction outside the Heartland in the early 'seventies was a sulfonation detergent plant in the free zone of Manaus in the North. In Alagoas, caustic soda and chlorine production is being expanded with the development of one of the world's largest such plants by Du Pont, utilizing the very pure salt deposits and ample hydroelectric power of Maceió.

In 1970 the petrochemical industry employed about 9 per cent of all the workers in manufacturing industry. It has had a marked effect on overall industrial growth through its strong forward and backward linkages. This can be seen in the plans for the União complex, which stimulated parallel investment of US$450 million, mostly in the plastics, dyestuffs and man-made textile fields.

REGIONAL DISPARITIES

Accelerating industrial development during the last decade has only exacerbated regional disparities, despite government efforts to encourage manufacturers to locate in the poorer parts of the country. Table 14 shows the increasing concentration of industrial workers in the Heartland and its Periphery and the declining proportion in the Northeast and Rimland, while the North remains virtually untouched by Brazil's industrial revolution. In 1969 the Heartland had 67 per cent of the total number of workers in manufacturing industry, although it contained only 36 per cent of the nation's population. At the same time the Northeast, where a quarter of Brazilians live, had only 9 per cent of the industrial workers. The Heartland states were responsible for 74 per cent of the value added in manufacturing and their industries consumed a similar proportion of the nation's electricity and attracted most of the foreign investment.[68] Table 15 shows in more detail the relative decline in industrial production since 1945 in the states most distant from São Paulo. Although in 1950 Paulista factories were more than a generation behind North America and Europe in technology,[69] the introduction of many foreign corporations producing goods such as motor vehicles, pharmaceuticals, tobacco, construction equipment and electronics led to an overall improvement in the level of industrial productivity. The industrial growth of São Paulo from 1953 to 1966 averaged 17·3 per cent per year for capital and consumer durable goods, reflecting the high purchasing power of the nation's biggest and richest city,[70] where 36 per cent of the nation's industrial workers produce 41 per cent of Brazil's total industrial output.

Greater Rio de Janeiro is second only to São Paulo City as an industrial centre, with most of Brazil's shipbuilding yards located around Guanabara Bay and much of the nation's petrochemical, machinery, tobacco, beverages, toiletries, pharmaceutical and publishing industries. Rio differs from São Paulo in having fewer heavy industries and a smaller variety of manufacturing. With the loss of its position as the nation's largest city in the 'fifties, however, and the transfer of the Federal capital to Brasília in 1960, the city lost some of its economic dynamism and its industrial labour force declined

TABLE 14

Regional Distribution of Manufacturing Establishments & Workers in Brazil, 1920–69

Region	1920		1940		1950 (Percentages)		1960		1969	
	Firms	Workers	Firms	Workers	Firms	Workers	Firms	Workers	Firms	Workers
North	1·86	1·41	1·93	1·57	1·44	1·22	1·59	1·00	2·44	1·20
Northeast	17·03	18·69	13·69	17·03	17·53	15·69	15·63	11·00	17·26	9·04
Periphery	14·69	11·11	15·97	11·82	16·21	12·55	16·77	14·06	18·47	14·00
Heartland	52·11	57·58	52·75	59·82	46·70	60·69	48·75	64·72	44·52	66·68
Rimland	14·39	11·19	15·66	9·75	18·11	9·85	17·26	9·21	17·31	9·07

Sources: Censo Industrial do Brazil, 1950, Anuário Estatístico do Brasil, 1964 and Sinopse Estatística do Brasil, 1971. Published by the Institute of Brazil of Geography and Statistics in Rio de Janeiro.

Table 15

Regional Distribution of the Value of Industrial Production in Brazil, 1920–68

Areal Unit	1920	1940	1950	1960	1968
			(Percentage)		
Rondônia	—	—	0·01	0·01	0·00
Acre	0·00	0·00	0·01	0·01	0·02
Amazonas	0·16	0·22	0·17	0·35	0·26
Pará	0·86	0·84	0·47	0·39	0·37
Roraima	—	—	0·00	0·00	0·00
NORTH	1·03	1·06	0·66	0·77	0·66
Ceará	0·80	0·58	0·76	0·77	0·89
Rio Grande do Norte	0·61	0·47	0·42	0·45	0·29
Paraíba	0·90	1·15	1·04	0·76	0·46
Pernambuco	3·52	4·73	4·16	2·83	2·53
Alagoas	1·42	1·05	0·78	0·50	0·50
Sergipe	1·02	0·57	0·43	0·24	0·19
Bahia	2·49	3·08	1·31	1·56	1·46
NORTHEAST	10·76	11·64	8·90	7·12	6·32
Espírito Santo	0·69	0·34	0·69	0·27	0·45
Rio de Janeiro	4·68	4·90	5·99	5·17	6·54
Paraná	3·42	2·17	2·94	4·16	3·23
Santa Catarina	2·01	1·76	2·55	2·04	2·12
PERIPHERY	10·81	9·18	12·17	11·65	12·34
Minas Gerais	6·15	6·37	7·06	5·93	6·00
Guanabara	23·49	16·70	13·79	9·87	9·44
São Paulo	34·71	44·66	47·75	56·02	57·53
Distrito Federal	—	—	—	—	0·01
HEARTLAND	64·36	67·74	68·61	71·82	72·98
Rio Grande do Sul	12·56	9·66	8·72	7·53	6·46
Mato Grosso	0·04	0·17	0·22	0·27	0·26
Goiás	0·12	0·21	0·42	0·44	0·64
Piauí	0·24	0·07	0·05	0·09	0·09
Maranhão	0·08	0·27	0·25	0·30	0·24
Amapá	—	0·00	0·00	0·01	0·02
RIMLAND	13·04	10·38	9·66	8·64	7·70

Sources: Censo Industrial do Brasil, 1950, Anuário Estatístico do Brasil, 1964 and Produção Industrial, 1968. All published by the Brazilian Institute of Geography and Statistics, Rio de Janeiro.

in size. In 1971 manufacturing industry in Guanabara grew only 1·7 per cent but incentives for new industries and the new port of Sepetiba led to a resurgence of industrial expansion. The growth rate of 34 per cent in 1973 particularly reflected the establishment of the motor vehicle industry in Guanabara.[71]

Running between Rio and São Paulo is the Paraíba Valley, which contains the second most important industrial zone in the state of São Paulo after the metropolitan area.[72] The valley forms a natural routeway between Brazil's two major industrial centres. Foodstuffs and textile industries are important, but with the establishment of the Volta Redonda steel works in the area the industrial base has broadened and many firms have been set up, such as those making vehicle parts, serving the industries of São Paulo and Rio de Janeiro.

The third state of the Heartland, Minas Gerais, produces one-fifth of the nation's metallurgical products by value and they account for 36 per cent of the state's industrial production. In addition to iron and steel the state also produces tin, bronze and aluminium. Minas Gerais is the nation's leading producer of cement, much of which is consumed in São Paulo. The state has almost half Brazil's sugar mills, although São Paulo produces more refined sugar. The creation of an industrial estate at Contagem, just outside Belo Horizonte, by the state government in 1941, and the provision of plentiful and cheap electricity encouraged industrial diversification. Some fifteen industries were established there by 1950 and 126 by 1963, giving Contagem the greatest concentration of industries in the state.[73] Growth has continued and in 1971 the Industrial Centre of Contagem signed an agreement with the National Economic Development Bank for eight million cruzeiros to set up 100 new industries creating 20,000 new jobs. Industry has also expanded in Belo Horizonte, which in 1970 was the third largest city in Brazil and one of the fastest growing. The number of industrial establishments in the city grew from 2,100 in 1952 to 4,093 in 1965. By 1968 the Belo Horizonte–Contagem area had engineering, chemical and electrical industries besides iron and steel, cement, textiles and foodstuffs.

Surrounding the Heartland are the states of the Periphery, Espírito Santo and Rio de Janeiro in the east and Paraná and Santa Catarina to the south. Together these states have 18 per cent of Brazil's manufacturing and employ 14 per cent of the nation's industrial workers. Their proportion of the nation's industries has grown steadily since 1920, reflecting spread effects from the major growth centres of the Heartland. Rio de Janeiro state accounts for two-fifths of both the workers and the value of production in the region, indicating the importance of the satellite cities of the Greater Rio de Janeiro industrial zone, which contain half the state's population. Espírito Santo is the most isolated and least industrialized state in the region, but industries such as meat-packing and steel making in Vitória are growing rapidly as both raw materials and markets become accessible with new roads linking the state to Salvador, Belo Horizonte and Rio de Janeiro. In the south of the Peripheral region the influence of São Paulo is dominant and industrial growth is directly related to distance from the Paulista metropolis. Paraná doubled its industrial employment between 1950 and 1960, whilst growth in the 'sixties was most rapid in Santa Catarina. Curitiba in Paraná and the German settlement area of Santa Catarina at Blumenau and Joinville are the main industrial centres, with textile, metallurgical and machinery industries. Outside these centres most industries are based on local timber supplies.

Elsewhere Brazil has two major regional industrial centres. In the extreme south of the country Rio Grande do Sul has 90 per cent of the Rimland's industrial workers, and since at least 1920 has been more important for industry than Minas Gerais. The capital city, Pôrto Alegre, has grown very rapidly in the last two decades as the centre of a highly productive agricultural region. In 1965 Pôrto Alegre had one-quarter of the state's industrial workers, most of them engaged in the metallurgical, machinery and publishing industries. Smaller centres often specialize in processing local raw materials, such as tobacco at Santa Cruz do Sul, and industries related to the skills of European immigrants, such as leather working at Novo Hamburgo. Although the importance of Rio Grande industries has declined since 1920 relative to Brazil as a whole, the technological level has risen remarkably. When one of the authors visited Caxias do Sul in 1945, a small firm specializing in silver harness ornaments and mate cutlery for the regional gaucho market refused a large order for such goods because the owner was not willing to expand production. Today this same firm is making electric motors for export.

The Northeast region's share of Brazil's industrial workforce has halved since 1920 but government programmes have helped to slow its decline in the last decade. Since 1959 some 234 industrial plants have been set up in the Northeast, creating about 190,000 new jobs; 149 more factories are under construction or in the planning stage, while some 127 have received SUDENE loans for modernization.[74] The regional industrial centre is Recife, the capital of Pernambuco. Recife has more industrial workers than Pôrto Alegre but less diversified industry, over half the labour force being employed in the textile and foodstuffs industries, a situation typical of most Northeastern cities.

Agglomeration and external economies make for the spatial concentration of growth around the initial starting points, and Hirschman has suggested that such regional inequalities are an inevitable concomitant and condition of growth itself.[75] It has been argued that the general economic policies of the Brazilian government, aimed at industrial growth behind a wall of import restrictions, have accentuated these regional imbalances.[76] In the raw material exporting regions of the North and Northeast, needed imports had to come from the high cost industries of the Heartland rather than from abroad. This resulted in a fiscal transfer from these backward regions to the most developed region. In addition most of the industrial projects undertaken by the Federal Government since 1940 have been located in the Heartland region despite the relatively long history of programmes aimed at the decentralization of industry.

Now, however, it is realized that only by exploiting resources in all parts of this vast country and increasing the size of the domestic market by raising per capita incomes can industry continue to expand at a rapid rate. Government agencies set up to co-ordinate the development of the lagging regions have encouraged some notable developments, such as the many light industries attracted to Manaus by its recently created free port status, the new modern jute mill at Santarém and the industrial estates growing up near the cities of Salvador and

Fortaleza. Yet the largest firms and the most up-to-date methods and machinery are still concentrated in the Heartland. The National Development Plan (1972–74) with its emphasis on improving infrastructure and creating growth centres in the Northeast, North and Central Plateau, and disciplining the economic growth of the Heartland, may have succeeded in encouraging some major decentralization of industry.

INDUSTRY IN THE ECONOMY

In 1967 the contribution of industry to the Brazilian national product exceeded that of agriculture for the first time. Government encouragement of private enterprise and foreign investment since 1964 has led to massive capital inflows, four-fifths of which have gone into manufacturing, but the government still controls twelve of the twenty biggest industrial enterprises and 400 of the thousand biggest firms in Brazil.[77] Industrial growth has first priority in national planning,[78] and the approval by the Council of Industrial Development of the Ministry of Industry and Commerce in 1970 of 860 new industrial projects involving an investment of US$1·3 thousand million indicates a continued high growth rate over the next decade. Manufacturers are being offered incentives to export in order to maintain the nation's annual growth rate[79] and exports of manufactured goods rose in value from US$140 million in 1967 to US$1,100 million in 1972, when they surpassed coffee exports for the first time.[80] The range of Brazil's customers has widened: the United States which took 36 per cent of all Brazil's manufactured exports in 1967 took only 20 per cent in 1970, whilst one-third went to LAFTA countries, and, also in 1970, Britain's trade with Brazil exceeded British trade with Argentina for the first time in history. Brazil is now one of the world's major exporters of finished goods and thus has taken a long step forward in the process of economic development.

REFERENCES

1. For example, see Furtado, Celso, *The Economic Growth of Brazil*, California, 1963.

2. Dean points out that because of the incomplete nature of the early industrial surveys 'the concept of *surtos industriális* or industrial surges, will thereby be appreciably diluted', especially with reference to the First World War. Dean, W., *The Industrialization of São Paulo, 1880–1945*, Texas, 1969, p. 93.

3. Leff, N. H. 'Long-term Brazilian Economic Development', *The Journal of Economic History*, XXIX (3), September 1969, p. 490.

4. Both ECLA and Huddle argue that contrary to Furtado's belief, exchange policy and selective control of imports probably reduced Brazil's rate of industrial development in the 1950s. See Donald Huddle, 'Furtado on Exchange control and Economic Development: An Evaluation and Reinterpretation of the Brazilian Case', *Economic Development and Cultural Change*, Vol. 15 (3), April 1967, pp. 269–285; and ECLA, *Economic Bulletin for Latin America*, December 1964, p. 156.

5. Baer, W. *Industrialization and Economic Development in Brazil*, Yale, 1965, pp. 110–135.

6. Huddle, D. 'The Brazilian Industrialization—Sources, Patterns and Policy Mix', *Economic Development and Cultural Change*, 15 (4), July 1967, p. 474.

7. Furtado, *op. cit.*, p. 240.

8. Huddle, April 1967, *op. cit.*, p. 279.

9. Santiago, Macario. 'Protectionism and Industrialization in Latin America', *Economic Bulletin for Latin America*, March 1964, pp. 61–103.

10. See, for example: Mandell, Paul I. 'The Development of the Southern Goiás–Brasília Region: Agricultural Development in a Land Rich Economy'. *Unpublished Ph.D. dissertation, Columbia University*, 1969. Nicholls, William H., 'The Brazilian Food Supply: Problems and Prospects', *Economic Development and Cultural Change*, 19 (3), April 1971.

11. Bergsman, J. *Brazil. Industrialization and Trade Policies*, Oxford, 1970, p. 157.

12. In gratitude for help against Napoleon the Portuguese Crown ordered the collection of duties of 15 per cent *ad valorem* on goods carried under the British flag when merchandise imported from Portugal had to pay duties of 16 per cent. This has been much criticized by some Brazilian economic historians. 'Brazil remained at the mercy of London, thanks to the commercial treaty of 1810—the fruit of true economic brutality'. Dorival Teixeira Vieira, 'Industrial Development in Brazil', in John Saunders, Ed., *Modern Brazil*, Florida, 1971, p. 157.

13. Martin, J. M. *Industrialization et developpment energetique du Brésil*, Paris, 1966, p. 83.

14. Baer, *op. cit.*, p. 13.

15. Between 1850 and 1870 the Baron attempted to diversify the Brazilian economy and promoted the building of railways, ports and textile

mills and founded several banking establishments, as well as a steel mill.

16. About 800,000 slaves were freed and most of them moved to the cities. Mortgages formerly secured partly by the value of the slave population of the fazendas were devalued thus reducing available credit. Many fazendeiros unable to cope with the problems of post-emancipation agriculture moved to the cities and turned their attention to industry and commerce.

17. Baer, *op. cit.*, p. 15.

18. Quoted in Saunders, *op. cit.*, p. 160.

19. Bello, José-Maria. *A History of Modern Brazil, 1889–1964*, Stanford, 1966, p. 199.

20. Bello, *op. cit.*, p. 200.

21. Martin, *op. cit.*, p. 87.

22. *Censo Industrial do Brasil, 1950*, I.B.G.E., Rio de Janeiro, 1957, p. 193.

23. Martin, *op. cit.*, p. 62.

24. Martin, *op. cit.*, p. 64.

25. *Censo Industrial do Brasil*, 1950, *op. cit.*, p. 191.

26. *Brazil, 1938*, I.B.G.E., Rio de Janeiro, 1939, p. 194. Of all the firms founded between 1910 and 1919 only 1,320 survived to be counted in the 1950 Industrial Census.

27. Baer, *op. cit.*, p. 16. In São Paulo industrial production rose by more than 25 per cent each year between 1914 and 1919. See Bergsman, *op. cit.*, p. 21.

28. Baer, *op. cit.*, p. 17.

29. Martin, *op. cit.*, p. 99.

30. Bergsman, *op. cit.*, p. 22.

31. Baer, *op. cit.*, p. 24.

32. Dulles, J. F. W. *Vargas of Brazil*, Texas, 1967, p. 505.

33. Dulles, *op. cit.*, p. 297.

34. Dulles, *op. cit.*, p. 206.

35. Baklanoff, E. N. 'Foreign Private Investment and Industrialization in Brazil', in Baklanoff, E. N., Ed., *New Perspectives of Brazil*, Vanderbilt, 1966, p. 110.

36. Furtado, Celso. *Diagnosis of the Brazilian Crisis*, London, 1965, p. 95.

37. *Sinopse Estatística do Brasil, 1971*. I.B.G.E., Rio de Janeiro, 1971, p. 134.

38. Martin, *op. cit.*, pp. 105–107.

39. Stein, Stanley J. 'Brazilian Cotton Textile Industry, 1850–1950', in S. Kuznets, W. E. Moore and J. J. Spengler, Eds., *Economic Growth: Brazil, India, Japan*, Duke University Press, 1959. Quoted in Bergsman, *op. cit.*, p. 136 note.

40. Bergsman, *op. cit.*, pp. 143–145.

41. *Sudene Informa*, Setembro–Otubro, 1971, pp. 22–23.

42. *Ibid.*

43. Bergsman, *op. cit.*, pp. 146–147.

44. *Alliance for Progress Weekly Newsletter*, Vol. VI (3), January 15, 1968.

45. *Produção Industrial, 1968*, I.B.G.E., Rio de Janeiro, 1970.

46. *Brazilian Bulletin*, March 1971.

47. *Brazilian Bulletin*, July 1966.

48. One-third of federal funds allocated to industry in 1960 was for steel production and by the late 'sixties approximately two-thirds of the industry was in government hands. See Martin, *op. cit.*, p. 143 and Baer, W. *The Development of the Brazilian Steel Industry*, Vanderbilt, 1969, p. 83.

49. Baer, 1969, *op. cit.*, p. 55.

50. For a detailed analysis of the industry in Minas Gerais see Dickenson, J. P., 'The Iron and Steel Industry in Minas Gerais, Brazil, 1695–1965', in R. W. Steel and R. Lawton, Eds., *Liverpool Essays in Geography*, London, 1967, pp. 407–422.

51. Baer, 1969, *op. cit.*, p. 56 gives 2,000 tons; Martin, *op. cit.*, p. 144, gives 775 tons; and Dickenson, *op. cit.*, p. 411, gives 4,000 tons.

52. Baer, 1969, *op. cit.*, p. 65.

53. *Rodovia*, No. 291, July–August 1971, p. 42.

54. *Brazil Herald* (Rio), April 13, 1972. Output goals have been revised upward.

55. The difference in cost between imported and national coal is large. Comparative costs for a ton at Usiminas in 1965 were US$42·45 for Santa Catarina coal and US$22·05 for imported American coal. Domestic coal is expensive because of its poor quality, inefficient mining operations and poor transport facilities. Brazilian iron ore deposits are so vast and of such high quality that they can be used to earn foreign exchange for the import of coal. In the Rio Doce ore trains bring back coal on their return journey. This area has been called the Brazilian Ruhr. See Baer, 1969, *op. cit.*, pp. 38–39.

56. Baer, 1969, *op. cit.*, p. 167.

57. *Brazil Herald* (Rio), February 24, 1972.

58. *New York Times*, October 28, 1961; and Embaixada do Brasil, *Boletim Informativo*, No. 99, June 7, 1962.

59. *Survey of the Brazilian Economy, 1966*, Washington, 1967, p. 147.

60. *O Dia* (Rio), May 22, 1971.

61. *Brazil Herald* (Rio), June 2, 1971.

62. *Survey of the Brazilian Economy, 1966, op. cit.*, p. 125.

63. Baklanoff, *op. cit.*, p. 112.

64. *Brazil Herald* (Rio), March 23, 1971.

65. *Survey of the Brazilian Economy, 1966, op. cit.*, p. 126.

66. *Brazil Herald* (Rio), May 21, 1968.

67. *Brazil Herald* (Rio), March 9, 1972.

68. *Atlas Nacional do Brasil*, I.B.G.E., Rio de Janeiro, 1966, Plate IV–11.

69. Dean, *op. cit.*, p. 238.

G

70. Bernardes, Nilo. 'The State of Espírito Santo in the Brazilian Macro-regional Background', in N. Bernardes, Ed., *A Case of Regional Inequality in Development: Espírito Santo State, Brazil*, Vol. 1, Rio de Janeiro, 1971, p. 9.

71. *O Globo* (Rio) March 4, 1974. Between 1969 and 1972 Guanabara's industrial production grew by only 7 per cent as compared to rates of 36·3 per cent and 47·9 per cent for São Paulo and Minas Gerais respectively. *Brazil Herald* (Rio), July 18, 1972.

72. Muller, Nice Lecocq. *Industrializaçao do Vale do Paraiba*, São Paulo, 1969, p. 1.

73. Dickenson, J. P. 'A geografia e o desenvolvimento industrial na parte central de Minas Gerais, Brasil', *Boletim Geografico I.B.G.*, No. 201, November–December 1967.

74. *Bolsa Review*, Vol. 5 (58), October 1971, p. 570.

75. Hirschman, A. O. *The Strategy of Economic Development*, Yale, 1958, p. 184.

76. Baer, 1965, *op. cit.*, pp. 174–185.

77. *Brazil Herald* (Rio), May 14, 1971.

78. *Brazil Herald* (Rio), May 18, 1972.

79. *Brazil Herald* (Rio), April 16, 1972.

80. Brazil is now selling watches to Switzerland, cutlery to West Germany, refrigerators to the United States, shoes to Italy, and photoelectric cells to the Netherlands. Private Brazilian firms are exporting 41 per cent of the total, government-owned firms 15 per cent and foreign-owned firms 44 per cent (see *Brazil Herald* (Rio), October 6, 1971). Exports of industrial goods rose by 72·1 per cent in 1972. Although coffee continues to be the major export product, its share of the value of total exports has been declining, from 35·2 per cent in 1969 to about 26 per cent in 1972. Among the industrial products, the main export items in 1972 were motor vehicles, soluble coffee, boilers and heating equipment, footwear and processed meat. *Bolsa Review*, Vol. 7 (76), April 1973, pp. 160–161.

CHAPTER 8

Infrastructure

Brazil, Love It or Leave It . . . and the last one to leave kindly turn off the lights at the airport. Political sticker and graffito at Rio de Janeiro's Galeão Airport

Among the non-political events that have most captured Brazil's imagination during the past dozen years, perhaps half had to do with the country's infrastructure. Although winning the World Cup for the third time in 1970 undoubtedly tops the list, closely followed by the construction of Brasília, competing for secondary honours with a Brazilian Miss Universe would very likely be the Trans-Amazon Highway, the Urubupungá hydroelectric project and the Belém–Brasília (Bernardo Sayão) Highway. The first three have undoubtedly prompted a certain unity among the people, but the last three have provided a practical means for attaining national development and regional integration. Much of Brazil's recent progress and dynamic growth rate has been possible only because of the rapid expansion of its power generating capacity and its growing capability for moving goods, people and ideas about the country, particularly by means of a greatly improved road network. For many, the lights of opportunity are only now beginning to flicker on, as physical unity becomes a reality for the first time in Brazil's long history.

RECENT GROWTH

In almost all phases of infrastructure development, the nation's capability has doubled or better during the inter-censal period 1961–70.[1] In transport, for instance, the Federal

Government's network of paved roads increased from 9,590 kilometres in 1961 to 24,150—nearly half the total Federally-maintained mileage—in 1970 and paving has been proceeding at a rate of about 4,000 kilometres a year. Another 24,000 kilometres of paved road was under state and municipal jurisdiction, for a national total of some 48,000 kilometres paved in 1970, which figure reached 56,200 kilometres at the end of 1972 and 71,000 by 15 March 1974, when President Médici left office. Road improvements were reflected in increased petrol consumption, which rose from 4,600 million litres in 1961 to 9,700 million in 1970. Diesel fuel consumption also increased, from 2,112 million litres to 6,515 over the same period.

Transport modernization also took place in the air and on the sea. Thus, although Brazil's consumption of aviation gasoline declined from 380 million litres in 1961 to 100 million in 1970, its use of jet fuel increased from 172 to 775 million litres during the same period. Similarly, whereas Brazil's merchant fleet was reduced from approximately 500, frequently exceedingly old, vessels in 1961 to about 325 in 1970, its tonnage increased from 1·3 million DWT to 2·5 million. This is expected to increase to about 5 million DWT by 1975, with over half of the new construction carried out in Brazilian yards.

In the realm of power generation, Table 16 shows that Brazil's installed capacity more than doubled between 1961 and 1970, with gains in both hydro- and thermo-electric capacities. These are expected to attain 18,000 MW (double the 1969 capacity) in 1975 and in the neighbourhood of 30,000 MW by 1980.

TABLE 16

Installed Electric Power Capacity, 1961 & 1970

Years	Hydroelectric, MW installed capacity	Thermo-electric, MW installed capacity	Total MW installed capacity
1961	3,809	1,396	5,205
1970	8,828	2,405	11,233

Source: Fundacão I.B.G.E., Sinopse Estatística do Brasil 1971, Instituto Brasileiro de Estatística, Rio de Janeiro, 1971, p. 209.

ELECTRIC POWER

Estimates of the regional distribution of Brazil's hydro-electric potential, which may be of the order of 150,000 MW, vary considerably. Probably one-third lies in the Amazon drainage basin, another 30 to 32 per cent in the Paraná system, where major recent power installations have been located, and approximately 10 per cent in that of the São Francisco, 'Brazil's Nile'. The remainder, or about one-fourth of the total, is provided by the relatively short, but steep and voluminous rivers which cross the rainy coastal ranges to flow into the Atlantic Ocean. A minor potential exists in the basin of the Uruguay River and a negligible amount in that of the Paraguay, although these are partially compensated for by the proximity of the southern Brazilian coalfields.

As shown in Table 17, the distribution of these potentials is not reflected in either present or projected hydroelectric

TABLE 17

Utilization of Hydroelectric Resources as of June 1970, in MW

Hydrographic basin	In operation	Under construction	Projected or under study	Scheduled for study	Total
Amazon*	0·7	60·0	599·6	5,657·1	6,317·4
São Francisco	1,114·9	1,492·6	8,406·8	2,557·5	14,571·8
Paraná	3,457·7	7,679·0	7,452·1	27,035·5	45,624·3
Eastern Seaboard	1,584·3	861·3	2,905·3	5,380·2	10,731·1
Uruguay	18·6	263·6	12·0	1,740·0	2,034·2
Paraguay	—	8·3	72·2	—	80·5
BRAZIL TOTAL	6,176·2	10,364·8	19,448·0	42,370·3	79,359·3

* Including the Tocantins-Araguaia.

Source: Ibid., p. 48.

installations, which, like the distribution of transport facilities, are singularly well developed in the Heartland and taper off in a sharp gradient towards the Northeast, the Periphery and especially the North. The most striking difference is between the Paraná basin and the meagre use, or even projected use, of the Amazon and its tributaries. Until Pará's 20 MW Curuá-Una plant went on stream in 1971 and 1972, Amazonia had no hydroelectric development except for minor installations in the Tocantins-Araguaia. On the other hand, expansion of capacities near the urban and industrial markets of the Heartland (Map 13) has required the use of increasingly distant power sources extending to the westernmost borders of São Paulo (Jupiá and Ilha Solteira) and Minas Gerais (Cachoeira Dourada), into the upper São Francisco (Três Marias) and, very soon, to the middle reaches of the Paraná on the Paraguayan border. In contrast, small diesel-powered generators are common in the smaller towns outside the Heartland and charcoal remains a widespread source of power in areas where forests are still abundant and transport is lacking or costly.

There are also striking disparities in the use of power by different sectors of the economy. The 37·6 MWh of electricity produced in 1970 was distributed among users as follows: industrial 19·4, residential 8·4, commercial 5·2, public lighting and government buildings 3·3, and 'other' 1·3.[2]

THERMAL & ATOMIC ENERGY. Of the 4 million metric tons of coal consumed in Brazil in 1970, 1·5 million was used for the production of thermo-electric power. The main generating stations are located, as might be expected, in places that are accessible to domestic or overseas supplies and where there is either a shortage or an overuse of nearby, readily developable hydroelectric sources. Thermo-electric plants are therefore concentrated on the plains of southern Rio Grande do Sul, along the Santos–São Paulo urban-industrial axis and around Guanabara Bay. Brazil's largest thermo-electric plant, with a capacity of 160 MW, is located at Santa Cruz, a suburb of Rio de Janeiro.

Brazil's first experimental nuclear reactor, of the 'Argonaut' type, was inaugurated in 1965 on Fundão Island in Guanabara Bay. The country's first nuclear power plant will not be too far away, at Angra dos Reis, 150 kilometres west of Rio on the coast. The signing of a contract with Westinghouse Electric Corporation in 1972 to build the plant, which is to be in operation in 1977 with a capacity of 626 MW, was preceded by five years of official studies, conflicting announcements and intense public controversy. Local opposition to the project centred on possible damage to land flora, air and water

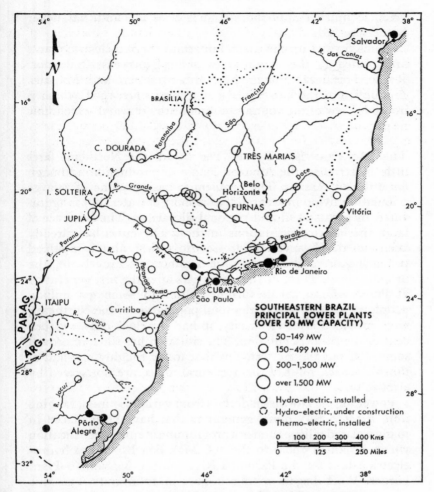

Map 13. PRINCIPAL POWER PLANTS OF SOUTHEASTERN BRAZIL

pollution, destruction of offshore fishing grounds and a decline in tourism because of the subconscious fear of radioactive contamination. As has become the well-nigh universal practice in such instances, assurances were given by government scientists that such fears were unfounded, and the project is going ahead. The question as to why the plant had to be located in such close proximity to this tourist and incipient industrial town, when so much empty shore-land is close at hand, has never been answered.

Much further up the coast, important thermo-electric plants are located in the major cities of the Northeast (Salvador, Recife, Fortaleza) and in the North at Belém and Manaus. Production at the last-named has trebled since 1968, which is ironic in view of the voluminous quantities of water which flow nearby.

THE SÃO FRANCISCO RIVER. Per capita the Northeast fares little better than the Amazon in power production, although for different reasons. The problem is basically one of a large population living in an area that is short of water, but is aggravated by great social and regional disparities. The existence of large thermo-electric stations in the major cities has already been noted. However, hydroelectric power also is destined primarily for, and formerly went almost exclusively to, the urban centres. Thus, in 1960, six years after the first generators at Paulo Afonso began turning, although some 3·5 million people, or 16 per cent of the total population of the Northeast, were provided with electricity, it had reached only 0·3 per cent of the rural population. The situation has since improved somewhat but the fact remains that today roughly one-half of the *Nordestinos*, most of them in rural areas, are not served by electricity.

Power for the Northeast derives from various sources, ranging from the 110 KW diesel generators that have been placed in many isolated villages under a programme of rural electrification which began in 1965, to the 108 MW Boa Esperança hydro-electric plant on the Parnaíba River on the Maranhão–Piauí border. Work began on this project in 1964 and when it is completed in 1976 it will have double the present capacity.

It is, however, the Paulo Afonso Dam on the São Francisco River which has for twenty years been the focus of attention for the power-hungry Northeast and is still considered[3] to be the key to its development. When the falls, which plunge nearly 100 metres off the lip of the plateau, were first harnessed in 1954 to provide a generating capacity of 200 MW, the region's power production approximately doubled, increasing the per capita consumption of electricity from 33 kwh per person to 74, although most of it was, in fact, destined for Recife and Salvador. Then in 1965 its capacity was increased to 310 MW and transmission lines were extended to Natal and Fortaleza; in 1968 the second stage of the plant's expansion was completed to provide a total of 615 MW. In February 1972, President Médici inaugurated the Paulo Afonso III plant which brought capacity to 1,259 MW, making it the third largest hydroelectric plant in Brazil. Transmission lines from Paulo Afonso now amount to 11,000 kilometres and serve seven of the Northeastern states. But much of it still passes over the surrounding rural area on its way to supplying the industries and the lights of the urban centres.

Other hydroelectric projects are planned for the middle reaches of the São Francisco, the most ambitious being the 750 MW capacity Sobradinho Barrage which will include locks that rise 32·5 metres to ensure the continuity of navigation on the river. It will also regulate the flow of the São Francisco, thereby making it possible further to increase the generating capacity at Paulo Afonso. In total, it is possible that the ultimate hydroelectric generating capacity of the São Francisco may amount to approximately 5 million kilowatts.

At present, the other major utilization of the river is in its upper reaches, at the Três Marias plant, which went on stream in 1962. Construction of this dam assisted in regulating the flow of the São Francisco and thereby made possible the expansion of the generating capacity at Paulo Afonso three years later, as well as providing flood control and improving year-round navigation conditions on the river. On the other hand, the power generated at Três Marias serves not the Northeast but the industrial Heartland to the south, as it is tied into the grid of the Central Electric Company of Minas Gerais (CEMIG), which also has three smaller plants on the Paraopeba, Jequitaí and Pandeiros Rivers, headwater tributaries of the São Francisco. The current capacity of Três Marias is 390 MW, but this is expected to reach 540 MW in the next few years.

THE EASTERN SEABOARD. As with the upper São Francisco, most of the power generated from the water courses which flow in an easterly direction from the Serra do Mar is destined for the cities and industries of the Heartland. It is, therefore, in the central part of this region that the major hydroelectric projects are concentrated, although some development extends fairly continuously from the Rio das Contas in central Bahia, where a 210 MW project is nearing completion, to the Itajaí Valley in central Santa Catarina, where a dam was begun in 1970 financed by British interests. Hydroelectric power is also provided by the upper Jacuí River where it flows over the Serra Geral in Rio Grande do Sul.

A high proportion of the rivers which flow off the seaward-facing slopes of the coastal escarpment are, however, too steep and short to be practical for development, or else they flow through sparsely populated areas. The most significant developments have therefore taken place along the Paraíba and the Rio Doce, both of which parallel the coast for considerable distances before breaking through the Serra do Mar. They also have the advantage of being accessible to centres of consumption and finance. Of the two, the Paraíba has had the longer history of exploitation. The last significant development on the river proper was the 210 MW Funil plant, completed in 1965, although a new project is planned which will divert water from the upper reaches of the river across the escarpment and down to a generating station at Caraguatatuba, on the coast, approximately 100 kilometres northeast of Santos. The latest installation on the Rio Doce was at the 2,000 foot Mascarenhas Dam, which came on stream in 1972 with a capacity of 115 MW, but a considerable potential remains along this river. The most significant developments of the eastern seaboard, then, have come not on the rivers which rise along the face of the Serra do Mar itself but rather along those which tap the slopes behind it, including those which rise along the rim of the escarpment and flow westward into the Paraná system.

One of the most imaginative feats in the annals of power plant engineering was the project now widely known, in which A. W. K. Billings, working for the Canadian-owned Brazilian Traction, Light and Power Company (the 'Light', as it is known locally), reversed the flow of the Tietê River with a series of dams and sent it down to a generating station at Cubatão at the base of the coastal escarpment. According to

Preston James, the people of São Paulo owe Billings 'a considerable debt of gratitude for the works which made possible the beginning of urban development'.[4] Since those early days, the capacity of this plant has been expanded so that it now stands at 864 MW.

THE PARANÁ RIVER BASIN. The core area of Brazil's hydroelectric development lies within a drainage basin comprising the Paraná River above its junction with the Iguaçu on the Argentine border and its headwater and east bank tributaries. The volumes of water and the gradients of the watercourses that follow the westerly dip of the plateau and their location with respect to the major industrial and urban markets of the Heartland[5] provide virtually ideal conditions for such enterprises. This is particularly true in the context of modern, large-scale dam construction, in which Brazil is conceptually and in individual projects, if not yet in total installed capacity, at par with the Soviet Union and the United States.

It is impossible, within the space available, to discuss in detail the antecedents and characteristics of all the hydroelectric installations located within the Paraná Basin, but a general picture can be obtained from the map on page 189, which shows the principal power plants and their approximate capacities at the time of publication. Their power is distributed through interconnecting transmission grids operated by a number of companies, the largest of which are the Rio and São Paulo 'Lights', now merged into a single Light S.A., the Centrais Elétricas de Minas Gerais S.A. (CEMIG),[6] and the Furnas Centrais Elétricas, whose interests extend from southern Minas Gerais to the Angra dos Reis nuclear power plant, and the state-controlled but publicly owned Centrais Elétricas de São Paulo (CESP). The last-named was formed in 1966 by the amalgamation of eleven separate power companies and is now the largest corporation in Latin America and the only one with a capital of over one billion dollars.

CESP is the largest shareholder in a consortium which includes CEMIG, Eletrobrás (the Federal power agency, which was established in 1962) and the states of Mato Grosso, Goiás, Santa Catarina, Paraná and Rio Grande do Sul, which was organized to construct Brazil's most ambitious project to date, the Urubupungá hydroelectric complex. This is located on the Paraná River below the confluence of the Paranaíba and the Rio Grande, on the São Paulo–Mato Grosso border, and when completed will be among the largest of its kind in the world, surpassed only by the Soviet plants at Krasnoyarsk and Bratsk. Urubupungá consists, in fact, of two dams located about 60 kilometres apart, one above the Urubupungá Falls at Ilha Solteira and the other below them at Jupiá. The principal contractor for the project was the Brazilian firm Construções e Comércio Camargo Corrêa, which was also involved in the construction of Brasília.

The first three 100 MW generators came on stream at Jupiá in 1969 and when that plant was completed in 1970 with a total capacity of 1,400 MW, it was the largest hydroelectric installation in Brazil. It will eventually be dwarfed, however, by the Ilha Solteira plant, which started initial operations at the end of 1973 and when fully operational in 1977 will have an installed capacity of 3,300 MW. The combined total annual output of these two plants that constitute the Urubupungá complex will amount to 26,000 million kwh when fully on stream, a figure which is equal to the total amount of power produced in Brazil at the time construction on them began in 1966. Indeed, an imaginative venture! Power from Urubupungá will serve an area of about one million square miles with a population of perhaps 60 million, being tied into the grids of the Heartland, the states of the South and southern Goiás and Mato Grosso. Ancillary benefits will include flood control on the Paraná, an estimated potential catch of 400,000 tons of fish annually from the lakes formed by the dams, irrigation works which will stimulate farming and stock raising in the not overly humid regions of western São Paulo and eastern Mato Grosso, a series of locks to provide river navigation in an area where this is not possible now and where there is a deficiency of other means of transport, and the attraction to the vicinity of industries that require cheap and abundant power.

The Brazilian imagination was not, however, content to stop with the launching of this signal feat of harnessing the Paraná and turned southward towards where the Centrais Eléctricas do Sul do Brasil SA had already begun work on a 700 MW project in the lower reaches of the Iguaçu River, to be completed in 1975 and tied into its existing grid with 1,000 kilometres of 230 kilovolt transmission lines. For some years attention had been focused on the stretch of water from the Iguaçu Falls to the mouth of that river and thence northward along the Paraná to the falls at Sete Quedas (known in Paraguay as the Guaíra Falls, near the town of that name, which marks the head of navigation on the Paraná). Development of the outstanding power potential of this section of the two rivers has, however, been complicated by the fact that it coincides with the international boundaries between Brazil, Argentina and Paraguay. Previous proposals for dams in this district by the Brazilians had invariably brought resounding denunciations from the Argentineans, who claimed that these would alter the course of the La Plata, disrupt navigation patterns at Argentine river ports, and cause other damage to the down-stream ecology.

These antagonisms came to a head during the latter part of 1972, about a year after Brazil and Paraguay issued a joint ceclaration that they would collaborate on building a 15,000 MW power plant at Sete Quedas, when Argentina brought the subject up at the United Nations, placing great stress on the ecological issue to take advantage of international interest then being focused, through the Stockholm Conference, on questions relating to preservation of the environment. A compromise accord was reached between the two main protagonists in September of that year under which they would consult before undertaking any projects on common rivers. This was followed later in the year by talks by the foreign ministers of Brazil, Argentina, Paraguay, Uraguay and Bolivia, aimed at discussing the use and valorization of the entire La Plata Basin, with a recent voluminous study by the Organization of American States on the subject[7] serving as a factual backdrop. It soon became clear that neither of the major powers in the basin had significantly altered its views on the question of damming the rivers and they reverted to their respective positions prior to the U.N. protocol, with Argentina insisting that dam construction on common rivers should not proceed without consultation and prior agreement between the countries affected, while Brazil maintained that this would interfere with national sovereignty.[8]

The smaller countries, in contrast, appeared to view the matter with greater equanimity, perhaps because of feelings of helplessness but more likely because they were hoping to gain from the development projects of their wealthy and more powerful neighbours. The President of Uruguay stated that he felt the main thrust should be towards, 'improving natural resources and using them to best advantage . . . as an expression of the maturity we have all attained'.[9] It is, of course, a moot point whether technological maturity is commonly matched by political maturity on the international level, as the continued squabbles over waterways and pipelines between those North American neighbours, Canada and the U.S.A., amply attest.

Be that as it may, in April 1973, Brazil signed an agreement with the more tractable Paraguayans, despite vigorous protests from Argentina, to build a dam not at Sete Quedas but further south at Itaipu, on the Paraná River about 15 kilometres above its confluence with the Iguaçu and the Argentine border. When completed by 1982, Itaipu will have a capacity of 11,700 MW (roughly Brazil's total hydroelectric capacity in 1972) and will have cost an estimated 3,000 million dollars.

There is an interesting financial aspect to the Itaipu project which is not only unique but which makes it the largest foreign aid project ever undertaken by one Latin American nation on behalf of another. This is, that although it is to be undertaken and later operated by a joint Paraguayan–Brazilian company, Brazil will underwrite all the construction costs. Paraguay is to repay its half of the obligation out of revenues—estimated at half that country's current GNP—obtained from the sale of power to Brazil. It will, therefore, cost Paraguay nothing, while providing it with an abundant source of revenue once the initial investment is paid back. In short, Brazil has been willing to pay a high price for harnessing the waters of this international river, and there is no doubt that Itaipu is viewed as only the first step in the development of the unrivalled hydroelectric potential that exists between the Iguaçu Falls and those at Sete Quedas.

A REGIONAL PERSPECTIVE. Cheap, abundant and suitably located hydroelectric power has undoubtedly been one of Brazil's major assets in its current phase of economic expansion, especially in view of the scarcity of exploitable oil and coal reserves. As has been shown, the country's installed capacity has risen rapidly not only to keep pace with, but to spark many of the changes that have taken place in recent years. Recent growth of the industry has been increasingly in the hands of public utility companies, and of an estimated increase in power capacity between 1970 and 1974 of 5,500 MW, approximately 2,500 will have been installed by Eletrobrás. The entire industry has been characterized by excellent planning, while the government-controlled power companies have operated efficiently and have been free from meddling or worse by political appointees. New projects, among which Itaipu and Urubupungá are only the most spectacular, are expected to raise the annual consumption of electricity from its 1970 level of 415 kwh per capita to 1,100 by 1980, although it is worth noting that the Heartland's 1974 power consumption is of the order of 1,400 kwh per capita, comparable to that of many a 'developed' country.

Nevertheless, in some of the centrally-located regions of Brazil the hydraulic power potential is already being used to full capacity so that new projects must be placed on the outer margins. This may, in the long run, have the desirable effect of promoting the dispersal of industrial and urban growth into the areas immediately adjacent to the Heartland and among the small cities within it, a trend which has for some years already been apparent from the growth of towns in the Paraíba Valley, the rapid development of Brasília, Goiânia and Anápolis on the Central Plateau, the rise of a number of dynamic centres in western São Paulo and Paraná, and the spectacular growth of such cities as Curitiba and Pôrto Alegre.

On the other hand, in the Northeast a critical shortage of power, which can hardly be met even with the maximum development of local hydraulic resources, continues to exist. There is, however, probably no good reason why, as penetration of the rainforest to the west proceeds along the Trans-Amazon and other highways, hydroelectric power could not be transported from at least the nearer of the Amazon's tributaries to the densely populated and urban areas of the Northeast even though the distance between, say, Salvador and the upper Araguaia is about 30 per cent further than that between São Paulo and Itaipu. The Amazon Basin itself, of course, has a tremendous potential for hydroelectric development and although immediate prospects will presumably have to await the valorization of that region, perhaps stimulated by the prospects and power needs of large-scale mineral exploitation, over the long term it certainly represents a power reserve that could be of great benefit to the nation. But in the meantime, ever more spectacular projects can be expected to rise along the watercourses that ring the Heartland as well as beside the principal harbours of the eastern seaboard.

PETROLEUM

In contrast to Brazil's abundant and rapidly developing hydroelectric power sources, the situation with regard to fossil fuels is not nearly as promising. The national coal fields would probably never have been of more than regional importance if it had not been for the quest to save on foreign exchange, the need for which has lessened in recent years, and petroleum production has as yet been unable to keep pace with rising demands, particularly as a result of the greatly increased use of motor vehicles over the past decade. There has, however, been an interesting shift in emphasis with respect to these two fuels in government policies. A quarter of a century ago the major emphasis was on disseminating the use of Brazilian coal, and laws were passed requiring it to be used in certain proportion to imported coal on the railways and in the steel mills. Today the almost single-minded drive is on discovering new reserves of oil.

A law passed in 1952 placed control of the petroleum industry in the hands of Petrobrás (Petróleo Brasileiro S.A.), a mixed corporation in which the Federal Government holds the controlling interest.[10] Full implementation of the law took some years, but today all oil exploration and production, the major share of its transport and refining, and some of its distribution and marketing are in the hands of Petrobrás.

At first inexperience, mismanagement and the appointment of political hacks to top posts made the company the butt of jokes and considerable grumbling. Nevertheless, Petrobrás has managed to overcome these growing pains to become one not only of Brazil's, but of South American's largest and most efficient enterprises. Operating at first with revenue from special government taxes, Petrobás has since 1960, when it began showing a significant profit, been financing 80 per cent of its projects with capital derived from its own operations. Since its inception, however, the company has consistently allocated one-third of its budget to exploration for new fields. Of a three-year investment programme budget of Cr$9,200 million, announced in March 1972, Petrobrás has allocated Cr$3,200 million to drilling exploratory wells, 108 of these to be on land and 104 on the continental shelf.

THE RESOURCE BASE. Oil was first discovered in Brazil in the Bahia Basin, just north of Salvador (Map 12, p. 112), in 1939 and commercial production began the following year. Fifteen years later, when Petrobrás took over its operation, it was yielding only 2 million barrels per annum. By 1961 that company had raised production in the Bahia Basin to 34·8 million barrels; but that rate of growth could not be maintained and the yield was about 50 million a year for the period 1970–72. Since 1968 the Bahia Basin has also been producing between 150,000 and 225,000 cubic metres (liquefied) of natural gas annually.

The continuous search for new oil fields was intensified during the 1960s and early 1970s. In 1962 non-commercial amounts of oil were discovered at Angra dos Reis, in southernmost Rio de Janeiro State, and again in 1965 in the São João district of Maranhão and, later, in Acre. The only new commercial wells, however, are in the Carmópolis district of Sergipe, where production commenced in 1965, and its extension on to the continental shelf off that state and Alagoas. This basin accounts for the remainder of Brazil's petroleum production, that is, 10 to 12 million barrels annually, although promising new fields have been located in the São Mateus district of Espírito Santo and offshore from Campos in the state of Rio.

Thus, despite Petrobrás' far-ranging search for new oil fields, which has covered some 3 million of Brazil's 5 million square kilometres of sedimentary formations, the results to date have been meagre. Whether private, foreign-owned companies would have had better results may soon be ascertained as Petrobrás was studying terms for their admission in 1975, a sign it might relinquish its monopoly on oil exploration.

It has been shown earlier that whereas Brazil's crude production somewhat less than doubled during the period 1961–70, its use of petroleum derivative fuels (diesel and fuel oil, petrol and jet fuel) increased at a higher rate. It was therefore necessary to raise imports of crude and partly refined petroleum from 7·5 million tons in 1961 to 18·8 million in 1970, a trend which must continue except for some unforeseen turn of events. The dilemma for Brazil is not, however, just a question of production but, rather, that whereas this increased by a factor of 30 during the period 1955–70, proven reserves approximately only doubled during the same period. These are now believed to be about 860 million barrels, or barely enough for the next decade without taking into account any coupling of increased consumer demand with further attempts at import substitution.

In reaction to the disappointing prospects for discovering new, productive oil fields and with the desire to guarantee meeting its future petroleum needs, in 1970 Petrobrás announced that it would seek exploration rights abroad and to this end, in February 1972, established a subsidiary, Petrobrás International S.A., known abroad as Bráspetro. Six months later the latter signed an agreement with Iraq to explore a 10,000 square kilometre area in the southwestern part of that country and subsequently entered an agreement with the Algerian national oil company, Sontarch, from which it had been purchasing crude oil since 1967 and for which Bráspetro acts as international agent in South America, for joint prospecting ventures. Bráspetro has also signed an exploration agreement with the Egyptian General Petroleum Corporation to prospect a 12,500 square kilometre area northeast of the Nile Valley on very favourable terms, with any profits to be shared 50–50. Other prospective exploration ventures for Petrobrás International are in in Angola, Mozambique, Nigeria, Mauritania, Colombia, Peru, Venezuela, with whom an agreement has been reached to transport crude oil to the United States in Petrobrás tankers, and Ecuador, where a joint technical commission has also been set up to study the feasibility of transporting crude oil down the Putumayo and Apa Rivers to a proposed refinery in the state of Amazonas.

There exists in Brazil an alternative source of oil and gas, however, in its domestic oil shales, the main formations of which occur in Bahia's Maraú Valley (an embayment that parallels the coast 100–130 kilometres SSW. of Salvador), in the Paraíba Valley centring on Pindamonhangaba, and in the Irati area of south-central Paraná. It has been reported[12] that Brazil has about 40 per cent of the world's oil shale deposits, containing a potential reserve of some 800,000 million barrels of crude.

Since 1961 there have been periodic announcements to the press by a Pindamonhangaba firm, Companhia Industrial de Rochas Bituminosas, that Soviet assistance is on its way to help develop the company's oil shale properties. In 1961 it was to receive $45 million, in 1965 $90 million and in 1969 $200 million, the latter for a plant which was to be operational in 1970 and to be producing 500,000 cubic metres of gas by 1971— yet in that year Brazil's total production was but one-third of that amount, all of it from the Bahia Basin. Press releases from Petrobrás, although more modest in their financial scope, were not far behind: in 1961 the U.S. was to loan $7 million towards building a plant at Irati; in 1963 successful trials had supposedly been conducted for processing the oil shales commercially; in 1966 Petrobrás was said to have spent $1·25 million on a pilot extraction plant at São Mateus do Sul, near Irati, and in the following year it was announced that a refinery was being built there which would have a capacity of 1,000 barrels of oil and 8 tons of liquid gas a day—but either of these has yet to appear in official statistics. A report that in 1970 Soviet experts had been assisting Brazil in a survey of some of its oil shales does, however, appear to be fairly reliable. Undoubtedly, possibilities exist for future development of these deposits, but, if the difficulties of trying to achieve commercial production of the Athabasca tar sands of Canada are any criterion, that day may be some years away for Brazil's oil shales despite renewed activity following the 1973–74 oil crisis.

REFINING & DISTRIBUTION. In contrast to a certain lack of success in developing its oil shales and finding new deposits of native crude, Brazil's refining and petroleum derivatives manufacturing have, as mentioned in the preceding chapter, been among the most dynamic groups of industries in recent years. This growth was sparked primarily by Petrobrás leadership, although, as pointed out in Chapter 7, the petro-chemicals industry was subsequently opened up to private, including foreign, investors. Oil refining remains, however, in the hands of Petrobrás.

When that company entered the refining business in 1954 Brazil's production amounted to but 2 million barrels annually, all of it from the Mataripe plant in Bahia. By 1971 production had risen to 155 million barrels, 65 million of it from domestic sources and 90 million from imported, and to over 200 million barrels in 1972. Eighty-five per cent of this was refined by Petrobrás at six refineries in Bahia, Rio de Janeiro, Minas Gerais, Rio Grande do Sul and two in São Paulo, the remainder coming from six privately-owned plants. The 1971–72 increase was due to two more Petrobrás installations coming on line: an additional unit at Cubatão on the São Paulo coast, which expanded the capacity of the existing refinery from 55,000 to 175,000 barrels a day, and a new refinery at Paulínia, near Campinas in São Paulo, which has a capacity of 126,000 barrels of crude oil a day supplied through a 225-kilometre, 24-inch pipeline from São Sebastião on the São Paulo coast. About 95 per cent of domestic needs for petroleum products are now met by Brazilian refineries.[13]

With the need to provide for the movement of these greatly increased quantities of petroleum and its derivatives, Petrobrás was obliged to concern itself with the infrastructure needed to transport them as well. In 1972 Petrobrás operated some 1,100 kilometres of oil pipelines, 400 kilometres of gas lines, thirty-two tankers and modern shipping terminals in five states. The company was also involved briefly in railroad building: in 1965, to transport crude oil from its Carmópolis field, it extended a local railway line in Sergipe to the Mataripe refinery in Bahia. In the same year, Petrobrás completed an oil pipeline from Rio de Janeiro to its Gabriel Passos refinery near Belo Horizonte, construction of which had begun in 1961 with the general objective of 'bringing progress and technology to the country's interior'.[14]

1965 was also the year in which Petrobrás for the first time took part in Brazil's shipbuilding renaissance, which had begun in 1958 (see Chapter 7), when it took delivery of three 10,500 DWT tankers from the Verolme yards at Angra dos Reis. The

Petrobrás fleet at this point totalled 640,000 DWT, spread over forty-seven ships; but in succeeding years, while the tonnage increased, the number of bottoms declined. Today, as mentioned, it operates thirty-two ships totalling 870,000 DWT, of which 800,000 tons represents seagoing tankers while the rest is distributed among those serving coastal and inland waterways. Some of the increased tonnage reflects the larger size of vessels built in national yards: two 15,000-ton tankers delivered in 1969 and four 26,400-tonners in 1972 and 1973, although Brazil's largest ship to date, and the largest built in Latin America, is the 53,000-ton grain carrier, the *Doceangra*, also from the Verolme yards. In any case, Petrobrás's main thrust has been through orders for supertankers placed abroad. The first two to be delivered were the 115,000 DWT sister ships *Hamilton Lopes* and *Horta Barbosa* from Denmark's Odense yards, which went into service in November 1969, and January 1970, respectively.

To accommodate these large ships and those of other flags serving Brazilian refineries with ever increasing quantities of oil, it became necessary for old terminals to be re-equipped and new ones built. The most ambitious of the latter was located at São Sebastião, a somnolent 300-year-old fishing village and minor tourist resort on the coast 100 kilometres east of Santos. Offshore is the resort island of the same name,[15] whose beaches had for many years been fouled by oil that was spilled when ocean-going tankers, anchored in the lee of the island, transferred their cargoes to smaller, shallow-draught vessels which completed the journey through the tricky estuarine channel leading to Santos and the Cubatão refinery. The annual cost of this transfer was estimated at over US$5 million.

In 1969 the São Sebastião terminal was officially opened, having cost US$17 million to build. It included a pier out to the natural, 20-metre deep channel which runs between the island and the mainland, where storage tanks were erected and connected through a pumping station to the end of the pier with 24-inch pipes. These could unload the 150,000-ton tankers which the pier could accommodate, at this first stage, in 24 hours. At the beginning, until a pipeline was completed to Cubatão (which was held up because of strife with the dock workers' union), the oil was pumped back into the coastal vessels. In February 1972, the second stage of development was initiated when Petrobrás signed a contract with Amsterdam Dredging N V. to deepen the channel over its 8 kilometre length to 25 metres and widen it to 300 metres, thereby providing access for tankers of up to 275,000 DWT. As noted above, this was also the year in which a second pipeline from São Sebastião, to the Paulínia refinery, came into use.

PETROBRÁS & PRIVATE ENTERPRISE. Starting from a very limited base, Petrobrás has become a giant enterprise, the largest of its kind in Latin America, coincidentally with a period of unprecedented national expansion in which energy and transport have played a vital role. Despite the opportunity and a mandate sufficiently open to have enabled Petrobrás to assume a monopolistic position beyond the immediate fields of finding, delivering and processing crude oil, it has exercised considerable restraint. It is true that until the early 1960s, when Brazil's mindless anti-colonial nationalism had its final fling, the corporation was tending to curtail private enterprise in the petrochemical field and was also heading in the direction of monopolizing the distribution of petroleum derivatives; but the military take-over of 1964 halted and then reversed these trends.

In 1970 General Ernesto Geisel, the then president of Petrobrás, said that the company did not intend to pursue a monoply position as an objective in its own right. Rather, he claimed, Petrobrás would merely maintain its monopoly in 'those sectors which are vital to the Brazilian economy—such as prospecting, refining imports and transport—areas in which the returns on investments are quite slow, in any case, and do not appeal to private companies', while leaving the latter to operate in such 'extremely lucrative' areas as the petrochemical industries and the distribution of gas and petroleum products, which are yielding the highest profits.[16] With respect to the last-named activity, at least, the truth of this statement is borne out by the figures given in Table 18.

TRANSPORT

The year 1960 represents a divide of sorts in the annals of surface transport in Brazil: it was the year in which railroad trackage was at its maximum before beginning a precipitous decline; it was also the year of Brasília's inauguration. The latter focused attention on the need to integrate the interior with the rest of the country and on the horrible condition of the few roads that led in that general direction.[17] Fundamental

TABLE 18

Distributors of Petroleum Derivatives, 1970 (per cent)

	All products	Petrol	Kerosene	Diesel	Fuel oil	Lubricants	Aviation fuel
Esso	27·7	27·5	39·1	23·6	29·0	21·7	43·0
Shell	24·1	22·5	19·2	19·4	28·4	19·8	44·1
PETRO-BRAS	17·8	6·8	7·5	14·5	37·7	—	12·9
Atlantic	9·1	13·6	11·3	13·9	0·3	12·0	—
Texaco	8·1	10·6	9·1	12·0	0·6	21·4	—
Ipiranga	6·1	9·8	4·0	8·6	0·4	8·5	—
Petrominas	1·6	2·9	0·7	1·8	—	0·3	—
Others	5·5	6·3	9·1	6·2	3·6	16·3	—
TOTAL	100·0	100·0	100·0	100·0	100·0	100·0	100·0

Source: Jornal do Brasil, March 26, 1971.

changes in both attitudes[18] and practices are clearly reflected in statistics on surface transport infrastructures across the following decade. From 1960 to 1970 the amount of railway line in use declined from a peak of 39,000 kilometres to about 32,000,[19] whereas the density of the road network rose from 56 kilometres per thousand square kilometres in 1960 to 123 in 1970, a commensurate extension of the amount of paving having already been noted at the start of this chapter.

THE RAILWAYS. In view of the essentially stagnant situation of Brazil's railways at present, little purpose would be served by detailing here this interesting, but primarily historical aspect of the country's regional economic development, especially as a considerable body of literature was published on the subject through the mid-1950s.[20] Suffice it to point out that the distribution of Brazil's railroads reflects the country's almost built-in regional economic disparities: 44 per cent of the trackage is in the Heartland and another 47 per cent is almost equally divided between the southern and northeastern states; a few long lines ribbon across the vastness of Mato Grosso and Goiás which, including the Federal District, account for a further 7 per cent of Brazil's trackage, while the remaining 2 per cent, totalling 678 kilometres, is tucked away in the North and includes the famed Madeira–Mamoré, now reduced to a single sightseeing train.

Of Brazil's 32,015 kilometres of track 25,313 are run by the Federal Government (Rêde Ferroviária Federal S.A.) and another 4,864 by the São Paulo state railways, Ferrovia Paulista. The latter was created only in 1971 through the amalgamation of five separate companies which only a dozen years before had, for the most part, been well-run and profitable enterprises. These two major systems are now both running large deficits, leaving the Victória-Minas Railway, operated by the Cia. Vale do Rio Doce, as the only profitable line remaining in the country, thanks to its role as a bulk ore carrier to the port of Tubarão.[21]

A recent report[22] states that the Brazilian railways have steadily been losing passengers—as, of course, have the railways of North America—and that although general freight increased by over 30 per cent between 1964 and 1970, this did not suffice to make the lines profitable and their actual share of the national traffic declined, until it now stands below 15 per cent. Obviously increased freight rates would reduce this share even further whereas, as the same study points out, 'the possibilities of attracting traffic through rate reduction and making the most of economies of scale are not worth consideration because of the low level of available equipment'.[23]

The Brazilian railways suffer from old equipment, poor and overdue maintenance and archaic operating systems which combine to make them unreliable and slow, a situation which is aggravated by the variety of gauges employed by the different lines. Undoubtedly renovation, standardization and electrification will continue to take place along those lines which fill a viable role in the nation's transport pattern: commuter services particularly around Rio de Janeiro, movement of bulk goods along corridors such as those between the Iron Quadrilateral and the steel mills and ore ports, and perhaps on long hauls like those between the industrial centres of the Heartland and distribution points in the Rimland. There is no doubt, however, that unremunerative local lines and those through intermediate points which are better served by the new and improved road network, will continue to be closed down. The great railroad era, begun when Brazil's raw materials exports were the foundation of its economy, lies in the past and, with the upgrading and internalizing of the national economy, the era of highway transport is well under way.

ROAD SYSTEMS. As shown in Table 19, Brazil has approximately one million kilometres of roadways, providing an overall density of about one kilometre for every eight square kilometres of land surface. This is distributed rather unevenly across the country, although, except for Amazonia, whose low density of 1 : 213 should properly include northern Mato Grosso and Goiás, not as unequally as might perhaps be expected. In the South a high density of small farms has made an abundance of roads both desirable and feasible. São Paulo has the most developed road network of any state with an average density of 1·5 kilometres of road per square kilometre, while the Heartland as a whole is also well served.

Another striking feature of the accompanying table is the extremely high proportion of municipal roads—about 90 per cent of the total. Only in the western and northern states does this figure drop down to about one-half of the overall mileage, with most of that located in the southern parts of Goiás and Mato Grosso and in Pará, which contains nearly 7,000 kilometres of the North's total municipal roads. Elsewhere in these two regions and in much of the *caatinga*, which is the major contributing factor to the Northeast's below-normal municipal and therefore total road density, a local road system is not required because most short-haul passenger and cargo traffic moves either by canoe and river boat or on horseback and by ox-cart.

On the other hand, in many parts of the country the distinction between an ox-cart trail and a municipal road may be difficult to make. The latter are commonly of very poor quality, which is borne out by the fact that, of the nearly one million kilometres of municipal roadway only a risible 3,610 kilometres were paved at the time these statistics were compiled and of these, 3,000 were located in São Paulo State. The situation with regards to state roads is somewhat better, with

16 per cent or about 21,000 kilometres paved. But even in this category two-thirds of the total was in the Heartland, with São Paulo contributing nearly 10,000 kilometres of it. These figures are in striking contrast to those, mentioned earlier, for the Federal highway system, of which nearly half (24,150 out of 50,101 kilometres) was already paved at the start of this decade.[24] In fact, except in São Paulo, where two-thirds of the state roads are paved, and to a lesser extent in the states of Rio de Janeiro and Guanabara, where one-third of such roads are paved, almost the only good, modern highways in the country are those built and maintained by the Federal Government, financed by a special tax on petrol and other petroleum products.

TABLE 19
Roads of Brazil

Region	Density: sq. kms. per km. of road	Total	Federal	State	Municipal
North	213·0	16,663	4,019	3,818	8,826
Northeast	6·3	243,442	14,224	39,649	199,569
Heartland plus R.J. and E.S.	2·2	410,463	15,262	39,374	355,827
Southern states	1·7	328,306	7,036	24,375	296,895
Western states incl. Fed. Dist.	23·3	80,578	9,560	24,100	46,918
BRAZIL	7·8	1,079,452	50,101	131,316	908,035

(Length of road systems, in kilometres spans Total, Federal, State, Municipal)

Source: Fundação I.B.G.E., Anuário Estatístico do Brasil, 1970, Instituto Brasileiro de Estatística, Rio de Janeiro, p. 399.

ROAD PATTERNS. Limitations imposed by map size make it impossible to detail here Brazil's municipal and state roads, or even the many connecting links in the Federal highway system. The accompanying schematic Map 14, however, provides an approximation of highway density patterns as well as the extent and location of construction and improvement projects during the past decade, and major new systems currently being constructed or planned by the Federal Government. The map also reflects, if imperfectly, the four principal types of road systems that developed in Brazil in the past and re-appear in the Federal programmes of the present time. These are: (1) export-import routes, which converge, fan-like, on certain ports or at the termini of 'route-zones',[25] (2) routes to establish effective control over the *sertão*, (3)routes to ensure the national presence at international frontiers and (4) routes for interregional connexion.

Sources: Rodovia, special edition 1972, and others.

Map 14. BRAZIL'S FEDERAL HIGHWAY SYSTEM IN 1972. B.H. = Belo Horizonte; G.V. = Governador Valadares.

(1) *Export-import Routes.* The Federal highway system of 1964 exhibited few patterns of this type, largely because their function of moving goods between coastal ports and the interior was being fulfilled, however inadequately, by existing state road systems. A few fan-like patterns do appear on the map, albeit in embryonic form, converging from five directions on São

Paulo, at the end of the route-zone to the port of Santos, and from three directions on Pôrto Alegre, Curitiba, Rio de Janeiro, Salvador, Maceió and Recife. These had all been intensified and expanded by 1972, with the two additional roads converging on Curitiba, the inland terminus for the route-zone to Paranaguá, being of particular interest.

This fan-and-route-zone pattern should be reinforced in coming years as the result of a joint plan proposed in 1972 by the ministers of planning, transport and finance, which is to focus investments in infrastructure development on certain export 'corridors' and their terminals. Special attention will be paid in the initial stages to the export corridors that terminate at Vitória-Tubarão, Santos, Paranaguá and Rio Grande, the inland termini for which are, respectively, Governador Vala-dares-Belo Horizonte, São Paulo, Curitiba and Pôrto Alegre, the last-named having effectively ceased to function as a deepwater port with the increasing tonnage of modern, bulk-cargo vessels.

(2) *Routes to Control the Backlands.* Historically, the organization of space around Brazil's ports, or in certain cases around centres on the eastern rim of the highlands, has been achieved in two ways: by developing local transport patterns as described above, commensurate with the needs of the time and the place, and by sending, not necessarily in the formal sense, exploratory ex-peditions into the *sertão*, or backlands. When the occasion warranted it, as for instance when the Crown in Rio de Janeiro wished to gain direct control over shipments of gold from Minas Gerais early in the nineteenth century (see also Chapter 3), roads were built in order to place these new lands and their resources within the political and financial jurisdiction of the coastal centres. Only in rare instances has the initiative originated from the interior or has the link been established primarily for the benefit of those inhabiting the *sertão*.

A recent illustration of this process is the fact that southern Goiás and southwestern Minas Gerais, two highly productive areas on the agricultural frontier, suffered from inadequate communications until the construction of Brasília, itself a product of the coastal imagination. It then became imperative to link the political resources of the new capital to the centres of power in Rio de Janeiro and São Paulo and the paved roads which were built into the area in the early 1960s are the direct result of this. The current road-building programme into the Amazon is, in part, an extension of this principle, since the idea originated in the nation's capital with the primary purpose of serving the economic interests of the Heartland and to act as an outlet for population pressures in the Northeast. These projects will certainly be of no benefit to the Amerindians who live in their path and the money and effort currently being expended on their execution are in sharp contrast to the previous lack of moral or financial support for projects, such as the road southward from Santarém, which evolved out of local demands.

(3) *Frontier Roads.* The road that is built to establish or consolidate the national presence along an international boundary also almost invariably originates with the central authorities, and it is probably safe to say that in Brazil most of those living along the frontier have tended to lose, rather than gain, by having a strong government presence among them to invigilate their activities. The earliest such routes to be built were across Rio Grande do Sul to counteract the Spanish presence in La Plata region. Brazil's southwestern border retains a similar interest today, although the gains it expects to register by road building are economic rather than military. Mention has been made of recent conflicts with Argentina over the use of the waters of the Paraná River, so it is probably more than coincidental that Brazil has built two bridges into Paraguay within six years. The first of these, the Friendship Bridge (Ponte da Amizade), inaugurated amidst great public fanfare in 1965, crosses the Paraná at Foz do Iguaçu and for the first time gives Paraguay a viable, albeit rather distant, outlet alternative to shipping its goods through Argentina, as it was given duty-free privileges at, and ultimately a first-class road to, Paranaguá, as shown on the accompanying map. In 1971 another bridge gave access to Paraguay, this time over the Apa River, which follows its border with Mato Grosso, linking up with a branch of the E. F. Noroeste do Brasil as well with a state highway. In the meantime, Brazil also built a bridge, inaugurated in 1968, over the Chuí River into Uruguay, tying that country into the new coastal highway through Rio Grande.

Overlapping in time, and perhaps to a certain extent in

concept, with recent bridge- and road-building activities along Brazil's traditional southern frontier with its Spanish-speaking neighbours, has been its drive to penetrate the Amazon with a road network that would attain its northern and western borders. Undoubtedly, the stated objective of national development has also been an important purpose, for, as one columnist put it,[26] 'The one permanent contribution that military rulers appear to make to economic development is the construction of roads. . . . To the simple, uncluttered military mind, anxious to bring order out of chaos, road-building is the obvious answer to charges of stagnation and neglect. In addition,' he goes on to say, 'new roads can serve an important strategic purpose. They often stretch into forgotten or virgin frontier lands where it is tempting for guerillas to congregate.' Here, certainly, is another reason which, when added to the desire to establish the national presence along these remote and long-neglected frontiers, may help to explain the extension of the new Amazonian highways into certain patently unremunerative corners of the Brazilian national space.

(4) *Routes for Inter-regional Connexion.* At a regional scale, with allowances made for the more fan-like pattern of highway dispersal and for distortions caused by the Serra do Mar and the resultant development of route-zones, the Brazilian road pattern fairly closely follows the model for transport expansion in underdeveloped countries proposed by Taaffe, Morrill and Gould from West African data.[27]

It is of interest to note that the Federal Government is now attempting to establish the connexions along the coast that are needed to complete the model and that have been lacking throughout the country's history, as the aforementioned authors have observed in a footnote.[28] At the time of writing, the remaining link of the quasi-coastal route between Salvador and Vitória had been completed and a major effort was being made to complete the remaining 257 kilometres of the 536-kilometre coastal road between Rio de Janeiro and Santos which was begun at a leisurely pace in 1963 as a scenic route ('Estrado do Tourismo').

In the context of Brazil's historical and economic regional geography, however, this and the other Rio–São Paulo highways must be viewed as inter-regional links rather than as part of intra-regional expansion patterns. There have, in the broadest sense, really been only three of the former, with each of the utmost importance to the particular stage of national development at which it occurred. The first of these was the eighteenth-century Rio–São Paulo road, nearly thirty years abuilding (1726–54), that linked the seaward-facing plantation region to the essentially independent, interior-oriented *bandeirante* culture that centred on São Paulo but encompassed Brazil's western and southern provinces as well.[29] This important link, which is essential to the maintenance of the Heartland as a viable regional concept, has continued to command official road- and railway-building interest to the present day, the most recent addition having been a four-lane, limited-access highway, completed in 1967, linking the two metropoli.

Two hundred years passed before the next inter-regional overland connexion was established, this time between the Heartland and the Northeast. This was triggered by World War II, when the sinking of Brazilian coastal vessels made it imperative to complete the railway line between these two regions, via Belo Horizonte and Salvador. This was superseded by a road, taking a route somewhat further to the east, which was paved in the early 1960s. The most recent, and final, inter-regional link-up was the Belém–Brasília highway which, as it connected with sketchy state roads leading in that direction, tied the Northeast as well as the Heartland into the North for the first time by an overland route. Amazonia itself was, of course, only intra-regionally linked by river (and air) transport, a fact which the east–west highways away from the main river are supposed to overcome, while roads leading southward from Santarém and Porto Velho tie the western Amazon in more closely with the Heartland.

THE AMAZON HIGHWAYS. As has been shown, there are good, or at least understandable, reasons for the recent expansion of the Brazilian highway system into Amazonia. A great deal of both national and international publicity has accompanied these ventures, although the latter has in recent years tended to emphasize, usually dramatically and often in ignorance of all the facts, the negative aspects, particularly with regard to supposed ecological damage and purported atrocities against the

Amerindians. This was not the case during the construction of the first of these routes, the 2,250-kilometre Bernado Sayão Highway,[30] more commonly known as the Belém–Brasília, although its southern terminus is, in fact, the old railhead town of Anápolis. This road took only two years to build (mid-1958 to mid-1960) and cost US $22 million, although the finishing touches such as bridge-building and paving, begun in 1968, have proved both more time-consuming and more costly.

One programme which was shelved for lack of funds envisaged fifty Federal agricultural colonies along the route. Instead, swarms of *grileiros*, or squatters, occupied the lands beside the highway unchecked and so rapidly that by 1962 it could be reported that 'there is practically no unclaimed land left along the road'.[31] A great deal has been written about this highway and about the people who gravitated towards it— lorry and bus drivers, carpetbaggers, traders, prostitutes, colonists and, with increasing frequency as travel conditions improved, tourists. Much of the frontier spirit remains, but the transients have moved on to new horizons to the north and west while the settlers have achieved a certain permanence and are gradually converting the landscape from forest to farmland, which has been described in considerable detail by Valverde and Dias.[32]

A road which received relatively little notice abroad, but which gained considerable attention from both the Brazilian business community and the public to whom it was billed by one magazine as 'the route of civilization'[33] to, one must suppose, the disgust of the residents of Acre and Rondônia, was built to link the uppermost Amazon through Cuiabá and thence by a much earlier route to southern Goiás and the eastern highway system. It is known as the Marshal Rondon Highway after the explorer who laid the telegraph line through then-unknown northern Mato Grosso (see also Chapter 2) to Acre, wrested from Bolivia only a short time before. Its various sections and branches were opened to traffic between 1965 and 1968 and were instrumental in sparking the tin mining boom in Rondônia, described in Chapter 6. After a suitable side road was built in 1972, it also provided access to the Aripuanã mine, the ore from which could now be shipped to smelters in Minas Gerais and São Paulo.

Truckers also 'pour into Acre . . . bringing in such articles as clothing and textiles, on which sellers make good profits. On their return, they take out loads of rubber, Brazil nuts and lumber, on which even more of a profit is made. . . . With a soil so fertile, in many parts, that 40-pound pineapples and yard long manioc tubers are common, farms and ranches are opening up as access to markets become easier'.³⁴ The first overland trade ever between Peru and Brazil took place when in August 1969, a Brazilian lorry left with a cargo of goods for Iberia, 70 kilometres beyond the Peruvian border. Eventually, the Rondon Highway is to continue on to Cruzeiro do Sul, in western Acre, and thence to connect to Pucallpa, to Peru's 'Jungle Highway' (Carretera da Selva) and to Lima.

It is not surprising, then, that with two examples of successful, if spontaneous and haphazard economic growth resulting from the introduction of highways into opposite corners of the Amazon Basin, the Federal Government should turn its attention to the gaping occupance void that lay between. More specifically, the idea of an east–west highway through the Amazon became 'President Médici's favourite project',³⁵ much as Brasília had been Kubitschek's a dozen years before. In June 1970, Médici signed a bill approving construction of the Trans-Amazon Highway as well as the Santarém–Cuiabá one, although this had, in fact, been started many years before but had languished because of lack of interest on the part of the central authorities. Both projects together are expected to cost about US$2,000 million. Construction of the 5,040-kilometre Trans-Amazon Highway (which equals the distance between New York and San Francisco with an additional 800 kilometres out into the sea) proceeded apace despite delays incurred during the rainy season. The first section, Estreito–Marabá, was in use by July 1971. In September 1972, President and Mrs. Médici inaugurated the completed second section, between Marabá and Itaituba, spending the night at an *agrovila* near Altamira, which is said to have been the first time in history that a Brazilian President has slept in the Amazonian rainforest. However, the former president did not realize his expectation that the entire Trans-Amazon Highway would be completed before his term expired in March 1974, when several hundred kilometres remained to be cut through the western jungles.

The completed portion of the highway is surfaced with gravel or packed earth, depending upon available materials. Trucks can traverse it safely at 40 miles per hour and passenger vehicles ('Any Brazilian can now drive his Volkswagen on the road', it is said) have been known to clip along at 70. Accessibility has already spawned the usual influx of people and the once-somnolent riverine towns through which the road passes have been greatly altered, doubling or tripling their populations in two years. Altamira is typical. Its population has risen from 6,000 to 14,000 and, in this frontier atmosphere, brawls and gunfights are frequent. In one instance, the militia was called in to quell an outbreak of violence between townsfolk and highway workers. Yet the mayor of Altamira points out that the highway has brought in not only more people, but 'more money, more shops and more goods in them. Two years ago there were 30 or 40 cars. Now there are 500. Before, there were hundreds of people who badly needed houses but had no money to build. Now buildings go up all over and Altamira is getting its first multi-storey blocks. There used to be an atmosphere of utter despair here. Today we have problems but the despair has gone. There is hope and the future seems very bright.'[36] In the rural areas bordering the Trans-Amazon, however, the spontaneous and explosive influx of settlers that accompanied the opening of the Belém–Brasília Highway is lacking[37] because of the Federal policy of regulated settlement, which is outlined in the following chapter.

It is, of course, too soon to pass judgement on the successes and failures of the Trans-Amazon Highway. Nevertheless, in 1972 President Médici announced a plan to build a 3,300-kilometre Northern Rim Road (Rodovia Perimetral Norte), proclaiming in a nationally televised speech that it 'will bring civilization to the part of Brazil north of the Amazon, a territory whose area is almost equal to the states of Minas Gerais, São Paulo, Paraná, Santa Catarina and Rio Grande do Sul put together'.[38] Construction on the Northern Rim Road began in July 1973; the eastern section as far as the Colombian border is expected to be completed in 1976, and the remainder by 1977.

The road will begin at kilometre 120 of the one between Macapá and the Serra do Navio, and skirt Brazil's northern border with the Guianas, Venezuela, Colombia and Peru, to link up eventually with the Trans-Amazon at Cruzeiro do Sul. It will cross the partially-completed road between Manaus and Boa Vista, which will be extended to the Venezuelan border. Early in 1973 the Venezuelan Minister of Transport announced that a connecting road to Caracas would be ready by the end of 1976. Another branch of the Boa Vista road will extend to the border of Guyana, there presumably to be linked to Lethem, in the Rupununi Savanna, which is already connected by a road of sorts to Georgetown. Finally, consideration is also being given to constructing a road from Santarém to Surinam, which would complete Brazil's connexions with the Guianas and, in fact, to all the countries which touch on its borders.

EPILOGUE

Early in 1967, one of the authors wrote:[39] 'There are as yet vast reservoirs of untapped and underutilized physical and human resources in Brazil. . . . Much of this . . . is due to regional differences which have been accentuated by minimal contacts and lack of integration between the regions. Yet the very emptiness and diversity, in which each unit of the Republic has its own special backlog of unused resources and skills, may ultimately prove to be among Brazil's greatest assets in an overcrowded, overused world. Improved communications and the beginnings of a modern scientific approach to resource utilization and regional integration represent the first steps towards as yet unrealized possibilities.' The key to this process is, unquestionably, the nation's infrastructure. Whatever shortcomings the military regime in Brazil may have exhibited, it has certainly improved communications and regional integration and it has also approached the problems of power resources, both hydroelectric and fossil fuel, in a rational and scientific manner. It remains to be seen whether Brazil's present form of government can do as well in mobilizing the nation's human resources for the task of national development that lies ahead.

REFERENCES

1. The figures that follow are from the Fundação I.B.G.E., *Sinopse Estatística do Brasil 1971*, Instituto Brasileiro de Estatística, Rio de Janeiro, 1971.

2. *Ibid.*, p. 350.

218 A GEOGRAPHY OF BRAZILIAN DEVELOPMENT

3. Address by Costa Cavalcanti, Minister of Mines and Power, *Brazilian Bulletin*, May 1968.

4. James, Preston E. *Latin America*, 4th edition, The Odyssey Press, New York, 1969, p. 796.

5. The demand for power of the State of São Paulo alone is about half that for all Brazil.

6. CEMIG serves all except the southernmost part of Minas Gerais, or an area about the size of France; its history and operations are described in Dickenson, J. P., 'Electric Power Development in Minas Gerais, Brazil', *Revista Geografica*, No. 70, June 1969, pp. 213–221.

7. Organization of American States, *Cuenca del Rio de la Plata, Estudio para su Planificacion y Desarollo*, 3 vols, maps, Washington, D.C., 1969–71.

8. *Brazil Herald*, December 7, 1972.

9. *Ibid.*, December 5, 1972.

10. Petrobrás was established during Getúlio Vargas' second term in office (1950–54) at the height of a wave of nationalism and denunciation of foreign economic exploitation. This period also saw the nationalization of the railways although the various expropriated lines were not put under a single government management as the Rêde Ferroviária Federal S.A. until 1957.

11. In 1971 a major effort to explore the Amazon Basin was to have been mounted with the assistance of a Japanese consortium. The scheme was shelved, however, when the latter backed out after a preliminary survey, on the grounds that the oil potential of the area was disappointing and the cost of exploration too high, a particularly discouraging verdict because that group has entered into exploration agreements with Colombia, Ecuador and Peru with regards to their share of Amazonia.

12. *The Journal of Commerce*, December 21, 1970.

13. According to the *Brazil Herald* (May 23, 1973), the rising demand for petroleum products will require a production increase of 450,000 barrels per day by 1980; this Petrobrás intends to meet by increasing its present processing capacity from 790,000 barrels per day to 1,282,000 by 1978, the first stage being the opening of the 126,000 barrels per day Araucaria refinery in Paraná scheduled for 1976.

14. Brazilian Embassy, *Boletím Especial*, Washington, D.C., December 2, 1965.

15. For a description of the island and adjacent mainland see França, Ary, *A Ilha de São Sebastião*, Universidade de São Paulo, 1954.

16. *Brazil Herald*, August 9, 1970.

17. Belo Horizonte, for instance, was not connected by a paved road to Rio de Janeiro until 1957 nor to São Paulo until 1960.

18. Compare, for instance, the views on highway development expressed by Silva, Moacir M. F. in *Kilometro Zero*, Oficina Tipografica São Bento, Rio de Janeiro, 1934, which was written during Brazil's first major period of road building that lasted until World War II, with those of Bittencourt, Edmundo Régis, *Brasil: Uma Política Rodoviaria*, Ministerio da Viação e Obras Públicas, Rio de Janeiro, 1960, at the start of

the current, second phase of highway expansion. A transitional stage in the actual planning of road construction can be observed in the Departamento Nacional de Estradas de Rodagem's *Plano Quinquenal de Obras Rodoviarias Federais—1956/1960*, M.V.O.P., Rio de Janeiro, 1956 (with maps).

19. There was some new rail laid down during this period to link up two segments of the Paraná system and to provide access to Brasília with a 246-kilometre branch line to the southern Goiás and São Paulo systems and a 400-kilometre line to Pirapora, at the head of navigation on the São Francisco, where it joins the Central Railway to Belo Horizonte and Rio de Janeiro.

20. Some relevant titles are: Alencar, Araripe, *Historia da Estrada de Ferro Vitória-Minas*, Cia.Vale do Rio Doce, Rio de Janeiro, 1954; Benevolo, Ademar, *Introdução a Historia Ferroviária do Brasil*, Ed. Folha da Manhá, Recife, 1953; Conselho Nacional de Geografia, *I Centenario das Ferrovias Brasileiras*, Serviço Gráfico do I.B.G.E., Rio de Janeiro, 1954; Gordilho, Osvaldo, *Os Transportes no Brasil*, M.V.O.P., Rio de Janeiro, 1956; Momsen, Richard P. Jr., *Routes over the Serra do Mar, op. cit.*, Chapter 1; Silva, Moacir M. F., *Geografia dos Transportes no Brasil*, Conselho Nacional de Geografia, Rio de Janeiro, 1949; Silva, Moacir M. F., *Pneu Versus Trilho*, Leo Reiter, Rio de Janeiro, 1937; Vasconcellos, Max, *Estrada de Ferro Central do Brasil*, Serviço Gráfico do I.B.G.E., Rio de Janeiro, 1947. A thumbnail sketch of the Brazilian railway system, past and present, will be found in *Communications in Brazil: making up for lost time*, The American Chamber of Commerce for Brazil, São Paulo, 1973, pp. 21–26.

21. See Chapter 6.

22. Bank of London and South America, *Bolsa Review*, Vol. 6, No. 70, October 1972.

23. *Ibid.*, p. 543.

24. It has been noted that the Federal road paving programme is proceeding at a rate of about 4,000 kilometres a year, so that at the time of publication perhaps 45,000 kilometres of the Federal road system will have been paved (there is no indication that the paving of state roads is proceeding at anything approaching that pace). On the other hand, new, unpaved road construction is also proceeding rapidly, especially in the Amazon drainage area, so that the ratio of paved to unpaved roads has probably not changed significantly. In 1972, for instance, although 3,700 kilometres of Federal highway were paved, the Government also constructed 5,200 kilometres of new roads.

25. For a discussion of this concept, see Momsen, *op. cit.*

26. Gott, Richard, 'The Military Way to National Progress', *Manchester Guardian Weekly*, July 25, 1968.

27. Taaffe, Edward J., Morrill, Richard L. and Gould, Peter R., 'Transport Expansion in Underdeveloped Countries: A Comparative Analysis', *The Geographical Review*, Vol. 53, No. 4, October, 1963, pp. 503–529. The distortions show up clearly in eastern São Paulo, whereas the road patterns to the west closely approximate the model as can be seen, for example, in Gauthier, Howard L. 'Transportation and the Growth

of the São Paulo Economy', *Journal of Regional Science*, Vol. 8, No. 1, 1968, pp. 77–94.

28. 'Cursory examination of the Brazilian pattern ... indicates a continued viability of some of the scattered ports in coastal commerce, due in part to weak lateral interconnection by land along the coast', Taafe, Morrill and Gould, *op. cit.*, p. 529.

29. For this reason, connexions between the São Paulo region and, later, that of Rio de Janeiro through southeastern Minas Gerais, to the West and South cannot be considered inter-regional as they represent only extensions of transport, through 'control routes to the backlands', from these centres.

30. Bernardo Sayão, who was killed by the branch of a falling tree while overseeing the construction of the road that has been named after him, was both a visionary and a very practical, energetic man who played many a leading role during the opening of the Goiás frontier in the 1940s and 50s: as director of Ceres, the Federal agricultural colony, as Vice-Governor and Governor of the State, as one of the prime movers in the construction of Brasília and as the principal promoter and planner of this first highway to the Amazon, which was deemed by many at the time to be an impractical, even an impossible undertaking.

31. Melo, Afrânio. 'Road of the Century', *Americas*, November 1962, p. 1.

32. Valverde, Orlando, and Dias, Catharina Vergolino. *A Rodovia Belém–Brasília, Estudo de Geografia Regional*, Fundação I.B.G.E., Rio de Janeiro, 1967. A more recent study is the Ph.D. Thesis of Allderdice, William Howard, 'The Expansion of Agriculture along the Belém–Brasília Road in Northern Goiás', Colombia University, 1972, 213 pp. (University Microfilms Order No. 73–8998).

33. 'O Caminho da Civilização', *O Cruzeiro*, July 21, 1971.

34. *Brazilian Bulletin*, May 1972.

35. *Brazil Herald*, September 26, 1972.

36. Quoted in *The Calgary Herald*, October 31, 1972.

37. The July 30, 1972, edition of the *Times of Brazil* gives a figure for that date of 8,000 families having been moved into the INCRA colonies at government expense.

38. *Brazil Herald*, October 31, 1972.

39. Momsen, Richard P. Jr. *Brazil: A Giant Stirs*, D. Van Nostrand Co. Inc., Princeton, 1968, p. 125.

CHAPTER 9

Demography and Development

*When St. Peter congratulated God upon the magnificent job He
had done in creating the land that was to become Brazil, the
Lord replied: 'Just wait until you see the people who will
be living there!'* Brazilian popular saying

Brazil not only has twice the population of any other Latin
American country but is also the only country on the continent
with an almost completely indigenous culture; what Wagley
calls 'a general framework of cultural uniformity, which
characterizes Brazil as a nation and as a distinct culture area'.[1]
Thus, unlike the countries of Hispanic America, Brazil has an
internal market that is both large and unified to support
rapid economic growth.

The first major group of colonists, many of whom were
convicts, arrived in Brazil in 1532. The failure of the Indian as
an agricultural labourer led to the introduction of African
slaves in 1538 and it is estimated that between 4 and 18 million
were brought in over the next three centuries.[2] As Gilberto
Freyre has pointed out miscegenation was more common in
Brazil than in other slave-owning colonies and today the
population of Brazil is a heterogeneous mixture of Negro, Indian
and Caucasian strains.[3] There has been some lightening of the
population between 1872 and 1950, perhaps as much in the
minds of the census takers as actual: the percentage of whites
rose from 38 to 62, whilst that of blacks and browns fell from
20 to 11 per cent and from 42 to 27 per cent respectively.
Regional differences are considerable, as illustrated in Figure 2.
Although the poor tend to be darker skinned than the rich,
overt discrimination is virtually unknown and vertical social

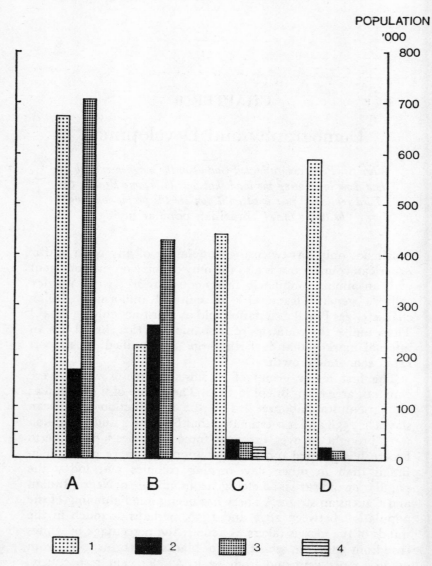

Figure 2. RACIAL COMPOSITION OF SELECTED AREAS. Key: (1) white, (2) Negro, (3) mixed, (4) yellow; Locations: A. coastal zone of Pernambuco, B. zone of the Recôncavo, C. northern Paraná. D. plains area of Rio Grande do Sul. Source: *Atlas Nacional do Brasil*, I.B.G.E., 1966, Plate V–1

and economic mobility is possible.[4] Even the isolated Indian tribes of Amazonia are now being brought into the national life, although not always with the happiest results.

Early settlement was along the coast of Northeastern Brazil, focused on the ports which provided the link with Europe. The transfer of the Vice-Regal capital in 1763 from Salvador to Rio de Janeiro recognized the change in the settlement pattern brought about by the migration towards the mines and new agricultural frontiers in the centre and south of the country. Two centuries later the creation of a new capital, Brasília, encouraged westward movement towards still newer frontiers. The coastal region is still the most densely peopled part of the country but the mean centre of population moved 182 miles south and west between 1872 and 1950.[5]

TABLE 20

Regional Population Distribution, 1872–1970

Region	1872	1890	1900	1920 (percentage)	1940	1950	1960	1970
North	3·35	3·32	3·99	4·70	3·55	3·55	3·67	3·86
Northeast	41·04	36·99	33·93	31·86	30·02	29·54	26·30	25·29
Heartland	31·75	35·52	38·34	38·00	38·09	37·15	36·97	35·90
Periphery	11·60	10·79	10·23	11·00	12·26	13·33	15·86	17·28
Rimland	12·26	13·38	13·51	14·34	16·08	16·43	17·20	17·67

Many of the migrants have come from the traditionally densely-populated Northeast and the proportion of the nation's population in this region has steadily declined since the first modern census in 1872 (Table 20), although in absolute numbers the population of the Northeast has increased from 4·1 million in 1872 to 23·8 million in 1971 and is adding a further one million people each year. In the early twentieth century many Northeasterners went to the Amazon hoping to participate in the rubber boom and it was at this time that the North attained its highest proportion of the nation's population (not including, of course, the pre-Columbian period). Around the turn of this century, as industrialization took root, the industrial Heartland became the most populous region of Brazil. By 1940 São Paulo had surpassed Minas Gerais in population to become the most populous state in the nation and has continued to grow relative to the other states. The spread of coffee into Paraná after the Second World War was accompanied by rapid population growth there, while the other states of the Periphery have also experienced steady growth, especially in the 'sixties. In the Rimland Rio Grande do Sul's proportion of Brazil's population has declined since 1940 but this has been more than balanced by rapid growth in the westerly states of the region. During the 'sixties the nation's fastest growing states were Mato Grosso, Goiás, the Federal District, Amapá and Paraná. Overall demographic density is very low at only 11 people per square kilometre, but it varies from 0·18 per square kilometre in Roraima to 368·552 people per square kilometre in Guanabara.

The 94·5 million Brazilians counted in the 1970 census made up 33·4 per cent of Latin America's population and 2·6 per cent of the world's population. In 1850 Brazil had only 21·5 per cent of Latin America's population and 0·6 per cent of the world's. In September 1972, when Brazil celebrated 150 years of independence, the population was estimated at 100 million, making Brazil the seventh most populous nation in the world after China, India, the Soviet Union, United States, Japan and Indonesia.

The rate of annual increase rose from 2·4 per cent in the period 1940–50 to 3·0 per cent in the decade 1950–60 and fell slightly to 2·9 per cent in the 'sixties. In the 'seventies the rate of natural increase has been estimated at 2·8 per cent which would lead to a doubling of the population in twenty-five years. The Federal Government opposes family planning since it feels that the population increase poses no problem as long as the rate of economic growth is over three times higher. This view, however, does not take into account regional variations, particularly such problem areas as the Northeast, where the population growth rate is above the national average but little economic growth is taking place.

Most of the population increase arises from a declining death-rate combined with a continuing high birthrate. Deathrates fell from more than 3·0 per cent to 0·9 per cent between 1850 and 1970. The birthrate, which had been as high as 4·5 per cent in 1960, did fall to 3·8 per cent in 1970, possibly reflecting the growing urbanization of the population.[6] The population remains a young one, slightly more than half of all Brazilians being under 20 years old and only 5 per cent being over 60 years of age.

HEALTH

The life expectancy of Brazilians has increased from 43 years in 1940 to 59 years in 1970. This relatively short average life span is largely the result of high child mortality. In Brazil 105 children in every 1,000 die before they reach five years of age as compared, for instance, to 7·4 per thousand in the Netherlands for the same age group. If a Brazilian reaches the age of 40 he has a high probability of living to the age of 75. Much of the effect of a higher average life expectancy on the economic life of the country, however, is vitiated if the vast proportion of the population is malnourished and suffering from various endemic parasitic diseases.

Some twenty-five years ago 80 per cent of the young men liable for military service were found to be unfit because of malnutrition and even today diets are deficient throughout most of the North and Northeast. These deficiencies reflect superstition and ignorance of dietary needs as well as poverty and food shortages. Between 1955 and 1967, however, there was a slight improvement in daily per capita intake of calories and proteins and in South America only Argentina, Uruguay and Chile exceeded Brazil in average dietary levels. Undernourished people fall prey to disease especially in areas without proper sanitary facilities. It was suggested in 1971 that only one-tenth of Brazil's population was not suffering from some sort of parasitic disease,[7] such as bilharzia, ameobic dysentery or Chagas disease. Medical services, potable water and modern sewage facilities are concentrated in the main cities and these have long been free of most tropical diseases.[8] Rural migrants moving to urban areas, however, have recently re-infected some metropolitan districts with bilharzia and Chagas disease.

The Federal Government has given high budgetary priority to the solving of the nation's health problems. Imaginative methods are being used to take medical services into isolated areas. Bus clinics and hospital ships are in operation in the North and Northeast and in 1967 Project Rondón was formed to take Brazilian university students out into the backlands as domestic 'Peace Corps' type volunteers to teach hygiene and provide medical assistance. Public health services are being improved, with special attention to the health of new settlers in the Amazon region, and considerable investments are being made in urban hospital facilities and the mass distribution of low cost medicines and nutritional supplements. Regional variations in the availability of medical services, however, are still marked. In the industrial core there is one hospital bed for every 200 persons and one doctor per 1,600 inhabitants, whereas the ratios for the Northeast are 630 and 5,700 respectively.

EDUCATION

Until recently the proportion of Brazilians able to read and write increased only slowly from 35 per cent in 1900 to 49 per cent in 1950. Education did not keep pace with population growth so that the absolute number of illiterates increased. In 1970, 37 per cent of the male and 40 per cent of the female population over five years of age was illiterate. Only Bolivia in South America had a lower literacy rate. Differences in literacy levels between the sexes, however, declined significantly during the 'sixties. Educational facilities are most easily available in urban areas and by 1964, 73 per cent of Brazil's urban population as compared to 33 per cent of the rural dwellers was able to read and write. This effect is clearly seen in the state of Amazonas, where only in the capital city, Manaus, did literacy exceed 50 per cent.[9] The literacy rate was lowest in the states of Alagoas, Piauí and Maranhão, with barely one-fifth of the population literate, while in Rio Grande do Sul, São Paulo and Santa Catarina over half and in Guanabara more than three-quarters of the population could read and write. Despite having had for many years the highest literacy rate in the nation, Guanabara State still contained over 40,000 illiterates in 1972.

A crash programme, the *Movimento Brasileiro de Alfabetização*, or *Mobral*, funded by revenue from the weekly national football pools and from private companies, who are allowed to earmark one per cent of their Federal income tax for this purpose, was established in 1970 to teach the illiterate 30 per cent of Brazilians over 15 years of age. In the first two years of operation *Mobral*

taught 2·3 million adults to read, write and do simple arith-
metic sufficient for participation in modern industrial society.
By the end of 1974, it is expected that the programme will have
reached 7·2 million people and by 1980 it is hoped that all those
capable of learning will be literate.

At the same time changes are being made in more conven-
tional education. With growing public interest, spending on
education has doubled and long-standing deficiencies are
finally being attacked by government. The proportion of school
teachers and pupils in the population doubled between 1958
and 1968, with Rio Grande do Sul having the highest figure for
primary students and Guanabara for secondary students. By
1972, 15 million children were in primary school, more than
double the number of a decade ago, but some 35 per cent of the
eligible children were still not in class. Of those who start
primary school, one-fifth enter secondary school and only 3·5
per cent finish, whilst a mere 1·1 per cent graduate from
university. Buildings are often inadequate and teachers un-
trained, especially in the rural areas, and there is a general
shortage both of teachers and of school and university places.
Consequently many students who pass the highly competitive
college entrance examinations cannot be admitted,[10] although
the number of students attending college increased five times
between 1963 and 1971. The curriculum is old-fashioned, little
science or technology is taught and teaching methods are
based on rote-learning. Teachers are badly paid and even
university professors hold other jobs to obtain an adequate
income. Reform of higher education was instituted in 1972.
The credit system and an optional twelve-month academic
year have been introduced and the '*campus avançado*', or branch
campus, is being used as a way of bringing higher education to
isolated areas. More emphasis is being put on advanced
technical and agricultural education[11] and the federal government has provided funds for universities to upgrade their most
important departments by offering professors salaries that are
high enough to allow them to work full time in the universities.
In the less-developed areas the development agencies have
channelled funds into education. In the Northeast, for example,
SUDENE between 1963 and 1968 trained 23,863 primary
teachers, built 2,934 classrooms and equipped a further 5,516.

The percentage of persons over six years of age in the region who could read and write increased from 32 per cent in 1958 to 49 per cent in 1968. Over the same period the number of high school diplomas gained increased by 203 per cent compared with the national average increase of 175 per cent and graduates of higher education increased by 238 per cent as compared with the national average of 155 per cent.[12]

EMPLOYMENT

Improvements in education have contributed to greater population mobility in both place of residence and employment. The proportion of the nation's workforce in agriculture fell from 52 per cent in 1960 to 46 per cent in 1970, whilst the share of the labour force in the service industries rose from 25 to 30 per cent, absorbing the greater part of the labour released by agriculture. Modern capital-intensive manufacturing provides limited job opportunities and only in São Paulo, Rio de Janeiro and Guanabara does the proportion of the workforce in this sector exceed that in agriculture. About one-third of the agricultural labour is provided by unpaid family workers and it is in this category that most of the women agricultural workers are found. Unemployment levels vary regionally from 3 per cent in Guanabara to 0·7 per cent in Maranhão, whilst underemployment averages 11 per cent and is highest in the Northeast and lowest in Paraná.[13] Product per person employed is less than the Latin American average[14] but the economic boom of the last decade is directly related to the existence of a tightly controlled labour force working long hours for low wages.

POPULATION MOVEMENT

RURAL-URBAN MIGRATION. This has become the dominant type of population movement, stimulated by improved communications, changes in the structure of the rural economy and a growing awareness of the higher levels of income and services available in urban areas. Much migration is step-wise from small town to regional centre, with the biggest cities attracting the greatest number of migrants. As in most parts of Latin America, rural migrants include a high proportion of women and are younger and have less education than city dwellers.

The first spurt of migration from the countryside to the towns came with the emancipation of the slaves in 1888. The consequent economic upheavals in rural areas led both masters and former slaves to move to the cities. In 1890 the present state of Guanabara had nearly half a million people, 30 per cent of whom were foreign born and 26 per cent migrants from various parts of Brazil. By 1950 the city of Rio de Janeiro had 2·3 million inhabitants, of whom only 9 per cent were foreign born whilst 40 per cent were migrants from elsewhere in Brazil. Nearly 17 per cent of these Brazilian migrants moved to Rio during the decade 1940–50. The effect of distance on this migration can be seen in both 1890 and 1950, when more than half the movers came from the neighbouring states of Rio de Janeiro and Minas Gerais, but the push effect of the intermittent droughts in the Northeast is also apparent, since this region supplied one-quarter of the immigrants in 1890 and one-fifth in 1950. According to the censuses of both 1950 and 1970 the states of the Northeast all had a net outmigration, as did Minas Gerais, Espírito Santo and Rio Grande do Sul. Minas Gerais had the highest number of outmigrants, whilst São Paulo attracted the greatest number of immigrants. In 1970 one-third of Brazil's population was living in a município other than that in which it had been born and migrants provided 57 per cent of the population increase, 1960–70, in Brazil's nine metropolitan areas.

Since 1950 changes in agriculture from traditional labour intensive crop production to livestock ranching demanding little labour have opened the way for increased rural-urban migration. During the 'fifties and 'sixties São Paulo became a major focus for migrants with more than one-quarter million arriving in some years. Virtually all the population growth of Brasília in the 'sixties was due to immigration from within Brazil, until the municipality of the Federal capital contained 524,315 urban dwellers in 1970. In that year 49 per cent of the nation's migrants had moved from urban to urban localities, 19 per cent from rural to urban and 6 per cent from urban to rural.

Daily movement or commuting is also becoming important as housing costs and shortages in the big cities force workers to live in distant suburbs, despite the fact that increasing traffic congestion slows the journey to work. In São Paulo it now takes an average of three hours to travel to and from work. Even in the planned city of Brasília some 60,703 commuters, mainly construction and service workers, travel as much as 130 kilometres round-trip on a four-hour journey to work from the satellite cities of the Federal District to the centre of Brasília. These commuters raise the population of the capital every day by almost one-third and are badly needed for the physical growth of the city. They cannot afford the capital's high rents for housing since they are usually paid only the minimum wage.[15]

RURAL-RURAL MIGRATION. The main movement within rural areas is towards the agricultural frontier by landless peasants in search of land and by large ranchers opening up new areas for commercial production. The severe drought of 1877–79 in the Northeast stimulated movement into the Amazon region with as many as 50,000 persons going in one year. These people became *seringueiros*, who collected the rubber on which the prosperity of Amazonia was based. By 1930 the rubber boom was over and the area lost whatever attraction it might have had to immigrants. In the next two decades the major movement was into the most westerly parts of São Paulo state. Between 1920 and 1939, 831,343 migrants went to work on farms in São Paulo, a high proportion coming from Bahia, Alagoas, Pernambuco, Sergipe and Ceará.[16] In the 'forties this movement spread into Paraná, following the expansion of coffee-growing into that state. Then came the opening up of the Rio Doce Valley and movement into Goiás and Maranhão. In the 'sixties the 'marcha para oeste' continued, with Brasília as a major focal point and much of Mato Grosso being opened up for large-scale ranching. The building of new roads has encouraged the movement to the frontier with some one million people settling along the Belém–Brasília highway.

Planned colonization, both private and government supported, has always played a part in this movement, especially in Paraná, where the British Paraná Company was responsible for much early development. In the 'seventies government colonization projects are becoming increasingly important, especially in the North. The World Bank has granted a £1 million credit for a SUDENE project to settle 5,000 Northeastern families on 200,000 hectares of fertile land in Maranhão,[17] but perhaps the most imaginative and biggest project of the decade is that in Amazonia. Along the Trans-Amazon highway the Federal Government has reserved to itself ownership of a strip of land 100 kilometres wide on either side of the road. Through INCRA (the National Institute of Colonization and Agrarian Reform) it has publicized this fact and even issued warnings against swindlers whose advertisements are appearing in newspapers offering land for sale in the Amazon region. Based on lessons learned from the Belém–Brasília Highway and from experence gained at the colonies it established along the highway through the rainforest in northern Maranhão, INCRA is planning to settle selected farmers, drawn mostly from the Northeast, on 100-hectare plots each with 500 metres of main road frontage, focusing on *agrovilas* located at 100-kilometre intervals along the highway. These contain a school, health post, research station and various government agencies, including an office of the extension service, as well as a brickworks and a sawmill. Potential colonists must be poor but with a good credit rating (how this is established is a cause for conjecture); they must also have a family workforce equivalent to at least $2\frac{1}{2}$ adults, farming experience and a 'capacity for work'. Those who meet these criteria are given free transport to their land, a small house and a loan, which may amount to as much as £1,000, to get them started. The government estimates that 18 million people will settle in the area in the next two decades. This may be over-optimistic as some disillusioned colonists are already leaving the area for the cattle ranches of Acre, Rondônia, Mato Grosso and Goiás, but INCRA insists that it will settle 500,000 colonists in the area by 1975 and the 1972 Federal budget allocated £1 million for land reform and irrigation projects and £0·8 million for colonization of the region.

Seasonal migration, associated with both shifting agriculture and transhumance, is also a way of life amongst Brazilian peasants. In addition, there is, in many areas, a seasonal flow of farm labour such as that from the semi-arid cotton-producing areas of the Northeastern *sertão* to work in the sugar cane or cocoa harvest on the coastal plantations.

FOREIGN IMMIGRATION. Immigration during the nineteenth

and twentieth centuries, mainly of European origin, played a major role in Brazil's development. Carneiro recognizes three main periods: from 1808 to 1886; from 1887 to 1930; and since 1930.[18] Immigration began after 1808 when Dom João granted foreigners rights to hold land in Brazil. Planned foreign immigration began in 1820 when a group of Swiss colonists founded the city of Novo Friburgo in the state of Rio de Janeiro. Elsewhere, the early colonies were on the coastal lowlands, but gradually colonization followed the river valleys into the highlands (Map 15). During this first period immigrants provided supplementary labour to that of the slaves and settled on small farms without slaves in southern Brazil. The flow of immigrants, mainly from Germany and northern Italy, was fairly small, eventually increasing to a peak of 30,747 in 1876.

In the decade following the American Civil War some 3,000 disillusioned Confederates left the American South for Brazil where they hoped to perpetuate the plantation way of life based on slave labour. Of the four colonies founded by this atypical group of immigrants, the three most northerly ones failed because of isolation and poverty but in Santa Barbara, São Paulo, where only colonists with capital could settle because of land prices, they were able to buy slaves and were accessible to a market. The colonists resisted assimilation for four generations but finally began to intermarry with Brazilians and to leave the colony for the city.

In the second period the post-emancipation demand for labour in the coffee plantations of São Paulo led to a high rate of immigration, reaching an all-time peak of 216,110 in 1891, when Brazil's population was only 15 million, with over half the immigrants from southern Italy and Sicily. Between half and two-thirds of the new settlers went to the state of São Paulo. Not until the First World War did the rate begin to decline, falling to 19,793 in 1918. During these years, however, the United States received about eight times as many immigrants as Brazil.

After 1930 restrictions were put on the naturalization of foreigners and somewhat later a quota system was introduced for all immigrants except the Portuguese. This ended the high rate of Japanese immigration which, although some Japanese

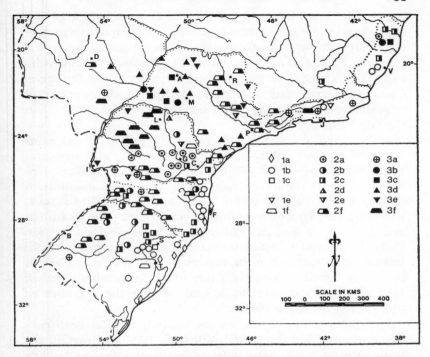

Map 15. ORGANIZED COLONIES OF SOUTHEASTERN BRAZIL. Vertical columns, (1) established before 1870, (2) established 1870–1930, (3) established after 1930; horizontal lines, 1a. Azorean, 2a. Slav, 3a. IBRA nucleus, 1–3b. German, 1–3c. Italian, 2–3d. Japanese, 1e. Swiss, 2–3e. others, including Brazilian nationals, 1–3f. mixed. Place names: A. Araçatuba; B. São Borja; C. Curitiba; D. Campo Grande; E. Florianópolis; G. Ponta Grossa; I. Foz do Iguaçu; J. Rio de Janeiro; L. Londrina; M. Marília; P. São Paulo; R. Ribeirão Preto; S. Caxias do Sul; T. Pôrto Alegre; V. Vitória. After: *Atlas Nacional do Brasil*, I.B.G.E., 1966, Plate III–6.

had entered as early as 1908, reached its peak in the late 'twenties and early 'thirties. This was also the major period of German immigration. There was little immigration during the War, when Brazil supported the Allies against the countries which had supplied so many of its new settlers. In 1950 half the naturalized Brazilians and three-fifths of the foreigners were living in the state of São Paulo. At that time there were over one million foreigners living in Brazil, of whom most were Portuguese, Italian, Japanese and Spanish, making up 2 per cent of the total population. There was a resurgence of immigration in the early 'fifties with 84,720 people arriving in 1952, but from 1955 to 1961 the flow averaged only about 50,000 per year. After this last date political and economic difficulties in Brazil coupled with growing opportunities in the European Common Market led to a rapid decline in the number of migrants going to Brazil, only about 6,000 per year arriving in the late 'sixties.

In the 150 years 1819 to 1969, 5·8 million immigrants entered Brazil, 3·9 million of them between 1887 and 1930 and 1·4 million between 1887 and 1898, of whom 0·8 million were Italian.[19] The national composition of the immigrants is dominated by two countries, Italy and Portugal. In 1902, however, the Italian government prohibited the recruiting and granting of free passage to immigrants destined for São Paulo because of complaints received about the treatment of Italian labourers on Paulista fazendas. The São Paulo government was forced to look elsewhere for its farm labour and in 1907 the state government agreed to pay the expenses of transporting Japanese to Brazil.

Portuguese immigration, on the other hand, has been consistent throughout the period, although total numbers in the peak year of 1913 were only 76,701 and only in the late 'fifties and early 'sixties, when many Azoreans were escaping the effects of a volcanic eruption, did it go against the general trend and increase. In the 150 years up to 1969 Portugal contributed 1·8 million people to Brazil's population, against 1·6 million from Italy, 0·7 million from Spain, 0·3 million from Japan and 0·2 million from Germany. Many Italians and Spaniards, however, moved on to Argentina or returned to Europe. There have undoubtedly been many immigrants from other South American countries who do not appear in the official statistics. In 1972, for the first time in over half a century, the Portuguese were not the largest immigrant group entering Brazil. The most numerous were the Koreans (1,895), followed by Portuguese (807), with Americans third (675). Chilean immigration, barely recorded in previous years, amounted to 224, reflecting opposition to the Marxist government in that country. Immigrants from the United States have never been numerically important but since 1960 their numbers have increased, perhaps related to dissatisfaction with contemporary life in the United States and the growth of American investment and firms in Brazil, so that, with the overall decline in foreign immigration, United States citizens made up almost one-fifth of the total flow during the 'sixties.

The immigrants have contributed to Brazil's culture and economy much more than their actual numbers would suggest. All of them have provided much needed labour to support Brazil's growth and because many of them came from more highly industrialized nations they were especially important in providing both entrepreneurship and skilled labour for Brazil's industrial revolution. The Germans in southern Brazil and to a lesser extent the Italians and Japanese in São Paulo have given these regions of Brazil a distinctive cultural ambiance. Those immigrants who settled on the land showed that family farms could be successful in Brazil. Foreign agricultural colonies were instrumental in settling the agricultural frontier.[20] Most such colonies were successful because they received financial assistance, usually in the form of free land, and the colonists often had a higher level of capital and skills than the Brazilian pioneer farmer. The immigrants introduced more modern intensive farming methods and new crops. The Swiss and Dutch developed commercial dairying, whilst the Japanese have led the way in the production of black pepper, jute, tea and silk. This latter group have tended to concentrate on market gardening close to cities, especially São Paulo, and have gained a virtual monopoly of vegetable and chicken production. They sell over 90 per cent of Brazil's commercial egg production and have formed large and successful production and marketing cooperatives. Immigrants have also been important in the development of specialized agro-industries such as wine, tobacco and leather, and São Paulo has the only saké plant in the southern hemisphere. Both Nippo-Brazilians and the Japanese Government are increasingly investing in industry. Tokyo is showing great interest in this country of vast unoccupied lands and unexploited resources with anticipated investment in the early 'seventies of £600 million in steel, petrochemicals and port installations.

TOURISM. During the decade of the 'sixties tourists became more numerous than immigrants. Their numbers increased from 53,314 in 1959 to 290,992 in 1971, and Brazil expects to welcome 2·5 million by 1980. South American countries, especially the relatively rich neighbouring nations of Argentina and Uruguay, supply the greatest number of tourists but the United States is rapidly becoming the most important single tourist source. The number of tourists from Western Europe, especially Germans, and from Japan has shown the most rapid rate of growth as new direct air links with Brazil have been developed.

Most tourists, 132,094 in 1971, arrive in Guanabara and 80 per cent of the nation's visitors spend at least one night there. There is a seasonal peak in the nation's tourist trade in January and February, coinciding with Carnival in Rio, with a secondary peak in July. The second most popular state of entry is Rio Grande do Sul where 68,277 visitors, predominantly Argentineans and Uruguayans, entered Brazil in 1971.

Brazil does have tourist attractions other than the *cidade maravilhosa* of Rio de Janeiro but the government is having difficulty attracting many tourists to other areas of the country. Many of the official tourist attractions are concentrated within a day's drive of Rio (Map 16). A new bridge to Niterói and Cabo Frio has reduced the travel time from Rio to many formerly almost inaccessible beach resorts. New and improved roads, increased car ownership and long distance bus services are opening up many areas for domestic holiday travel. Land speculation is rife and much farmland in coastal Rio de Janeiro state is being subdivided for weekend homes.

The national tourist agency is encouraging investment in tourism by granting fiscal incentives to both corporations and private individuals. At the end of the 'sixties there were 8,324 hotels in Brazil but only forty-three were of luxury-class standard and occupancy rates were low. Both foreign hotel chains and local investors are building many new top-class hotels and in 1972 the largest hotel in Latin America was opened in Rio de Janeiro. In the Northeast and North, with the help of their respective development agencies, modern hotels are being built in all the major cities. The hotel industry had a relatively low labour input employing only 1 person per 2·7 guest rooms as compared to an average of one employee per 0·6 guest rooms in the Caribbean.[21] Yet in 1969 tourism earned Brazil only £1 million in foreign exchange, whilst Brazilian travellers spent more than four times as much abroad.

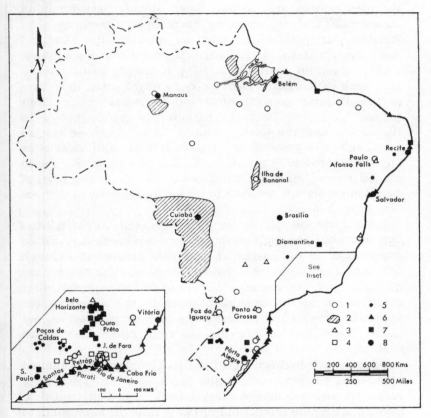

Map 16. TOURIST ATTRACTIONS. (1) national or state park; (2) hunting area; (3) natural scenic attraction; (4) mountain resort; (5) spa; (6) beach resort; (7) historical city; (8) capital city. After: *Atlas Nacional do Brasil*, I.B.G.E., 1966, Plate V–6; Benham, F. C., *Turismo e Veraneio nas Regiões periféricas da metrópole Carioca*, Universidade Federal do Rio de Janeiro, Rio, 1971, maps facing pp. 8, 50 and 54; and *Brazilian Bulletin*, September 1968, p. 7.

URBANIZATION

In Brazil, as in many other parts of the world, people are being increasingly attracted to the cities. It has been estimated that if the world's biggest cities go on growing at their present rate, by that ominous year 1984 São Paulo could be one of the largest cities in the world.[22] This is a very disturbing prospect as the metropolitan area of São Paulo already has $9\frac{1}{2}$ million inhabitants and is becoming increasingly unmanageable. Reservoirs are polluted, there are no fish in the Rio Tietê and roads are congested. It has been suggested that the subway, which came into operation in 1975, is already inadequate to cope with its passenger load. Cubatão near Santos, the centre of the Paulista petrochemical industry, has the dubious honour of having both the highest per capita income in the nation and the worst pollution. A rising crime rate in São Paulo city resulted in 11,400 robberies and assaults in 1971 compared to 3,750 in 1968. But as long as São Paulo can offer more attractive job opportunities than most parts of Brazil migrants will continue to trudge into the city at the rate of 150 per hour.

Early towns founded in Brazil were generally at coastal sites and not until the eighteenth century was there any urban development in the interior. Towns grew up around a church or a fort and combined defensive functions with the typical administrative and commercial ones of colonial times. Unlike the situation in the Spanish colonies in the Americas, the upper-class Portuguese settlers lived on their plantations, not in the towns, and colonial life was rural rather than urban centred.

Where routes between a port and its hinterland were limited by natural barriers, such as the Serra do Mar, it has been suggested that a complementary inland settlement tended to develop at the convergence of routeways from the hinterland, as in the juxtaposition of Santos and São Paulo.[23] The critical moment when São Paulo's growth overtook that of its port came when its trade with the hinterland surpassed its overseas trade channelled through Santos. This model suggests comparisons with other 'coupled nuclei' such as Barra Mansa–Angra dos Reis and Curitiba–Paranaguá and has successfully predicted the growth of Governador Valadares which, in the 1970 census for the first time recorded a larger population than its port Vitória.

As urban growth has become more closely linked to industrialization, the ports and administrative centres of colonial times have declined in relative importance (Table 21). The cities of the industrial Heartland have increasingly come to dominate the nation's urban hierarchy, although there are signs that this trend may be slowing. Between 1960 and 1970 regional centres of the Northeast and the Rimland, such as Feira de Santana and Campo Grande, joined the ranks of Brazil's fifty largest cities but at the same time the number of Paulista cities in this category increased from 12 to 14. In the 'sixties São Paulo usurped Rio's traditional position as the most populous city in Brazil, but growth was especially rapid in the industrialized satellite cities of both of these major metropoli. Meanwhile, the more functionally specialized cities, such as the resort town of Petrópolis and the steel town of Volta Redonda, grew less rapidly.

TABLE 21

Location of the Fifty Largest Cities in Brazil, 1940–70

Characteristic	1940	1950	1960	1970
Coastal	18	17	16	14
Heartland	21	24	26	26
State capitals	19	20	21	21
Non-state capitals outside Heartland	11	8	8	8
Non-state capitals north of Minas Gerais	5	3	2	3

After: Santos, Milton, 'Croissance nationale et nouvelle armature urbaine au Brésil', *Annales de Géographie*, 77 (419), 1968, pp. 37–63 and I.B.G.E., 1971, *op. cit.*

In 1970 for the first time there were more Brazilians living in towns than in rural areas. The urban proportion of the population increased from 31 per cent in 1940 to 56 per cent in 1970 while the number of town dwellers rose from 12·9 million to 52·9 million. Yet in only seven states and the two city states of Guanabara and the Federal District did the urban population exceed the rural population. In São Paulo State four-fifths, and in Rio de Janeiro State 77 per cent, of the population was urban whilst urban dwellers also outnumbered the rural populace in Minas Gerais, Rio Grande do Sul, Pernambuco and the two sparsely-populated Rimland mining territories of Amapá and Rondônia. Geiger and Oxnard detect four major patterns in recent population changes: in metropolitan areas there is both suburban population growth and increasing rural density near the city; urban growth is greatest in cities located in developing agricultural regions and in the higher ranking cities in the central place hierarchy; in São Paulo there is a trend towards an absolute decline of the rural population; and in southern Brazil the patterns of rural and urban growth reflect differences between ranching and cropland farming, between old colonial areas and pioneer zones and between cities with some industrialization and those with none.[24]

The urban network is most complete in the Heartland and in Rio Grande do Sul, where it is based on industrial growth spread through Canoas, Esteio, São Leopoldo and Novo Hamburgo, all of which are municipalities of the metropolitan area of Pôrto Alegre. In Mato Grosso and Goiás the urban network reached a better balance during the 'sixties following the catalytic development of Brasília, the Federal capital, which grew from 92,761 to 268,615, at an annual rate of 14·4 per cent, to become in 1970 the nation's eleventh largest urban municipality. In the Northeast, which has traditionally been characterized by large coastal cities such as Recife and Salvador, both of which had over one million people in 1970, and small inland towns, the 'sixties saw the growth of a number of medium sized cities such as Sobral and Caruaru as interior regional centres. In the North Belém and Manaus continued to dominate, containing over half the region's urban population in 1970, the next two largest towns, Santarém and Macapá, having only 52,000 inhabitants each by this date

In 1940 there were twenty-two towns of over 50,000 people but by 1970 there were 115. The bigger cities have tended to grow more rapidly than the smaller ones. In the 'sixties the annual population growth rate for cities of less than 10,000 inhabitants was only 2·3 per cent but was 6·1 per cent for larger cities. The proportion of the urban population living in cities of over 10,000 increased from 58 per cent in 1940 to 79 per cent in 1970. Of the nation's eleven largest urban municipalities only in Guanabara, where migrants tended to settle in the satellite towns of Greater Rio rather than in the city itself, was the annual population growth rate less than the rate for the country as a whole.

Inequalities in the distribution of economic development and particularly of industrialization have led to irregularities in the rank-size hierarchy, in particular to the overwhelming dominance of the two primate cities of São Paulo and Rio, which in 1970 contained 11 per cent of the nation's population. The irregularities are most marked in the outlying areas of the Northeast, North and West, where cities are characterized by a population growth out of proportion to their socio-economic status.[25] Modern industrialization has become concentrated in the metropolitan areas of São Paulo, Rio, Belo Horizonte, Recife and Pôrto Alegre and is associated with a wide range of functions and industrial activities, a high proportion of people over 14 years because of selective migration, and greater regional accessibility. Outside the major metropolitan centres there is a dynamic peripheral group of cities stretching from Santa Maria in Rio Grande do Sul, to Ponta Grossa in Paraná, Campo Grande in Mato Grosso, Uberaba-Uberlândia in Minas Gerais and Vitória in Espírito Santo. These cities are characterized by a more limited commercial structure and lower levels of accessibility but high population growth rates.[26]

The rapid rate of growth of the cities has led to an inevitable deterioration in the quality of urban life. Municipal government is notoriously inefficient.[27] After a heavy rainstorm in Rio de Janeiro *favelas* slide down hillsides, drinking water is polluted, and power and telephones are cut off for days. Beaches such as Copacabana have become polluted because of untreated sewage dumped in the sea too close to shore. Most of the large cities of Brazil have reached saturation point in terms of traffic. The rapid spread of motor vehicles amongst a populace many of whom are little educated, and on to a highway system designed for much lower traffic densities has given Brazil one of the highest rates of traffic fatalities in the world. In 1972 one-third of the nation's deaths resulting from traffic accidents occurred in the city of São Paulo. This was an increase of 28 per cent over the previous year with only one-tenth more vehicles on São Paulo's streets.[28] Migrants to the city bring with them little but disease. In São Paulo State one-sixth of the population was born outside the state and one-quarter of these migrants is illiterate. It is becoming increasingly difficult for modern urban economies to absorb unskilled and uneducated workers. Many migrants are forced to turn to the so-called 'service' industries of shoe-shining, prostitution and begging. Faced with shops full of unobtainable consumer goods some turn to crime to survive. Family structures break down and children are abandoned in the streets. The state orphanages cannot cope with the numbers of such children and so many become juvenile gangsters. In this situation it is easy for urban guerillas to find a niche.

Attempts are being made to improve the urban environment, as when the floating shanties of Manaus were removed in 1965. Forty-one *favelas* have been bulldozed from the steep hillsides of southern Guanabara, to be replaced by neat public housing developments in the smoggy suburbs, where there is less community spirit and the journey to work is longer and more expensive. On the other hand, about 40 per cent of the country's vacant houses are located in the Heartland, and Guanabara and São Paulo have the lowest average number of persons per occupied dwelling. The National Housing Bank has built over 700,000 low cost housing units since it was set up in 1965, but estimates that it has satisfied only about one-tenth of existing demand. The Bank is financed by an 8 per cent payroll tax and lends the money back to the workers to finance the purchase of houses, and also supplies working capital for the building materials industry. It is planned to build two million houses in the next ten years to be sold to low-income families at monthly instalment rates of not more than 20 per cent of the legal minimum wage.[29] There is a growing feeling that the reasonably liveable *favelas* should not be destroyed. The housing may be substandard and the crime rate high but television aerials abound, and these slums are the homes of the celebrated samba schools and a strong popular culture.

The Bank is now turning its attention to improving the availability of urban services. In 1950, 39·5 per cent of urban houses had piped water compared to 1·4 per cent in rural areas. By 1970, 53 per cent of the people who lived in Brazil's cities had piped water and one-quarter had access to the public sewage system. The Bank aims to bring sanitation and potable water to four-fifths of the urban population by 1980. In practice the big cities will subsidize the small towns with a maximum limit on the water rates of 5 per cent of the legal minimum wage.

Many cities in Brazil are world-renowned for their beauty; either natural as, for example, Rio and Salvador, or architectural, notably Niemeyer's Brasília[30] or the colonial splendours of Ouro Prêto. If these attributes are to survive then the urban explosion must be contained. The development of new towns and secondary industrial complexes, as in the Paraíba Valley, is one way of diverting population from the big cities. Brazil has a long history of the successful creation of planned new towns. In addition to the well-known example of Brasília, Belo Horizonte, now the third largest city in Brazil, was established less than one hundred years ago as the state capital of Minas Gerais, and Goiânia, now bigger than the neighbouring Federal capital, was established in 1939, replacing an isolated former mining centre as the capital of the state of Goiás. In the 'seventies the opening up of the Amazon is being accompanied by the creation of 'instant cities', such as Pacaraima on the Brazilian–Venezuelan border and the so-called science town of Humboldt, 800 kilometres north of Cuiabá in Mato Grosso. Rural electrification programmes and the improvement of urban facilities in small towns, especially in the Northeast,[31] may help to stem the flow of migrants to the major metropoli. In the long run the urban problem is one of creating more jobs and curbing the birthrate which has yet to show any major decline among the urban population.

The pressures of the transition to a modern industrial society are destroying traditional settlement patterns. Changes in the rural economy produce the migrant flood which is drowning the old urban environment. For the first time Brazilians have become an urban people but the concomitant transference of surplus agricultural labour into manufacturing on the classical model is not taking place. Inequities in the distribution of income, education and services must be overcome if one hundred million Brazilians are to participate fully in their nation's developing economy.

REFERENCES

1. Wagley, Charles. *Contemporary Cultures and Societies of Latin America* Random House, 1965, p. 130.
2. Marcondes, J. V. Freitas. 'The Evolution of Labour Legislation in Brazil', in *Modern Brazil, op. cit.*, p. 134.
3. Freyre, G. *Casa Grande e Senzala*, 2nd edition, Rio, 1936.
4. There has been a mulatto President, Nilo Peçanha, 1910–14, and in 1969 a Nippo-Brazilian, Fabio Yassuda, was appointed Federal minister of industry and commerce.
5. Neft, David S. *Statistical Analysis for Areal Distribution*, Regional Science Research Institute, Philadelphia, 1966, pp. 51–52.
6. 70 per cent of women in the city of São Paulo do not want more than two or three children according to a social survey carried out in 1971. *Brazil Herald*, October 24, 1971. The average family among the rural population of the Northeast and Amazonia contains fifteen to eighteen children. *Brazil Herald*, November 30, 1972.
7. *Brazil Herald*, July 10, 1971.
8. One of the authors holds the doubtful honour of having been the last recorded case of yellow fever in the city of Rio de Janeiro in 1933. In 1972 the World Health Organization announced that small pox was no longer endemic in Brazil.
9. Govêrno do Estado do Amazonas. *Atlas geoeconômico do estado do Amazonas*, Manaus, 1966, p. 32.
10. In 1968 there were 227,786 eligible students for 102,020 first-year university places, I.B.G.E., *Annuário Estatística, 1970*. Rio, 1970, p. 681. This situation led to student riots. There has been some broadening of the student intake, however, as 40 per cent of the students at São Paulo University are the children of illiterate parents. *Report on Brazilian Higher Education Reform*, Washington, D.C., 1972, p. 8.
11. A US$45·4 million programme, largely funded by international agencies such as the International Development Bank, was set up in 1967 to expand and improve the teaching of basic science and technology and agriculture in nine universities of which seven were in the Heartland and one each in Pernambuco and Ceará.
12. Kleinpenning J. M. G. 'Objectives and results of development policy in Northeast Brazil', *Tijdschrift voor economische en sociale geografie*, 42 (5), 1971, p. 277.
13. I.B.G.E., 1970, *op. cit.*; ECLA, *Economic Survey of Latin America*, 1970, New York, 1972.
14. ECLA, 1972, *op. cit.*, Table 25.
15. Paviani, Aldo. 'Les Migrations Journalières de Travailleurs à Brasília', paper read at *22nd I.G.U. Montreal, 1972*, mimeo, 5 p.
16. Smith, T. Lynn, *op. cit.*, p. 177.
17. *Brazil Herald*, June 20, 1972.
18. Carneiro, J. Fernando. *Imigração e colonização no Brasil*, Rio, 1950.

19. These figures are based on data gathered by Carneiro, *op. cit.*, for the period 1819 to 1947. There are many, generally minor, discrepancies with data quoted in T. Lynn Smith, *op. cit.*, pp. 122–123, but the general outline of the movement is essentially the same. Later figures are taken from various volumes of the official *Annuário Estatístico do Brasil*.

20. Augelli, J. P. 'The Latvians of Varpa', *Geographical Review*, 48 (3), 1958, pp. 356–387. Also see Henshall, J. D., 'Japanese Pioneers in Brazil', *Geographical Magazine*, 40 (16), pp. 1366–1373.

21. In Brazil waiters usually work 16 hours a day and many hotels economize on labour by not operating all their lifts. In Montserrat, in the Eastern Caribbean, chamber maids refuse to work more than a four-hour day and so two shifts of maids have to be employed.

22. Special issue of *Realidades*, 'Nossas Cidades', May 1972.

23. Momsen, R. P. Jr., 1963, *op. cit.*, pp. 143–165.

24. Geiger, Pedro P. and Oxnard, Susan. 'Aspects of Population Growth in Brazil', *Revista Geografica*, 70, June 1969, pp. 7–28.

25. Geiger, Pedro, P. 'Cities of the Northeast. Factor Analysis applied in the study of Northeastern cities', in *Quantitative Geography in Brazil*, Ed. Marilia Velloso Galvão, Rio, 1971.

26. Faissol, Speridião. 'The Big Brazilian Cities. Basic dimensions of differentiation and relations with the economical development. A study of factor analysis', in *Quantitative Geography in Brazil*, *op. cit.*

27. In the historic tourist centre of Petrópolis municipal government virtually stopped in 1972 after officials had not been paid for four months. *Brazil Herald*, January 30, 1973. In 1973 eight metropolitan regions were established to help streamline urban planning in Brazil's major cities.

28. *Brazil Herald*, January 6, 1973. Brazil has 33 traffic fatalities per 10,000 vehicles compared to 6 per 10,000 in the United States. *Brazil Herald*, May 19, 1973.

29. *Brazil Herald*, January 25, 1973.

30. The final date for the installation of all foreign embassies in Brasília and thus its full recognition as Federal capital, was September 7, 1972. However, the diplomats complained of high rents, traffic congestion and lack of recreation facilities. In 1972, it was necessary to build a new suburb, Ceilândia, 20 miles from the city centre, to house the 80,000 occupants of shanty towns within Brasília itself. Rapid population growth and bureaucratic red tape have combined to create such problems that its two founder architects Lucio Costa and Oscar Niemeyer both declared in 1972 that they would have nothing further to do with projects in Brasília. This loss may destroy the city as an architectural monument and throws doubt on the fate of urban improvement projects in general, since this city was built from scratch along modern functional lines.

31. See Neves, Jorge. *Northeastern Brazil, Urbanization and the Spatial Development Strategy*, Fortaleza, 1973.

CHAPTER 10

Brazilian Development: Myth and Reality

The significance of our government's policies as to the country's future is to continue building a free, prosperous, strong and independent nation, with a prominent place among the other great nations. President Médici as quoted in the *Brazil Herald*, April 1, 1973

From 1967 to 1974 Brazil had an annual growth rate of at least 9 per cent and thus has become one of the world's fastest growing nations.[1] However, the short run cumulative effect of making optimal decisions for rapid economic development is to exacerbate inequalities in the distribution of the benefits of modernization both between social classes and between regions.[2] Income differentials in Brazil are above the Latin American average[3] and appear to be increasing. In 1970, 38 per cent of the national income went to the richest 5 per cent of the population as compared to a share of 29 per cent in 1960. Over the same period the proportion received by the poorest two-fifths of the population fell from 10 per cent to 8 per cent.[4] Between 1964 and 1967 real minimum wages declined 20 per cent[5] and polarization of income groups increased over the decade.[6] Sectoral differences also widened during the 'sixties, with the mean reported census income in agriculture in 1970 only US$282 as compared to an average non-agricultural income of US$992.[7]

Sectoral and class inequalities are overlain by traditional regional income disparities, and Brazil may be seen as the classic case of a country in which technological dualism takes the form of regional dualism.[8] Of the poorest fifth of the population 41 per cent live in the Northeast, 40 per cent in the

East, and 15 per cent in the South, while the bulk of the richest 5 per cent live in the South (46 per cent) and East (40 per cent) with only 8 per cent in the Northeast.[9] Half of the low income group is engaged in traditional subsistence agriculture in the backward areas of the Northeast and East and another quarter in primitive non-agricultural activities in the same regions.[10] This distribution reflects the marked concentration of modernization in the southern part of the country.

Within Brazil the problem of regional inequalities is claiming increasing public attention. As a recent editorial put it:

> Concentration of progress within one limited area will not lead to harmonious expansion of the nation's productive energies. The old thesis, accepted at the beginning of the (Brazilian) industrialization era, that one dynamic centre was enough to irradiate progress over the entire nation, is no longer viable. Old regional disparities have not been removed and new critical areas are arising to aggravate the imbalance of development. This is not only an economic problem, but . . . areas of poverty also provoke psychological and social tensions throughout the entire nation.[11]

The question, then, is not the existence of the problem of spatial mal-distribution, but rather what can best be done to resolve it.

REGIONAL DEVELOPMENT PROGRAMMES

Many solutions have been sought and applied to Brazil's regional disparities, particularly during the past ten or twenty years. These have included building Brasília (essentially a political solution), drives to reduce illiteracy and ill health (social solutions), subsidizing of industrial plants outside the Heartland (an urban/economic solution), introducing agrarian reforms and land use legislation (economic solutions for the rural sector) and, lately, promoting highway construction and improvements on an unprecedented scale (solution through upgrading the infrastructure). Organizational solutions have been sought with the establishment of regional administrative entities such as SUDENE, SUDAM and SUFRONTE. Fiscal solutions have also been applied, including the allocation of a proportion of Federal tax receipts to development projects in the more backward areas and of giving tax incentives to private individuals and firms to encourage the transfer of capital to the poorer regions.

In contrast to the make-work projects and improvisations of previous periods, beginning with Goulart's Plano Triennal in the early 1960s government policies have reflected a concerted attempt to reduce, perhaps even to reverse, the historic pattern of regional disparities. The conceptual culmination of this policy has been the Plano de Integracão Nacional (PIN), which was promulgated in 1970. It involves taking funds from the more affluent sectors of the regional economy and transferring them to projects in the less developed areas when extra support is needed. For instance, the Fundação I.B.G.E. has received supplements to its normal budget for equipment to be used in its geodesic and other surveys in the North and the Rimland. The D.N.E.R. (National Highways Department), even though it is one of Brazil's more affluent public agencies, has also received additional PIN funds for the construction of the Trans-Amazon Highway and the Northern Rim Road.

Government efforts to spread the effects of economic growth during the past decade have, however, revolved for the most part around a variety of sectoral and regional development programmes, channelled through a plethora of public bodies. The Federal sectoral agencies range in their interests from mining to petroleum and from agriculture to fisheries, with frequent duplications within the state goverments. In the areal context, public bodies include those supervising urban projects and municipal public works, state planning agencies, regional (usually river basin) development commissions such as those for the Alto Araguaia-Tocantins, the Jaguaribe, the São Francisco, the Paraíba and the Paraná-Paraguay, and culminate in the supervisory agencies in charge of large segments of the national territory (i.e. SUDENE, SUDAM, SUFRONTE, and, most recently, PROESTE).

The major regional schemes vary considerably in the area they encompass, in boldness of concept, in degree of innovation and in significance. SUFRONTE, for example, which was aimed at the development of the southern part of the Rimland (Map 4), has had limited impact because it has done little more than attempt to systematize a process of spontaneous colonization and urban growth that had already outstripped the scope of the official measures which were set in motion over a decade ago. It is probable that the PROESTE programme, announced by President Médici in late 1971 for the purpose of developing the rural environment of the middle Rimland— Goiás, Mato Grosso and northwestern Minas Gerais (this last fiscally but not conceptually a separate entity)—will fall into the same category, since the northern part of this region is, as the former director of the Fundação I.B.G.E. has suggested,[12] 'undergoing the same process now which was described by Preston James decades ago for the Pioneer Fringe of western São Paulo.' In fact, as will be shown in a later section, it is precisely the southern and middle Rimland which have exhibited the greatest absolute improvements in per capita agricultural productivity and in education over the past decade. Nevertheless, these areas may be expected to benefit from official attention to the extent of receiving infrastructure works and a greater amount of technical assistance for farmers and ranchers than might have been the case if development had been left entirely in state or private hands.

The two regions encompassed by SUDENE and SUDAM, the Northeast and the North, have attracted the greatest official and unofficial attention. This has been due primarily to the magnitude rather than to the nature of their problems, which are in no way unique within Brazil. The low level of human resources development because of disease, malnutrition and insufficient education is widespread throughout the country and is simply more ubiquitous in the densely-populated Northeast. There are also many empty or poorly-utilized areas in Brazil, but in the Amazon this void assumes major proportions. Nor are the measures proposed for the solution of the problems of the North or Northeast particularly innovative, as most have been previously applied elsewhere, if on a smaller scale. They include road building programmes, power-plant construction, installation of sanitary facilities, school construction, the establishment of new industries, agricultural colonization, and mining and port development. H. O'R. Sternberg has pointed out[13] that, particularly in the frontier areas, 'there is much of the *déjà vu* in current patterns of investment, settlement, ecological impact and other features of change; but now the scale is much greater.' It is this last which makes the SUDAM and SUDENE programmes worthy of special attention.

THE NORTHEAST

The history of Federal intervention with projects in the Northeast dates back to the drought relief programmes of the 1930s. Under the National Department of Anti-drought Works (DNOCS) dams and roads were constructed in the Drought Polygon, an area roughly coincident with the *caatinga* (Map 1). The most significant result of this was to retain a portion of the rural labour force in the region which might otherwise have fled during periods of drought. In consort with the DNER and the Army, DNOCS reverted to public make-work projects during the severe drought of 1970, building roads which either were of no particular utility or were laid down with such poor engineering standards that they subsequently became unusable. According to a local informant, the two cruzeiros (about 12 pence) per day which the workers on these projects received sufficed 'to keep the peasants from revolting'.

Nevertheless, in recent years the normal remedial policies of DNOCS, which continues to operate in the Drought Polygon under SUDENE's supervision, have altered radically. Its projects now place particular emphasis on better agricultural use of the water impounded in the existing reservoirs, many of which it had previously built. Under SUDENE's 4th Guidance Plan,[14] 54 per cent of the DNOCS budget was for irrigation works with another 9 per cent allocated to other types of agricultural, storage and distribution projects, for a total of 63 per cent. A seemingly high 32·5 per cent was given over to administrative costs, with but 3 per cent for road construction, one of its principal activities in the past. The remaining 1·5 per cent was to go into minor programmes in natural resources development and education.

In 1945 the São Francisco Hydroelectric Company (CHESF) was established to provide, along lines derived from the TVA in the United States, a programme that was conceptually and spatially more broadly based than that of DNOCS. It was to focus on hydroelectric and ancillary developments from harnessing the Paulo Afonso Falls, spread over an area that included both the Drought Polygon and a region extending to the coast between Fortaleza and Salvador. But, as has been noted in an earlier chapter, the benefits from this project have gone principally to those urban areas where the wealth and productivity of the Northeast were already concentrated. To plug some of the resulting gaps, another agency was founded, which later came under SUDENE's jurisdiction, the Superintendency for the São Francisco Valley (SUVALE). Despite its resounding name, its scope was limited to 'carrying out studies and research into the use of the hydroelectric potential of the great river and its tributaries in the Middle São Francisco,' including only 'that area not served by the CHESF or CEMIG systems'.[15] In fact, its budget for 1968–73 did not reflect even these objectives to an significant degree, being allocated as follows: agriculture, storage and distribution 47 per cent; administration 16 per cent; power 11 per cent; transport 10 per cent; health 6 per cent; education 4·5 per cent; sanitation 4 per cent and natural resources development 1·5 per cent.[16] In short, SUVALE essentially duplicates in a more restricted area the types of projects already supposedly being undertaken by SUDENE over the entire region, but with the notable exception of an industrial development component.

The Superintendency for the Development of the Northeast (SUDENE) was established in 1959 with overall authority for development planning within the area of its jurisdiction, the objective being to achieve an integrated approach to Northeastern development. However, it lacked the conceptual framework for truly integrated regional planning and has functioned primarily in the sense indicated by its name, as a superintending agency attempting to bring order to a rather inchoate mass of federal, regional, state and local agencies, even though it does conduct research and is involved in the initiation, financing and implementation of specific projects. As N. Bernardes has pointed out, 'SUDENE is not really a regional organization, but rather a supervisory body for an illogical area which comprises an agglomeration of states or portions thereof with a wide variety of physical and human settings'.[17] As such, it has had a difficult task to perform and there is therefore some justification for a certain lack of consistency in its programmes, both spatially and temporally. In the latter sense, it is of interest to compare the shift in budget allocations between SUDENE's 1st and 4th Guidance Plans, for 1961–65 and 1969–73 respectively, as shown in Table 22.[18]

The accompanying table shows that SUDENE's emphasis has shifted from an infrastructural orientation in its early days, when two-thirds of the budget was allocated to road and power projects, some of which involved taking over those which other agencies had abandoned in mid-construction, to a more diversified approach to upgrading the Northeastern milieu. The concomitant increases in the other categories were spread fairly evenly across the various sectors, that for human welfare, for instance, rising from 15·3 per cent of the total to 21·2 per cent. Among them, the largest gains were registered in natural resources development and industrialization, both of which increased approximately five-fold. Nevertheless, industrial development inputs appear to be rather limited, which is at odds with the great emphasis that has been placed upon that aspect of Northeastern development since the 1960s in a vain attempt to achieve the 'take-off' promised by North American economists. The reason for this is simple: SUDENE acts only as a clearing-house for industrial investment programmes in the Northeast, the main source of funds being the '34/18' tax incentives plan[19] and Bank of Brazil financing. Thus, the 4th Plan took into account, but did not include, a projected NCr$3,000 million which was to come from these two sources, as compared to only NCr$66 million from SUDENE's own support programmes. The former figure, incidentally, amounted to more than twice SUDENE's total budget of NCr$1,342 million.

One Federal minister not too long ago described this emphasis on industrial investment in the Northeast as 'naïve',[20] and as early as 1967 an editorial commented that 'SUDENE attributed almost exclusive importance to industrialization . . . and . . . its managers thought only in terms of machinery without being aware of the population explosion involving increasing offering of unskilled labour, neglecting agriculture which should deserve major attention'.[21] In a study of the industrialization process in Fortaleza, Cruz Lima points out that, 'Given

TABLE 22

SUDENE Development Programmes for the Northeast
Investments and Costs as per cent of Total Budget

	1st Guidance Plan 1961–65	4th Guidance Plan 1969–73
Power	37·8	19·5
Transport and Communications[1]	30·6	14·5
Agriculture and Ranching	6·4	11·8
Storage and Distribution	2·7	5·1
Industry[2]	1·0	4·9
Natural Resources[3]	1·8	9·8
Basic Sanitation		11·2
Education	15·3	6·6
Health		2·2
Housing	0·0	1·2
Special Programmes	4·4[4]	4·2[5]
Administration	—	9·0
	100·0%	100·0%

1. 1st Plan, roads only.
2. Expenses of industrial support programmes only, does not include Bank of Brazil or tax incentive funds.
3. 1st Plan, mining only.
4. Colonization programmes, hydrologic surveys and cartography.
5. Programmes for administrative reform and for the rationalization of the sugar industry.

Sources: SUDENE, *I* and *IV Plano Director de Desenvolvimento Economico e Social do Nordeste*, Ministério do Interior, Recife, 1966 [*sic*] and 1968 respectively.

the economic status of the region and the lack of technical-educational resources and adequate relationships with the country's decision-making centres, the work force that has come from the rural areas, expelled by the semi-feudal structure and by climatic crises, has been subject in the city to the speculations of incipient industries many of which are also of rural origins and belong to traditional families with an inadequate entrepreneurial mentality. This has led to an excess of workers over demand, the lowering of wages and an irrational use of the labour force.'[22] He goes on to say[23] that, on the basis of prevailing piece-work rates, industrial workers are unable to earn even the minimum wage[24] without working 10 or 11 hours a day and that because of the low educational level of most of these transplanted workers and the fact that over 90 per cent have had no previous training, there is a high turnover in the work force. Skilled jobs in the more sophisticated industries are filled by workers from the industrialized regions.

This does not necessarily mean that the Northeast has failed to benefit from SUDENE's industrial development programme, which has brought about a rise in per capita wage levels and has provided a measure of alternative employment to at least a portion of the rural populace. However, besides the industrial structure and employment shortcomings mentioned above, to fundamentally change the centuries-old programme has had the two important negative effects of building up over-expectations and of diverting attention from the overall needs of the region centring on the depressed conditions of the rural areas. SUDENE planning has, furthermore, failed to come to grips with the basic problem: the necessity to change fundamentally the centuries-old social and economic structure of the region, without which no development effort in the Northeast will be truly effective. It does not appear that the present government shows any tendency towards embarking upon or encouraging any such new direction. On the contrary, a statement issued by thirteen Northeastern bishops and archbishops on May 6, 1973, takes the government to task not only for its repression and use of torture, but also accuses it, perhaps somewhat unfairly given the long-standing nature of these ills, of being responsible for poverty, starvation wages, unemployment, high infant mortality and illiteracy.[25]

On the other hand, in the past few years the Federal Government has come to realize that its industrialization programme for the Northeast has not lived up to early expectations and that more emphasis should be placed upon improvements in the rural sector. To this end a new programme, the *Proterra Plan*, aimed at upgrading the agricultural interior, was instituted in 1972. Although it is too early to judge the effectiveness of this in terms of specific achievements, it falls short on overall conceptual grounds, firstly because it merely represents a sectoral shift in emphasis from industry to agriculture and does not therefore come to grips with the need for overall regional planning and, secondly it is to operate independently of SUDENE. This, taken with the existence of other independent, or nearly independent bodies operating in the Northeast, such as DNOCS, CHESF, SUVALE and the various state development agencies, leaves SUDENE in an administrative morass which can only diminish both its operational and possible innovative roles. Nor, as SUDENE itself has become more bureaucratized and hierarchical, does there seem to be any immediate hope that sectoral interests will be put aside and a search for new regional methodologies undertaken, to the detriment of its future effectiveness. One recent editorial has taken the stand that, 'Many decisions concerning the Northeast—the Trans-Amazon Highway, Proterra, Provale —are being made without any participation by SUDENE. This explains the fears that SUDENE will gradually lose all its influence. The danger cannot be ignored. Already today, SUDENE is a body without major decision making powers. For several years it has also suffered from the flight of influential politicians and technicians and this has produced a climate of indifference and apathy within that body. It is not known, for the time being, what the plans of the government are with regard to SUDENE, but its growing lack of influence may herald its eventual extinction.'[26]

There can be little doubt that SUDENE has failed to live up to the hopes and expectations of its early days, when it attracted many of Brazil's great minds and most energetic idealists. Perhaps they expected too much, or perhaps the theoretical basis for such a vast human undertaking is not yet available and the practical problems are too complex to be grasped readily and reduced to operable formulae. On the other hand there have been positive accomplishments: in education, in transport, in health and sanitation, and in providing at least a somewhat higher level of employment opportunity. No doubt, 'much is being done to improve things, although often without planning. Government authorities are determined to solve the problems of the Northeast, but in many cases they do not know where to begin.'[27] In this respect, the Northeast of Brazil is not unlike most of the world's underdeveloped areas; and if that country has failed to discover the key to unlocking this ubiquitous enigma, it can at least take some comfort from knowing that it is not alone. It is to be hoped, for the sake of the *Nordestinos*, that officialdom will not now be distracted from this task by the spell cast by new horizons opening up in Amazonia, though such a distraction would certainly be in the tradition of Brazil's history of economic development.

THE NORTH

The first federal Amazonian development agency, SPVEA (Superintendency of the Plan for the Economic Valorization of the Amazon), preceded SUDENE by six years. It was established in 1953 as an autonomous agency for the purpose of promoting fuller occupancy of the Amazon Basin, upgrading its economy and integrating that more fully into the Brazilian economy. Its programmes differed in concept, if not in execution, from those of SUDENE which were subdivided sectorially, whereas SPVEA focused its attentions on small, non-contiguous regional units, 28 in all, the more effectively to use the limited funds at its disposal. For the next decade interest centred primarily on public works. However, in 1962 the idea of attracting industry to the region also took hold and tax exemptions were granted for 5 to 20 years to plants processing local raw materials, but without notable success except for two large plywood and veneer plants established in Amapá.

In 1966 SPVEA was superseded by SUDAM, the Superintendency for the Development of the Amazon, the terms of reference for which were similar to those for SUDENE—that is, for a broader, co-ordinative role over development efforts in the Amazon. This region was also to benefit from '34/18' and to receive 3 per cent of the Federal Government's tax revenues. Of the latter, two-thirds was to go to the public sector and the remainder was to be used to back private investments, although these were not placed under SUDAM but under a separate agency, FIDAM, the Private Fund for Amazon Development.

These moves naturally led to more emphasis being placed on industrialization, even though the North had neither the numerous established and well-placed urban centres of the Northeast nor the labour surplus which made such a programme a virtual necessity within the SUDENE sphere of influence, whatever the shortcomings in execution might have been.

Only two Amazon cities, Manaus and Belém, were in a position to benefit more than peripherally from any immediate moves to promote industrialization, and Belém was already undergoing a revitalization as a result of its terminal position on the Bernardo Sayão Highway. In fact, by the end of the 1960s that city's renewal and prosperity could be discerned in the highrise buildings that dotted the downtown area and was supported by reliable reports that Belém had ceased to be the smuggling capital of Brazil.

This dubious distinction has fallen to Manaus since 1967, when that city, with a surrounding 6,000 square mile area extending 30 miles upstream and 45 miles down, was declared a free-trade zone. This was to be administered by yet another autonomous body under the Ministry of the Interior, SUFRAMA (Superintendency of the Free Zone of Manaus). Imported goods for use by local industries were exempt from import duties and overseas exports from Manaus were likewise exempt from export taxes. Furthermore, Brazilians were permitted to take the equivalent of US$100-worth of goods with them to other parts of the country upon leaving the city, anything above that amount being supposedly subject to regular import duties.

Within a year of the establishment of the free port at Manaus, thirty industries had been built or were under construction and another dozen projects were awaiting approval. However, few were of any significance except for an oil refinery and a small (20,000 tons annual capacity) charcoal-fired steel mill. In contrast, 1,200 new commercial firms sprang up in the city, as well as fourteen new credit companies where only six had existed before. By the end of 1968 imports of electrical appliances, radios, record-players and television sets were proceeding at a rate of US$250,000 per month. Shops were generously stocked with everything from cheap plastic toys from Hong Kong to a varied selection of foreign cars and including such things as imported tinned foods, whiskies and perfumes, Swiss watches, Japanese motorcycles and huge American outboard motors. The stores did not, however, confine themselves to luxury items, mostly for re-export to other parts of Brazil, and imports of everyday consumer items such as razor blades (which could be purchased more cheaply than in U.S. drugstores) and staples, as well as baby foods, frozen pizzas and American ice-cream caused the cost of living in Manaus to drop by 30 per cent. One local economist claimed that within a few years, 'there will be no Brazilian goods for sale here at all'.[28]

Between 1967 and 1968, 3,000 new jobs were created in Manaus, absorbing virtually all the surplus labour force, and new construction was proceeding at such a pace that during the same period cement imports rose ten-fold. At present SUFRAMA is co-ordinating the construction of an industrial park adjacent to the city. It may well be that, when the impact of the Trans-Amazon Highway and its extensions are felt in this part of the North, Manaus may become the hub of a new and dynamic area of commercial and industrial growth, as occurred in Belém with the Brasília road a decade earlier. In that case, the prediction that Manaus would boast a population of over a million by the end of this decade[29] may not be entirely unfounded, but it will take more than the establishment of a duty-free zone to provide the required impetus for growth of that order.

Some recent and prospective developments in rural Amazonia have been mentioned in previous chapters: highway construction, mineral discoveries and their development, and agricultural colonization, both spontaneous and of the controlled type sponsored by INCRA. There is, however, another kind of occupance which is proceeding very rapidly and causing considerable alarm among environmentalist circles, and that is the proliferation of large ranching operations particularly along the southern, most readily accessible margins of the Amazon Basin from Maranhão to Rondônia, with a heavy concentration in northern Goiás and Mato Grosso. This activity receives approval from SUDAM which qualifies the large private, often corporate investors for benefits under the '34/18' and for other forms of government assistance. The private capital comes from investors in São Paulo and southern Brazil for the most part, but some has also come from the United States and West Germany. The ranches are often vast, in some cases embracing a thousand or more square miles, and many have built their own roads into the area or have 'loaned' heavy earth-moving equipment to the government so that it could build the roads for them.

The largest spreads have already cleared several hundreds

of thousands of acres of forest land apiece and are running tens of thousands of head of cattle. Clearing is done by migrant labour from the Northeast at predictably low wages and, as the ranches employ relatively few hands in their actual operations, a residue of squatters remains. As yet, the latter have not developed into a major problem probably because of adverse conditions of land tenure, the existence of opportunities at new clearing operations further along the retreating fringe of the forest, and the retention of law enforcement in the hands of the ranchers or their deputies.

The squatters are not, of course, protected by the decree that was passed in 1971 to safeguard the rights of settlers and to establish rules for the operation of colonization companies. Actually, the days when the establishment of private agricultural colonies was an attractive investment are probably over because of the drying-up of the supply of immigrants for whom they were best suited, the greater return on investment capital achieved by ranching, and the relatively unencumbered fiscal and managerial practices required for the success of the latter. It is not appropriate to enter further into the details of these ranching operations here; suffice it to point out that they clearly represent much of the *déjà vu* of Brazil's frontier settlement in terms of the privilege they impart to the already influential, the exploitation of human resources which accompanies them, and the destruction of the forest environment which is proceeding at an accelerated rate.

It is the last of these three major negative aspects of the grazing land expansion which has attracted the attention of academics both in Brazil and abroad. On the other hand the first two—privilege and human exploitation—are largely ignored by the latter group except on the rare occasions when exploitation takes the form of a particularly odious incident involving one of the few remaining Amerindian tribes in the area. Brazilian officialdom, meanwhile, either supports or ignores these negative aspects of the process in the interests of progress. There are many, both in and outside the country, who regard this process of 'rolling back the jungle' and 'challenging the last frontier'[30] as an admirable one in the best tradition of the American West, whether North or South.

The environmentalists' rightful concern over the large-scale destruction of the Amazon forest by the ranching interests has, particularly by foreigners writing on the subject, unfortunately been extended to include all types of settlement and even road building and mineral exploitation in the region. Such extremist views have virtually destroyed their credibility in Brazil and, by association, also reduced the effectiveness of those Brazilians who are espousing stricter environmental controls. Both the nature and the tenor of foreign writings on the subject, at least from the geographers' point of view, are succinctly expressed in a recent article by Denevan,[31] the very title of which—Development and the Imminent Demise of the Amazon Rain Forest—conveys the essentially negative and alarmist approach which is anathema to those who espouse the taming of Brazil's last *sertão*.

An entire volume could, of course, be devoted to an examination of the pros and cons of the various types of Amazonian development practices and their impact on the environment. Although this is impossible in the context of this book, a capsule of the issues raised by the environmentalists, after Denevan, and some of the arguments against them are of sufficient importance to merit summary attention. Among the principal areas of concern are the *climatic effects* that might follow a postulated destruction of the forest. Denevan himself points out that these are speculative[32] and he does not go as far as some authors whose exaggerated claims about depletion of the earth's oxygen supply have since been disproved; but current knowledge obviously provides a poor basis upon which to recommend that the Brazilians cease burning the forests, especially while the industrialized nations continue to pour pollutants into the atmosphere from factories, power plants, and automobiles.

Second is the problem of *soil deterioration*. Although this problem is a very real one, there are two fallacies in its presentation, namely, the use of the worst possible examples of soil deterioration in small areas that have been subjected to intensive and long standing misuses, which could hardly apply throughout the Amazon unless the population attained many tens, perhaps even hundreds of millions, and the assumption that such downgraded soils would exhibit properties like those beneath the natural savannas despite the fact that the latter are the result of quite different natural processes, exist under different physical conditions and are, in fact, retreating before the advance of the forest.[33]

In the realm of biota, the *decimation or extinction of wildlife* as a distinct and, in some few cases, not too distant possibility has not gone unrecognized and the Brazilian Government has placed restrictions on exports of skins and wild animals; but to restrict settlement in order to preserve the fauna is ridiculous in the Brazilian context, as is the idea (perhaps hinted at although not explicitly stated by Denevan) that settlers be prevented from hunting animals for food. Even were such a regulation enforceable, it would be nutritionally calamitous until such a day as it becomes possible for the *caboclo* to obtain his meat from a local supermarket at prices which he can afford.

The *preservation of genetic material* as a reservoir for future evolution is another concept now much in vogue; but it has not been satisfactorily explained why a million square miles of forest are needed for this dim and speculative eventuality, nor has a cost-benefit analysis been prepared to balance the possible value of such a reservoir against the needs of Brazil's extant and future human genetic material. This question is related to that of preserving the Amazon for its *scientific value*; but one must question the academic imperialism that is implicit in the statement that biological knowledge will suffer 'if the jungle is destroyed before we have had a chance to study it'[34] and ask how many generations of presumably foreign biologists will be required to accomplish this task before a surfeit of information would permit occupation of the basin by ordinary mortals?

Finally, there is perhaps the most resented argument of all based upon the *esthetics* of 'the jungle' which is characterized as 'a place of mystery and beauty'[35] and thereby intrinsically worthy of preservation—virtually *in toto* if some of the more extreme conservationists were to be heeded. The Brazilian ambassador to the United States has said that such views 'seemed to suggest that the Amazon region was untouchable in order to be preserved as a refuge for frustrated wealthy people,'[36] indeed, probably only for the very wealthy, since the average tourist seems quite content with a day's motor launch journey around the environs of Belém or Manaus. The reasoning, particularly of the North American environmentalists, has generally failed to take into account three very important factors in any promotion of a pristine Amazon. Firstly, the esthetics of suburbia are not necessarily duplicated in the attitudes of those who must contend with the rain forest environment on a day-to-day basis. Secondly, the position held by this environment is in no way comparable to the role that is played by the U.S. desert, the Canadian Arctic, or even the Scottish moors in the sense of being different and at best only marginally useful places to the people of those countries; rather, it is an integral part of Brazil's useable space, an extension of already settled areas, occupied and occupiable under existing techniques and within current economic norms. And, finally, the Brazilians are not unaware of scientific, esthetic and recreational values, as witness the Xingú and other national parks, and can be relied upon to preserve a sufficiency of Amazonia to meet their needs and interests well before the imminency of its demise is approached.

The cause of the environmentalists would undoubtedly be far better served if, instead of pursuing a myth of their own affluent, middle-class, academic creation, they recognized the reality of Amazonia in its Brazilian context and brought their expertise and good intentions to bear on apposite issues, if only so that future problems might be diminished. There are, to be sure, sufficient of these as the development of this region gains momentum, with three major ones in the realms of ranching, farming and urbanization which demand attention.

Certainly one can agree with Denevan that 'massive forest destruction . . . may serve the interest of immediate development but will be self defeating in the long run' if it leads only to 'extensive ranching of mediocre cattle, with relatively high living standards but few people benefiting'.[37] It does seem anomalous that government agencies should provide financial incentives for this kind of activity, which is infinitely more destructive of the environment than a horde of colonists would be, without placing on it the restrictions which it imposes on the latter both with regard to their selection for personal qualities and their freedom to cut down the forest on their properties. It is probably unrealistic to suggest a cessation of the activities that are rapidly turning vast tracts of forest into grazing land, especially in view of Brazil's long ranching tradition, the economic and political power of the large land-owners, and the rising world prices for beef; however, some control would certainly be desirable, and infractions of a spatial nature could be monitored accurately and at relatively low cost through currently available satellite imagery such as that provided by ERTS (Earth Resources Technology Satellite) or EROS (Earth Resources Observation Satellites) in which programmes Brazilian scientists are already participating.

Attention should also be paid to the problem, which appears to be built into the government's colonization schemes, of producing in the Amazon only 'labour-intensive forms of agriculture supporting fairly dense rural populations . . . at bare subsistence levels'.[38] A moratorium on new settlements of small farmers would be unrealistic, but much could be done to improve both human and ecological conditions if more atten-tion were paid to upgrading the farming practices of the colon-ists and the economic climate in which they function. If the new settlers could at least approximate the technology and work norms of the Japanese colonists on lands similar to those now being opened up, both the cause of ecology and of higher living standards would be well served. A consultant with INPA (Instituto Nacional de Pesquisas da Amazônia) has suggested[39] that 'the old "colonial" system of destructive agricultural exploitation of ever larger areas' should be replaced by 'smaller plots which can be cultivated with greater zeal . . . combined with an equally intensive raising of animals.' But, he points out, 'in order to replace the inorganic nutrients . . . which are removed from the soil by the harvests and through other losses . . . most of the animal feed should be imported'.[40] Although he suggests that this feed would be brought in primarily from southern Brazil, an interesting opportunity might be opened up for the Northeast as a result of a process recently developed in Barbados that produces cattle fodder at competitive prices from bagasse with a urea additive. Im-proved water and highway transport between the North of Brazil and other regions might now make such a system feasible, while growing urban and other markets within the region should provide outlets for an agricultural system functioning above the quasi-subsistence level.

Finally, the environmentalists appear to overlook the fact that, as commercial, industrial, and mining activities increase, so will the proportion of the population in urban centres. Not only should this somewhat mitigate the fears of those who foresee the forests disappearing before a tidal wave of unchecked rural humanity, but it also presents a new set of problems—urban blight and pollution—which are perhaps not sufficiently appreciated against the backdrop of the empty lands and voluminous rivers of Amazonia. As one editorial has pointed out, 'Currently fish are dying out in the sparsely inhabited swamp regions of Mato Grosso due to pollution of rivers, while salmon are now reappearing in the formerly polluted Thames River of England. . . . Brazil should learn from the experience of nations now compelled to incur enormous expenses in tackling a problem largely caused by ignorance and which could have been settled early at smaller costs.'[41]

This may become a problem even for the Amazon and its major tributaries. For how much longer can 'huge volumes keep the rivers so pure that even just below Manaus the water is as pure as any tap water in the United States'?[42] In that city, steps have been taken to eliminate the picturesque, if unsanitary water-borne shanty-town; but this will be of little consequence if the problem is simply transferred to dry land. Certainly the proliferation of *favelas* in urban centres throughout the country, to say nothing of ever-increasing traffic problems, should provide a stimulus to rational urban planning in the new or rejuvenated towns and cities of Amazonia. As can be seen from Table 23, with the exception of Acre and Maranhão (without which the proportion of urban dwellers would rise to 44 per cent), the northern and adjacent states and territories are already quite highly urbanized. The trend is undoubtedly towards an intensification of this situation, as demonstrated by Amapá. In 1950, before the development of its manganese mines, Amapá had a population of 37,477 of which only 37 per cent was urban, compared to its present population of almost 120,000 with 55 per cent urban. Thus, of the nearly 80,000 new inhabitants attracted to Amapá by opportunities in mining, transport, manufacturing and commerce about 50,000, or 63 per cent, settled in urban centres. It seems logical to suppose that similar trends will prevail elsewhere in the basin and that problems of urban blight and pollution will arise years before the jungles are all stripped and their soils exhausted.

From the foregoing and, indeed, from earlier chapters, it is clear that despite the government's recent efforts aimed at reducing inequalities, Brazil's marginal regions—the North, the Northeast and the Rimland—retain many of the social and economic characteristics that have long distinguished them from the Heartland. Nevertheless, changes have been taking place within these areas, quite significant in the southern part of the Rimland but only very recent and localized in the Amazon. The question that needs to be answered is whether, in fact, these changes are such that Brazil's new prosperity is being more evenly shared out among its regional components or whether, despite the government's efforts, there is merely an intensification of the old inequalities, as economic theory tells us should be the case.

TABLE 23

Populations of Brazil's Northern and Adjacent States, according to the 1970 Census

	Urban	Rural	Total	% Urban
Rondônia	60,541	56,079	116,620	52
Acre	60,557	157,449	218,006	28
Amazonas	409,278	551,656	960,934	43
Roraima	17,929	23,709	41,638	43
Pará	1,037,340	1,159,732	2,197,072	47
Amapá	63,785	52,695	116,480	55
Maranhão	771,790	2,265,345	3,037,135	25
Mato Grosso	699,661	923,957	1,623,618	43
Goiás	1,269,035	1,728,535	2,997,570	42
TOTAL	4,389,916	6,919,157	11,309,073	39

Source: Fundação I.B.G.E., Sinopse Estatística do Brasil, 1971, Instituto Brasileiro de Estatística, Rio de Janeiro, 1971, pp. 61–62.

A NEW ERA OF CHANGE?

In order to provide a quantitative measure of relative and absolute changes in the level of regional disparities, data covering thirty-three aspects of the demographic, production, services, communications and consumption patterns of the twenty-six units of the Brazilian federation were analysed. Principal components analysis was utilized to examine the situation at the beginning of the 'sixties and at the end of the decade and the results compared to give a picture of the changes that occurred during the 'sixties.[43]

An 'R'-mode principal components analysis produced five components with eigenvalues greater than one, explaining 87·6 per cent of the original variance for the 1960 data; and six components explaining 91·1 per cent for 1970. Varimax rotation of the components was carried out to isolate the separate dimensions of the data.[44] In the analysis of the 1960 data the following components were identified; modernization, industrialization, growth, education and agriculture. For 1970 the components identified were similar, with the addition of a sixth dimension, a mortality factor, suggesting that inter-relationships between mortality rates and other variables are becoming more complex.[45]

Coefficients of congruence were used to test the stability of the components over the decade. The modernization component which explained 40 per cent of the total variance in 1960 and only 24 per cent ten years later, was virtually identical in the two analyses with a coefficient of congruence of 0·94. This factor has high loadings for population density, per capita productivity, communications and per capita availability of sewage connections and hospital beds. The declining contribution of this factor to the overall variance indicates that as spread effects come into operation the modern/traditional dichotomy becomes less important as a major element in Brazil's spatial differentiation. The second dimension, which isolates the variables associated with industry, has a coefficient of congruence of 0·78. Its contribution to the total variation rose from 18 per cent in 1960 to 24 per cent in 1970, emphasizing the growing importance of sectoral income differences.

The growth component is related to the physical expansion of urban areas with high loadings for cement and petrol consumption, levels of urbanization, building permits and minimum wage variables. This factor shows quite high stability across the decade with a coefficient of congruence of 0·79. However, the growth component in the 1970 analysis is also very similar to the modernization component in the 1960 analysis.

The contribution of the growth factor to the overall variance rose from 13 per cent in 1960 to 21 per cent in the later study. The variables for urban population and building permits, which in the analysis of the 1960 data had their highest loadings on the modernization factor, had, by the end of the decade, become more closely associated with the growth factor. These changes seem to indicate that as the most basic attributes of modernization such as piped water, sewage connections and secondary education facilities become available outside the major cities the heartland/hinterland pattern becomes more closely associated with a dynamism/stagnation dichotomy than with a modern/traditional one.

The remaining dimensions are of minor importance, explaining only 18 per cent of the variance amongst the input variables for 1960 and 22 per cent ten years later and they show less stability over the decade than the first three components. However, their changes reveal certain aspects of the development process during the decade. In the analysis of the earlier data the primary education variables are linked mainly with agricultural productivity whilst in 1970 the link between primary and secondary education is more clearly marked suggesting that secondary schools became more widespread during the 'sixties. The agriculture factor is bipolar, with highest loadings for the variable of rice yields (positive) and proportion of the state's population in the capital city (negative), indicating that modern agriculture is associated with states having a balanced urban network providing services to the rural areas. Using the 1970 data the variables for per capita net domestic product in agriculture and road density have their highest loadings on this factor, providing a clearer identification of this component which recognizes a rural modern/traditional element. Mortality as identified by the variables for infant mortality and overall death rates, loads negatively on the 1960 growth component, suggesting that at that period mortality rates were highest in the stagnating areas. In the 1970 analysis the presence of the variables for proportion of the population in the state capital on the mortality component indicates an urban-rural differential in death rates. These relationships should not be emphasized, however, as the mortality statistics are notoriously unreliable.

REGIONAL PATTERNS

Relative changes in the socio-economic levels of the various states between 1960 and 1970 are shown by their scores on the components. In Figure 3 scores for the 26 units of the federation on the modernization and industrialization components, which together account for approximately half the total variance, are plotted against each other. São Paulo and Guanabara retained their dominance of the industrial and modernization components respectively although Guanabara became relatively more industrialized and São Paulo scored lower on the modernization scale at the end of the decade, reflecting both the continued concentration of industrial activity in the Heartland and the declining quality of life in São Paulo as migrants put excessive pressure on urban facilities. The secondary industrial centre of Rio Grande do Sul declined on both components during the 'sixties relative to the states of the Periphery, emphasizing the importance of spread effects from the Heartland. The marked change in the position of the Federal District illustrates the transformation of Brasília from a city under construction in 1960 to a functioning Federal capital in 1970, purposefully planned to be virtually without industry.

During the 'sixties the socio-economic gap between the Heartland and the Northern and Northeastern ('standard') regions widened. The concentration of these two major less-developed regions in the lower left-hand quadrant of Figure 3 became more marked, with Bahia and Amapá showing relative declines on the industrialization and modernization axes respectively, where in 1960 they had scored positively. In the North, Amazonas became the most highly modernized state as a result of the free port status of Manaus; and the development of tin mining in Rondônia led to an improved position on the industrial dimension for this territory. At the same time the regional identities of the individual states became stronger, with the Northern states continuing to have relatively fewer industries than the Northeast. In the Rimland states regional identity declined, with the central states of Mato Grosso and Goiás feeling the effect of improved communications with the Heartland whilst the northern states stagnated.

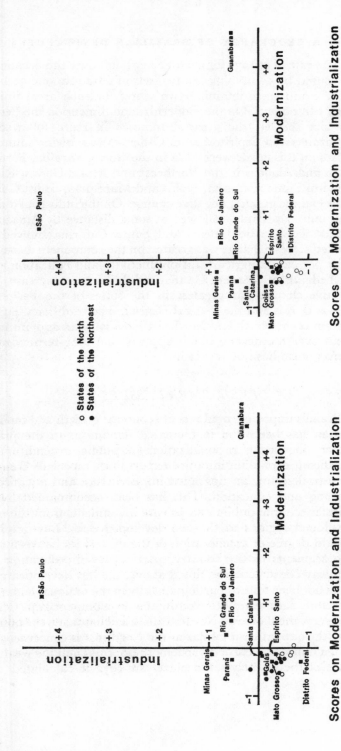

Regional Economic Structure of Brazil 1960 and 1970

Figure 3

Scores on Modernization and Industrialization Components for 1960

Scores on Modernization and Industrialization Components for 1970

○ States of the North
● States of the Northeast

Industrialization
Modernization

São Paulo
Guanabara
Rio Grande do Sul
Rio de Janiero
Santa Catarina
Espírito Santo
Minas Gerais
Paraná
Goiás
Mato Grosso
Distrito Federal

The rate of change for each Federal unit over the decade was measured by combining the two sets of data into one 52 by 33 matrix and thus obtaining two scores for each areal unit on each component. On the modernization dimension the Federal District showed the greatest increase in score followed by Amazonas and Espírito Santo. Other states showing improved scores on this factor were Pará in the North, Paraíba, Pernambuco and Alagoas in the Northeast and Minas Gerais, Rio de Janeiro, Santa Catarina, Goiás and Maranhão, whilst Guanabara had the greatest negative change. On the industrial dimension only São Paulo, followed at some distance by Amazonas, Rondônia, Rio de Janeiro and Santa Catarina showed improved scores. Change was greatest on the component associated with per capita agricultural productivity and education, with all Federal units except Guanabara showing an increase. This positive change was greatest in the states of the Periphery, Minas Gerais and the Federal District. The traditional lagging regions of the North and Northeast show some areas of improvement over the decade but it appears that long-term regional convergence has not yet set in.

BRAZILIAN DEVELOPMENT ISSUES

Brazil's unprecedented recent economic growth and modernization has been due to increased dynamism in the private sector, increasing rationalization of public expenditures, a significant expansion into new export lines, especially from the industrial sector, an upgraded infrastructure and advances in housing and education. This has been accompanied by the transfer of some public and private investments from the more developed regions to the less developed ones. But despite a certain degree of amelioration of the disparities between these two segments of the country, particularly in education and highway construction as noted above, the less developed areas have not been able to participate fully in the national boom and therefore significantly to narrow the development gap. On the contrary, the Banco do Nordeste do Brazil has taken the position that the gap, at least insofar as the Northeast is concerned, will widen unless a massive diversion of resources from the wealthier parts of the country takes place. In 1972 it calculated that, whereas the per capita incomes for Brazil as a whole would rise from US $442 to $838 by 1980, the Northeast would decline relatively unless it could attain an annual growth rate of at least 10 per cent, compared to its 1965–69 rate of 8·1 per cent.[46] Such overall figures furthermore obscure the fact that internal disparities between the rich and the poor segments of society are much greater in the less than in the more developed parts of the country. Therefore, while rising living standards in the developed regions have been reasonably evenly distributed among the populace for some years, in the less developed areas this has not been the case and probably will not be until fundamental and far-reaching changes occur in their social and economic structures. This would presumably have to take place at the expense not only of the economy of the wealthier parts of the country but probably also of the entire nation's political structures. While the present regime has shown itself amenable to at least a certain juggling of the regional distribution of Brazilian wealth, it is presumably not prepared to entertain any fundamental economic and political changes in the structure of Brazilian society. On the contrary, it goes to considerable pains to emphasize that whatever steps towards change may be necessary are, in fact, being undertaken.

Although the 'simple, uncluttered military mind, anxious to bring order out of chaos',[47] may be tending to oversimplify Brazil's problems and especially the means for their solution, this does not mean that the so-called revolutionary regime, and its civilian participants,[48] are unaware of current problems and those that lie ahead. President Medíci's oft-quoted statement that the economy is doing well but the people are doing badly (*a economia vai bem, é o povo que vai mal*), is perhaps indicative of this concern. Despite certain excesses[49] and dogmatisms it cannot be overlooked that, by Third World standards and, indeed, compared with the Russian and Chinese Revolutions, the American Civil War or the strife that shook Europe during the Industrial Revolution, which preceded fundamental economic shifts in much of the presently 'developed' world, change is taking place in Brazil by relatively peaceful means. If the current rate of progress can continue and the objectives of the government can be achieved within a reasonable period of time, Brazil may well be able take its place in world councils as an advanced country at very low social cost.

Although former Minister of the Interior, Costa Cavalcanti, has stated that 'inter-regional inequalities now place Brazil in a position intermediate between development and underdevelopment,'[50] many Brazilians would argue that the country is already developed.[51] Certainly, many of the problems which Brazil is attempting to deal with today are those which are of particular concern to the so-called developed, rather than the underdeveloped worlds (the quality, rather than just the maintenance of life, better income and services distribution, city management and the preservation of at least selected parts of the environment for recreation, to name only a few). Furthermore, a certain degree of advancement and prosperity is necessary before a country can turn its attention from the mere struggle for economic or even physical survival to that of a more equitable distribution of its wealth. In this respect, Brazil's conscious attempt to ameliorate the plight of its own internally less developed areas has more in common with the regional incentives programmes of Britain, Canada, the United States or the Soviet Union than with the policies that prevail in most of the Third World.

Costa Cavalcanti has on separate occasions summed up these major lines of current Brazilian concern—in ascending order of officially perceived importance: environmental degradation, poverty and regional disparities. 'The deterioration of the environment,' he declared, 'goes further than industrial pollution. There are other forms of degradation, which consist of the pollution of poverty or of underdevelopment.'[52] But, he has pointed out,[53] the major problems that currently confront Brazil are regional in nature: (1) the Northeast with its large population and lack of employment, (2) the Amazon, which must be occupied and its resources mobilized within the next few years, (3) the not fully occupied West, which must absorb some of the excess population from the Northeast and appropriate to itself some of the inputs destined for the North and (4) the industrial Central-South which needs to be strengthened by the expansion of internal markets that, in turn, can be accomplished only by increasing the purchasing power of the rest of the country.

The ability to overcome these problems and attain the national goal of full, rather than just selective, development must, then, go beyond the very real sectoral accomplishments that have been registered during the past decade or more in upgrading the infrastructure, multiplying the production of power, developing a viable export industry, making inroads upon the rationalization of agriculture and extending education and health measures to a higher proportion of the population. The full development of Brazil hinges upon its ability not only to overcome the regional disparities but to integrate the country in such a manner that every part thereof has a positive, rather than a negative relationship to the overall achievements to which the nation aspires. There can be no doubt that 'today, under a strong central government, the various bits and pieces are being locked together'[54] and that to develop these an 'appropriate technology' is being 'designed through pooled efforts by people who know their environment extremely well'.[55] If these efforts appear to the Anglo-Saxon reader to be coming down too unilaterally from above and without sufficient public participation, it may well be because, as Nilo Bernardes has said, 'in Brazil, an individual's interest stops at his garden gate —everything beyond belongs to the government'.[56]

The government does have two very important geographical assets working for it. In physical terms, although the 'monotonous tropical mediocrity' described in Chapter 1 may not seem to be the most propitious environment for development, it does have the advantage that the Brazilians are used to dealing with it on their own terms and that the techniques devised for this are to a great extent transferable from one locale to another. Brazil also boasts a cultural uniformity, mentioned in Chapter 9, which has proved to be one of its major assets throughout history, both in maintaining its national integrity, in contrast to the fragmentation which beset the former Spanish colonies on the continent, and by providing a vehicle for the diffusion of ideas and innovations readily throughout the nation.

There are, therefore, no significant physical or cultural barriers standing in the way of a nationwide extension of the current processes of modernization, which are themselves breaking down the spatial barriers that as yet divide the country into clearly defined developed and underdeveloped, economic geographic regions. It will be interesting in the years ahead to observe whether, in fact, Brazil is able to overcome this fundamental, if relative, problem in the geography of development where all the other countries of the world except the very small or the very poor have failed.

REFERENCES

1. The 11·3 per cent increase in GDP, in real terms, in 1971, declined slightly in 1972 to 10·4 per cent. However, industrial production rose by 13·9 per cent in 1972 as compared to 11·2 per cent in 1971, while the annual growth rate of agricultural production fell from 14·3 per cent in 1971 to 4·1 per cent in 1972 primarily because of a poor wheat crop, *Bolsa Review*, Vol. 7 (74), 1973, p. 53.

2. As in the Brazilian Finance Minister's aphorism '*crescer e concentrar*, —to grow is to concentrate'.

3. Economic Commission for Latin America, *Income Distribution in Latin America*, United Nations, New York, 1971, p. 36.

4. According to Robert McNamara, President of the World Bank, in his address to the 1972 UNCTAD Conference as reported in the *Survey of International Development*. Vol. 9 (4). 1972.
   Brazilian economists dispute the exact figures but agree with the general trends seen by the World Bank. See *The Economist*, 'The Moving Frontier: A Survey of Brazil', September 2, 1972. Fishlow states that in 1970 the upper 3·2 per cent of the labour force commanded 33·1 per cent of the national income as compared to only 27 per cent in 1960. He also suggests that since rapid growth only occurred in the final three years of the decade that stabilization following the 1964 revolution was more responsible for the widening inequalities in the 'sixties than was economic growth. See Fishlow, Albert, 'Brazilian Size Distribution of Income', *American Economic Review*, Vol. 62 (2), 1972, p. 401.

5. *Ibid.*

6. Between 1960 and 1970 the share of the national income going to the people earning either less than US $40 a month or more than US $90 a month increased while the proportion earned by the intermediate group of workers fell from 32 to 18 per cent. Economist Survey, *op. cit.*, p. 34.

7. Fishlow, *op. cit.*, p. 401.

8. Higgins, B. 'Regional interaction, the frontier and economic growth', in A. R. Kuklinski, Ed., *Growth Poles and Growth Centres in Regional Planning*, United Nations, Geneva, 1972, p. 285.

9. ECLA, 1971, *op. cit.*, p. 122. São Paulo State is here included in the South.

10. ECLA, 1971, *op. cit.*, p. 72. Fishlow, *op. cit.*, p. 394, suggests that 60 per cent of the Brazilian poor live in rural areas.

11. '*O Globo*', quoted in the *Brazil Herald*, March 1, 1973.

12. Lima, Miguel Alves de, personal communication, June 1973.

13. Sternberg, Hilgard O'Reilly, seminar held at the University of Calgary (Canada), September 1972.

14. SUDENE, *IV Plano Diretor de Desenvolvimento Econômico e Social do Nordeste, 1969–1973*, Ministério do Interior, Recife, 1968, pp. 281–282, and un-numbered appendix.

15. *Ibid.*, p. 298.

16. *Ibid.*, un-numbered appendix.

17. Bernardes, Nilo, discussion at the II Congresso Brasileiro de Geógrafos, Rio de Janeiro, 1965.

18. The First Plan was actually aborted in 1962 as a result of political upheavals. It was followed by a Second Plan which lasted from 1963 to 1965 and by a Third which covered the years 1966–68.

19. This is referred to as the '34/18' after the articles in the laws which instituted the programme. Under it, corporations in Brazil may deposit up to 50 per cent of their annual income tax obligation in a blocked account at the Banco do Nordeste do Brasil (BNB), the regional development bank. Within certain time limitations, the depositors then have a choice of investing these funds in their own or other projects approved by SUDENE either as a loan or as equity. The ratio of '34/18' funds, repayable five years after the start of production, to other sources of private capital varies between 25 and 75 per cent, depending upon the number of points accumulated under a system which takes into account the importance of the project to the industrial development of the region, the number of jobs created, the proportion of regional raw materials used, the degree of import substitution of goods or raw materials from outside the region, and the probability of success in exporting the finished product to other Brazilian or overseas markets. Additional incentives are provided by full or partial exemption from federal and in some cases state and local taxes as well, and from certain customs duties.

20. *Brazil Herald*, August 5, 1971.

21. *Jornal do Commercio*, quoted in the *Brazil Herald*, December 16, 1967.

22. Lima, Luiz Cruz. 'Composição da Mão-de-Obra Industrial numa Zona Urbana de Fortaleza, Ceará', paper presented at the Conference of Latin Americanist Geographers, Calgary, 1973, mimeo., p. 3.

23. *Ibid.*, pp. 6 & 7.

24. The official monthly minimum wage, which varies regionally and is changed periodically in response to inflation of the currency, provides the basis for many calculations in Brazil. In May 1971, this ranged from a high of Cr$225·60 in Guanabara and the urban areas of São Paulo and Rio de Janeiro states down to Cr$172·80 in the Amazon and the two principal cities of the Northeast, Recife and Salvador, and to only Cr$151·20, the figure in force at the time of the Cruz Lima survey, throughout the rest of the Northeast. On May 1, 1973, minimum wages were set in the range Cr$312·00 and Cr$213·60 for the highest and lowest regions respectively, thereby maintaining essentially constant ratios between them across the two-year time span.

25. *Latin America*, Vol. VII, No. 21 (London), May 25, 1973, p. 166.

26. *O Estado de São Paulo*, as quoted in the *Brazil Herald*, March 8, 1972.

27. *O Estado de São Paulo*, as quoted in the *Brazil Herald*, December 5, 1971.

28. Saul Benchimol, as quoted in *The Miami Herald*, July 12, 1968.

29. *Brazil Herald*, May 13, 1969.

30. Lead headlines over articles on Brazil in *The New York Times* of January 17, 1966, and July 7, 1970. The Brazilian ambassador in Washington, in refutation of an article in an American weekly magazine which had criticized his government's plans for developing the Amazon region because of the ecological dangers involved, said that 'the Amazon project recalls the feats of the pioneers of the Far West in U.S. history', *Brazil Herald*, July 12, 1972. A fuller discussion of the economic and spiritual significance of the 'Amazonic Epic' and its popular appeal will be found in *Brazil—The Take-off is Now*, American Chamber of Commerce for Brazil, São Paulo, 1971, pp. 19–22.

31. Denevan, W. M. 'Development and the Imminent Demise of the Amazon Rain Forest', *The Professional Geographer*, Vol. 25, No. 2, May 1973, pp. 130–135

32. *Ibid.*, p. 131.

33. For a brief sketch and example of these conditions and processes see Momsen, R. P., Jr., 'The Forest-Grassland Boundary between Jaraguá, Anápolis and Goiânia on the Central Plateau of Brazil', *Comptes Rendus du XVIII Congres International de Géographie*, Vol. III, International Geographical Union, Rio de Janeiro, 1965, pp. 82–89.

34. Denevan, *op. cit.*, p. 132.

35. *Ibid.* p. 132. A similar mystique is also prevalent anthropically *vis-à-vis* the tribal natives who 'extreme conservationists (are) anxious to maintain . . . in their pristine state like so many flies in amber', Hugh O'Shaughnessy in a report to the Minority Rights Group as quoted in the *Brazil Herald*, July 22, 1973 (see also footnote 29 in Chapter 2).

36. As quoted in the *Brazil Herald*, July 12, 1972

37. Denevan, *op. cit.*, p. 133.

38. *Ibid.*

39. Sioli, Harald, 'Ecologia de Paisagem e Agricultura Racional na Amazonia Brasileira', proceedings of the *II Simposio y Foro de Biologia Tropical Amazonica*, Florencia and Leticia, Colombia, 1969, pp. 268–279.

40. *Ibid.*, pp. 274–276. See also Davenport, William A. 'Photosynthesis/Respiration Ratios and their Relationship to Organic Matter in Tropical Soils under Cultivation', in *Geographical Analysis for Development in Latin America and the Caribbean*, C.L.A.G. Publications, Inc., Chapel Hill, North Carolina, 1975, pp. 132–139.

41. *Jornal da Tarde*, as quoted in the *Brazil Herald*, December 14, 1971.

42. Sternberg, Hilgard O'Reilly, discussion at the II Congresso Brasileiro de Geógrafos, Rio de Janeiro, 1965.

43. A fuller version of this study was presented at the Annual Meeting of the Institute of British Geographers, Birmingham, 1973.

44. Since orthogonality between the factors could not be assumed, an oblique rotation was also applied to the data. There was little substantive difference between the results of the two rotations, indicating a basic dimensional stability. Comparison of the results for the two rota-

tions shows greatest consistency for the education and agriculture components and least for the modernization component. Coefficients of congruence are higher in the oblique solution for the components associated with industry, education and agriculture and lower for the modernization and growth components. In the 1960 analysis the highest correlation (0·42) was between the factors linked with industry and primary education due to the presence of state and company-run schools in the industrialized states. With the establishment of more schools by the federal government this link had become less noticeable by the end of the decade, although Amapá, where company operated schools are still an important element in the educational system, moved from second to first position in the nation in terms of numbers of students in primary education relative to the total population. In the 1970 analysis the strongest link between the obliquely rotated components was that between the modernization and growth components.

45. With the exclusion of the extreme values for the states of São Paulo Minas Gerais, Guanabara and Distrito Federal analysis of the resultant 22 by 33 data matrix for 1960 showed greater complexity than in the study for the whole country, with seven components being identified. On the other hand, at the end of the decade regional variation was reduced with the extraction of only five meaningful components. The major areal pattern revealed was the division between the north and the south of Brazil. Rural-urban contrasts were important in differentiating between states. This analysis also showed greater within-region variation, recognizing, in particular, the states containing the major urban growth poles of the North and Northeast.

46. BNB, *Revista Econômica*, Vol. III, No. 11, Jun/March 1972, pp. 17–21.

47. Gott, Richard, as quoted in Chapter 8.

48. The importance of this participation must be emphasized. As a special study group from the Instituto Iberoamericano de la Universidad Sofia (*Boletim Informativo*, No. 12, Tokyo, March 1973, p. 1) pointed out on its return from Brazil, 'whereas political decisions are in the hands of the military, economic planning is carried out by technocrats, in contrast to the Peruvian structure where both the key political and economic posts are in the hands of the military'. It should be added that a high proportion of the Brazilian technocrats, as well as many of its upper-echelon military personnel, are well-trained, competent and hard-working individuals.

49. See, for example, Commission Interamericaine des Droits de l'Homme *Rapport sur l'œuvre Accomplie par la Commission Interamericaine des Droits de l'Homme au Cours de la Vingt-Septiemme Session (28 fevrier–8 mars 1972)*, O.A.S., Washington, D.C., 1973, which states in the section on Brazil (pp. 18–29) that: 'il est impossible d'invoquer de telles voies de recours (de la juridiction interne du Brésil) allors qu'elles n'existent pas'. Internal criticism of government practices, which has been sporadically voiced by certain leaders in the Church hierarchy of this, the world's largest Roman Catholic country, came to a head during the 13th General Assembly of The National Conference of Brazilian Bishops in February 1973, which resulted in a document stating the Church's position on human rights in the country and challenging the authorities to improve the situation. Among the rights which were said to be 'least

278 A GEOGRAPHY OF BRAZILIAN DEVELOPMENT

respected' were those of liberty and physical integrity, of political participation especially among the opposition, of free association especially
in labour unions, of legal defence, in view of the absence of habeas
corpus provisions, and of expression and information, *The New York
Times*, March 18, 1973.

50. *Brazil Herald*, March 5, 1971.

51. One public display of this attitude has been Brazil's siding with the
developed nations at recent UNCTAD deliberations.

52. *The Economist, op. cit.*, p. 16.

53. Brazilian Embassy, *Boletim Especial*, No. 7, Washington, D.C., January
13, 1970.

54. *The Economist, op. cit.*, p. 15.

55. Brown, Harrison. 'The Fall of the Deus ex Machina', *Ceres*, March–
April 1973, p. 39.

56. Bernardes, Nilo, *op. cit.*

List of Acronyms

BNDE	National Economic Development Bank
CEMIG	Central Electric Company of Minas Gerais
CEPLAC	Plan for the Economic Recovery of Cacao Cultivation
CESP	Central Electric Company of São Paulo
CHESF	São Francisco Hydroelectric Company
CPRM	Federal Minerals Research and Resources Company
DNER	National Highways Department
DNOCS	National Department of Anti-Drought Works
DNPM	National Department of Mineral Production
FIDAM	Private Fund for Amazon Development
IBGE	Brazilian Institute of Geography and Statistics
IBRA	Brazilian Institute of Agrarian Reform
INCRA	National Institute of Colonization and Agrarian Reform
INDA	National Institute of Agrarian Development
INPA	National Institute for Amazonian Research
MOBRAL	Brazilian Literacy Movement
PIN	Plan for National Integration
PROESTE	Programme for the Development of the West
PROTERRA	Programme for the Redistribution of Land and the Stimulation of the Agro-Industries of the North and Northeast
SPVEA	Superintendency of the Plan for the Economic Valorization of the Amazon
SUDAM	Superintendency for the Development of the Amazon
SUDEC	Superintendency for the Development of Ceará
SUDECO	Superintendency for the Development of the Central-West
SUDENE	Superintendency for the Development of the Northeast
SUFRAMA	Superintendency of the Free Zone of Manaus
SUFRONTE	Superintendency of the Plan for the Economic Development of the Southwestern Frontier
SUVALE	Superintendency for the São Francisco Valley

Index